The Agricultural Holdings (Scotland) Act 1991

The Agricultural Holdings (Scotland) Act 1991

A. G. M. DUNCAN, M.A., LL.B., W.S.

W GREEN/Sweet & Maxwell

EDINBURGH

1991

ISBN 0 414 00986 X

A catalogue record for this
book is available from the
British Library.

Typeset by MFK Typesetting Ltd., Hitchin
Printed and bound in Great Britain by
Butler & Tanner Ltd, Frome and London

CONTENTS

CONTENTS

TABLE OF CASES

References are to section and Schedule number

Where a section number appears followed by (N), this refers to the notes for that particular section or subsection.

e.g. s.115(N) refers to the General Note following s.115
      s.115(5N) refers to the notes for subs. (5) of s.115

AGRICULTURAL HOLDINGS (SCOTLAND) ACT 1991*

(1991 c. 55)

[A table showing the derivation of the provisions of this Consolidation Act will be found at the end of the Act. The table has no official status.]

ARRANGEMENT OF SECTIONS

PART I

AGRICULTURAL HOLDINGS

PART II

TERMS OF LEASES AND VARIATIONS THEREOF

Variation of rent

Termination of tenancy

PART III

NOTICE TO QUIT AND NOTICE OF INTENTION TO QUIT

PART IV

COMPENSATION FOR IMPROVEMENTS

---

* Annotations by A.G.M. Duncan, M.A., LL.B., W.S.

Part V

Other Provisions Regarding Compensation

Market gardens

Miscellaneous

Part VI

Additional Payments

Part VII

Arbitration and Other Proceedings

Sheep stock valuation

Part VIII

Miscellaneous

An Act to consolidate the Agricultural Holdings (Scotland) Act 1949 and other enactments relating to agricultural holdings in Scotland.

[25th July 1991]

PARLIAMENTARY DEBATES
Hansard, H.L. Vol. 527, col. 296; Vol. 528, col. 1357; Vol. 529, col. 111; H.C. Vol. 195, col. 1115.

INTRODUCTION AND GENERAL NOTE

The Agricultural Holdings (Scotland) Act 1949 consolidated the statutory provisions affecting agricultural tenancies (other than those of crofts and smallholdings) as contained in the Agriculture (Scotland) Act 1948 and earlier Acts. In the period of more than 40 years which has elapsed since that consolidation there have been a number of significant developments requiring radical amendment of the 1949 provisions. It appears that there are prospects of further changes involving a greater measure of freedom of contract in the landlord-tenant relationship. It is, however, appropriate that any such developments there may be should have been preceded by a much-needed consolidation of the statutory provisions in force, which provisions may be expected to continue to apply to tenancy contracts entered into before further changes are enacted.

The 1948 provisions, as re-enacted in the 1949 Act, may be said to have represented a high-water mark in the protection of tenants' interests. Subsequent legislation has maintained a somewhat fluctuating balance as between the respective interests of landlord and tenant. The Agricultural Act of 1958 struck a blow for landlords in enabling them, by taking action within time limits prescribed, to enforce compliance with a Notice to Quit given to a successor of a deceased tenant without having to seek consent from the appropriate authority. The same Act effected a transfer of certain quasi-judicial functions, including the granting of consent for the operation of Notices to Quit, from the Secretary of State to the Scottish Land Court. It also contained provisions making clear that an open market basis was to be the sole criterion in the review of rents under the statutory machinery. The Succession (Scotland) Act 1964 assimilating succession rights in heritage and moveables itself contains certain provisions referring to agricultural holdings as well as amending the provisions of the 1949 Act to take account of the replacement of the tenant's heir at law by an acquirer from his executor. A more significant change affecting the succession to tenancies is, however, contained in the Agriculture (Miscellaneous Provisions) Act 1968, which makes a distinction between near relative successors (*i.e.* spouses and children of a deceased tenant) and other successors testate or intestate. Reversing to this extent the effect of the 1958 Act, the 1968 Act gave the near relative successor a continuation of the security of tenure of his predecessor subject only to the right of the landlord, if taking action within time limits prescribed, to invoke any one of certain special grounds in applying for consent to the operation of the notice to quit. The 1968 Act also created what is known as reorganisation compensation, being additional payments due to tenant farmers by landlords, who without being able to establish personal hardship, are recovering possession in order to use the land for a non-agricultural purpose. The same Act entitles tenants who have part of their holdings resumed on short notice to compensation for loss of profits. Again, important amendments to the 1949 provisions were made by the Agricultural Holdings (Amendment) (Scotland) Act 1983. This Act extended and amended for tenancies originating from 1984 onwards the special grounds for Land Court consent to a Notice to Quit given to a near relative successor. The Act's most significant effect was, however, its modification of the statutory directions for review of rents as contained in the 1949 Act as amended by the 1958 Act. A lack of comparable lettings of farms had made it difficult in many cases to apply the open market basis. Where this situation arises the arbiter or the Land Court is permitted to take into account a number of external factors instead of proceeding on the basis of a market distorted by the element of scarcity. The 1983 Act also created for the Land Court a special appellate jurisdiction applicable to rent reviews carried out by arbiters officially appointed and reduces from five to three years the minimum period between rent reviews.

The present Act incorporates in ss.68–72 and Scheds. 9 and 10 the provisions for valuation of bound sheep stocks previously dealt with in other legislation. However, for the rules of good husbandry and good estate management, matters central to the landlord and tenant relationship, we have still to refer to the Agriculture (Scotland) Act 1948, of which only a few provisions of significance now remain in force. Among provisions of the 1949 Act which have been omitted from the present Act as being unnecessary or spent is s.100. It provided that apart from express provision nothing in the 1949 Act should prejudicially affect any power, right or remedy of a landlord, tenant or other person derived from any other Act or law or any custom of the country or otherwise. The corresponding provision continues to appear in English legislation (see the Agricultural Holdings Act 1986, s.97) and references in Scottish text books indicate that the section was not without potential significance (see Gill, *The Law of Agricultural Holdings in Scotland* (2nd ed.), paras. 10, 177, 439 and 554 and Connell, *The Agricultural Holdings (Scotland) Acts* (6th ed.), pp. 206/7). Accordingly its omission seems surprising with the saving provisions in s.87 of and Sched. 12 to this Act applying only to rights of statutory origin.

While this Act has been described in Parliament as being pure consolidation, it contains much redrafting and rearrangement of the existing legislation. Instances of this are referred to in the annotations which follow. It would appear that certain drafting errors might have been avoided by closer adherence to the wording of the existing provisions (see ss.46(3) and 56(2)).

For the most part the content of provisos as appearing in the 1949 Act has been reproduced in separate subsections. With the possible exception of s.55(7), as commented on in the relative annotation, this change does not appear to have altered the meaning or effect of the proviso.

In some respects, however, the rearrangement of sections within this Act seems unfortunate. For example, certain matters which the 1949 Act conveniently dealt with together and in sequence in ss.4, 5 and 6 are now distributed between ss.4, 5, 14 and 46, with s.46(3) apparently ignoring the fact that s.6(2) of the 1949 Act has been treated as spent. Again we have the complex and interrelated provisions of ss.13 and 14 of the Agriculture (Miscellaneous Provisions) Act 1976 dealing with demands on tenants to remedy defects in fixed equipment and Notices to Quit following thereon, covered in reverse order by ss.32 and 66 of this Act.

It appears that consideration was given to the omission of the provisions for compensation for old improvements which in practice are not often invoked. The possibility had, however, to be envisaged of claims for long-standing improvements of the more permanent type arising, particularly in cases of tenancies passing by succession. The 1949 Act contained separate provisions for old and new improvements. The form of the relative Schedules has been retained but Pt. IV of this Act consists of sections dealing with both categories of improvements. The 1949 arrangement, although involving some repetition, had the advantage of ready reference to the rules applicable in a particular case.

In the annotation of each section the sections of the 1949 Act or other Acts from which it is derived are noted. References have also been made to the appropriate paragraphs in Gill, *Law of Agricultural Holdings in Scotland* (2nd ed. 1990), which forms an up-to-date and definitive treatment of the law as it stood prior to the present consolidation. Again, there have been inserted, so far as possible, references to the corresponding statutory provisions as operating in England. The interpretation of these provisions by the English courts can be helpful in resolving some problems of construction on which Scottish authority may be lacking. The significance of English decisions is exemplified by the frequent references made in Scotland to the ruling of the House of Lords in *Johnson* v. *Moreton* [1980] A.C. 87, demonstrating the public interest aspect of the agricultural holdings legislation as affecting attempts to circumvent or contract out of its effects.

ABBREVIATIONS
1886 Act: Removal Terms (Scotland) Act 1886
1907 Act: Sheriff Courts (Scotland) Act 1907
1923 Act: Agricultural Holdings (Scotland) Act 1923
1931 Act: Small Landholders and Agricultural Holdings (Scotland) Act 1931
1937 Act: Sheep Stocks Valuation (Scotland) Act 1937
1946 Act: Hill Farming Act 1946
1948 Act: Agriculture (Scotland) Act 1948
1949 Act: Agricultural Holdings (Scotland) Act 1949
1958 Act: Agriculture Act 1958
1963 Act: Agriculture (Miscellaneous Provisions) Act 1963
1964 Act: Succession (Scotland) Act 1964
1968 Act: Agriculture (Miscellaneous Provisions) Act 1968
1973 Act: Local Government (Scotland) Act 1973

1976 Act: Agriculture (Miscellaneous Provisions) Act 1976
1983 Act: Agricultural Holdings (Amendment) (Scotland) Act 1983
1986 Act: The Agriculture Act 1986
Connell: The Agricultural Holdings (Scotland) Acts (6th ed.)
Gill: The Law of Agricultural Holdings in Scotland (2nd ed.)

PART I

AGRICULTURAL HOLDINGS

Meaning of "agricultural holding" and "agricultural land"

1.—(1) In this Act (except sections 68 to 72) "agricultural holding" means
the aggregate of the agricultural land comprised in a lease, not being a lease
under which the land is let to the tenant during his continuance in any office,
appointment or employment held under the landlord.

(2) In this section and in section 2 of this Act, "agricultural land" means
land used for agriculture for the purposes of a trade or business, and includes
any other land which, by virtue of a designation of the Secretary of State
under section 86(1) of the Agriculture (Scotland) Act 1948, is agricultural
land within the meaning of that Act.

DEFINITIONS
"agriculture": s.85(1).
"landlord": s.85(1).
"lease": s.85(1).
"tenant": s.85(1).

DERIVATIONS
Agriculture Act 1958, s.9(1).
Agricultural Holdings (Scotland) Act 1949, s.1.

GENERAL NOTE
See Gill, Chap. 2. (For the corresponding English provision see the Agricultural Holdings
Act 1986, s.1).

Subs. (1)
Sections 68 to 72 relating to valuation of sheep stocks are excepted because their application
is restricted to holdings wholly or partially pastoral (see s.72(a)). "The aggregate of agricultural
land" has reference to the wide variety of activities coming within the definition of "agriculture"
contained in s.85(1). There is no minimum size for the agricultural holding (see *Stevens* v.
Sedgeman [1951] 2 K.B. 434 and *Malcolm* v. *Dougall* [1916] S.C. 283). Corresponding provisions at one time operative in England have been held to result that a dwelling-house or
building, if used for agriculture, may itself constitute agricultural land (see *Blackmore* v. *Butler*
[1954] 2 Q.B. 171).
The exception of a let to the tenant during employment with the landlord may be taken as
relating to what is known as a service occupancy rather than a tenancy in the proper sense. The
status of the tenant or occupier in any particular case will be a matter of proof (see, *e.g.*
Dunbar's Trustees v. *Bruce* [1900] 3F 137 and *McGregor* v. *Dunnett* [1949] S.C. 510).

Subs. (2)
It is a question of fact whether land is being used for trade or business (see *Blackmore* v.
Butler [1954] 2 Q.B. 171, at pp. 175 and 181). The use must be a lawful one permitted by the
lease, but it has been held that the trade or business need not be an agricultural one (*Rutherford*
v. *Maurer* [1962] 1 Q.B. 16 and *Crawford* v. *Dun*, 1981 S.L.T. (Sh. Ct.) 66 and see notes on
s.85(1)(b). In cases of mixed agricultural and non-agricultural use the predominant use will
determine whether or not the tenancy as a whole constitutes an agricultural holding. A decision
of the Land Court in *McGhie* v. *Lang*, 1953 S.L.C.R. 22 that the non-agricultural part of a
mixed holding should be excised, leaving the remainder as the agricultural holding, is unlikely
to be followed (see Gill, paras. 17–19 and the case of *Cameron* v. *Duke of Argyll's Trustees*,
1981 S.L.T. (Land Ct.) 2 at p. 7). However, in terms of s.49(3)(4), where the non-agricultural
element in a holding predominates, the agricultural element is treated for compensation
purposes as a separate agricultural holding, unless the parties agree otherwise. The power of

the Secretary of State under s.86(1) of the Agriculture (Scotland) Act 1948 to designate land as agricultural land has for long been unused.

Leases for less then year to year

2.—(1) Subject to subsection (2) below, where, under a lease entered into on or after November 1, 1948, land is let for use as agricultural land for a shorter period than from year to year, and the circumstances are such that if the lease were from year to year the land would be an agricultural holding, then, unless the letting was approved by the Secretary of State before the lease was entered into, the lease shall take effect, with the necessary modifications, as if it were a lease of the land from year to year.

(2) Subsection (1) above shall not apply to—

(a) a lease entered into (whether or not the lease expressly so provides) in contemplation of the use of the land only for grazing or mowing during some specified period of the year;

(b) a lease granted by a person whose interest in the land is that of a tenant under a lease for a shorter period than from year to year which has not by virtue of that subsection taken effect as a lease from year to year.

(3) Any question arising as to the operation of this section in relation to any lease shall be determined by arbitration.

DEFINITIONS
"agricultural holding": s.1(1).
"agricultural land": s.1(2).
"lease": s.85(1).
"tenant": s.85(1).

DERIVATION
Agricultural Holdings (Scotland) Act 1949, s.2.

GENERAL NOTE
See Gill, pp. 62–83. (For the corresponding English provision see the Agricultural Holdings Act 1986, s.2).

Subs. (1)
This is a vitally important provision preventing the avoidance of security of tenure by the use of short-term lets, whether for one period or for successive periods (*Rutherford* v. *Maurer* [1962] 1 Q.B. 16). By making such lets operative as year-to-year tenancies it brings them within the definition of a lease in s.85(1) and makes them subject to tacit relocation in terms of s.3. The rule has been held to apply to a lease for a fixed term of one year as being less then from year to year (*Bernays* v. *Prosser* [1963] 2 Q.B. 592).

The phrase "with the necessary modifications" covers only modifications consistent with the terms of the lease, which must remain "recognisably the same agreement" in contrast with "a transformation. . .into something radically different" (see *Harrison-Broadley* v. *Smith* [1964] 1 W.L.R. 456 at p. 467) and *Bahamas International Trust Co.* v. *Threadgold* [1974] 1 W.L.R. 1514, C.A.).

For the Secretary of State's approval to a short-term lease to be obtained, the Department of Agriculture, to whom there must be submitted a plan of the ground with duration and dates of the short-term let and the reasons for proposing it, has to be satisfied that the granting of a normal agricultural tenancy is unreasonable or impracticable, *e.g.* because proposed developments will take the land out of agricultural use in the fairly near future. (Other examples of special circumstances in which consent has been given are to be found in Gill, para. 64.) The Secretary of State is not concerned with the terms of the proposed let but has to decide whether in principle the land should be let on a short-term basis. To be effective, the approval must precede the lease, but the lease must be entered into before the duration of the approval expires (*Secretary of State for Social Services* v. *Beavington* (1982) 262 E.G. 551). Again the approval must apply to the whole subjects of let (*NCB* v. *Drysdale*, 1989 S.L.T. 825) but it appears to be undecided whether the lease must be of an area which has been the subject of specific prior approval or whether it is sufficient that it relates to part of a larger area covered by a prior approval (see *NCB* v. *Drysdale* (above) and Gill, para. 65).

Subs. (2)(a)

To be excepted from the application of security of tenure, both the duration of the lease and the parties' contemplation of the use of the subjects must comply with the statutory requirements. In the case of verbal lets, as often occurring with seasonal or short-term tenancies, it may be difficult to establish the purpose of the tenancy as contemplated by the parties at its commencement. Again, if there is a formal lease not containing express provisions as regards purpose and/or duration, there may be doubts as to whether extrinsic evidence on these matters is admissible. The tenant's facilities should be confined to grazing animals or mowing grass. Any form of cultivation or cropping during the seasonal let will normally involve security of tenure for the tenant but in one unusual case the tenant's ploughing operations were treated as ancillary to his use of the grassland (*Sanson* v. *Chalmers*, 1965 S.L.C.R., p. 135). An obligation on the tenant to maintain fixed equipment and grassland is not inconsistent with a grazing let (*Mackenzie* v. *Laird* (1959) S.C. 266).

The "period of the year" does not need to be defined by specific dates but can be described in general terms such as "grazing season" or "growing season," the meaning of which, as sometimes varying according to district, will be known to parties likely to be concerned (*Mackenzie* v. *Laird*; *Gairneybridge Farm* v. *King*, 1974 S.L.T. (Land Ct.) 8). The period may be as long as 364 days (*Reid* v. *Dawson* [1955] 1 Q.B. 214). A single contract for a succession of seasonal grazing lets over a period of years, which may be indefinite, is within the terms of this subsection (*Mackenzie* v. *Laird*). Successive periods of let involving continuous occupation for a year or more can however, give rise to difficulty, and the safe course is for the landlord to insist on a temporary removal of the stock, even though the subjects are being relet to the existing tenant (see *Rutherford* v. *Maurer* [1962] 1 Q.B. 16 and *per contra Scene Estate* v. *Amos* [1957] 2 Q.B. 205).

For the significance of grazing lets under s.2(2)(a) in transactions in milk quotas, see Gill, para. 73.

Subs. (2)(b)

As a sub-tenant can have no better right than the tenant as his author, the sub-tenant in a tenancy within the terms of subs. (2)(a) has himself no security of tenure. In any event, sub-letting in such seasonal tenancies, as in agricultural tenancies generally, is not permissible without the landlord's consent.

Subs. (3)

Arbitration is here being applied to the operation of the section as opposed to its application. In the past, however, the effect of the distinction, as interpreted by the courts, has not been entirely clear or consistent (for a full discussion of the matter see Gill, paras. 76–83).

The Scottish Courts have taken the view that the question of whether the approval of the Secretary of State has been given as provided for in subs. (1) is a matter for arbitration (*NCB* v. *Drysdale*, 1989 S.L.T. 825) but under the corresponding provision in the English legislation the matter has been treated as within the jurisdiction of the courts (see, for example, *Epsom and Ewell Borough Council* v. *Bell (C.) (Tadworth)* [1983] 1 W.L.R. 379). In both countries, however, it appears to be accepted that if the question is whether there was agreement between the parties or whether such agreement could take effect as a year-to-year let under subs. (1) it is a matter for the courts. In England it also appears to be accepted that any question as to whether a particular contract falls within the equivalent of subs. (2) is one for the courts (*Goldsack* v. *Shore* [1950] 1 K.B. 708), but Scottish decisions on this matter give conflicting views (*Love* v. *Montgomerie & Logan*, 1982 S.L.T. Sh. Ct. 60) following the English view but earlier decisions such as *Gairneybridge Farm* v. *King*, 1974 S.L.T. (Land Ct.) 8 and *Maclean* v. *Galloway*, 1979 S.L.T. (Sh. Ct.) 32 being to the opposite effect.

In consistency with the reference in this subsection to the operation of the section, the better view would appear to be that the only function of arbitration in such cases should be to determine the consequential modifications of a lease which the court has decided should be enlarged from a short-term tenancy to a year-to-year tenancy.

Leases to be continued by tacit relocation

3. Notwithstanding any agreement or any provision in the lease to the contrary, the tenancy of an agricultural holding shall not come to an end on the termination of the stipulated endurance of the lease, but shall be continued in force by tacit relocation for another year and thereafter from year to year, unless notice to quit has been given by the landlord or notice of intention to quit has been given by the tenant.

DEFINITIONS
"agricultural holding": s.1(1).
"landlord": s.85(1).
"notice of intention to quit": s.21(2).
"notice to quit": s.21(2).
"tenant": s.85(1).
"termination": s.85(1).

DERIVATIONS
Agricultural Holdings (Scotland) Act 1949, ss.3, 24(1).

GENERAL NOTE
See Gill, Chap. 5. (For the corresponding English provision see the Agricultural Holdings Act 1986, s.3).

The section, which should be read along with s.21 applies the common-law rule of tacit relocation, subject only to the modification that to prevent the tenancy continuing after the expiry of its duration, notice of not less than one year nor more than two years must be given by one party to the other, these being the maximum and minimum periods prescribed by s.21(3). The opening words of the section make it clear that contracting out is prohibited. As to the meaning of "agreement" in this context, see the note to s.21(1).

The section applies to leases generally and so in terms of s.85(1) includes a lease for a term of years. A lease for 18 months is in that category and thus would not escape security of tenure as it did in the English case of *Gladstone* v. *Bower* [1960] 2 Q.B. 384, C.A., decided under reference to a statutory provision for prolongation of a tenancy applying only to tenancies of two years or more. The section does not apply to seasonal lets, which are unaffected by the doctrine of tacit relocation (see Rankine, *Leases* (3rd ed.), p. 599; *Secretary of State for Air* v. *Davidson* (1950) 66 Sh.Ct.Rep. 59).

PART II

TERMS OF LEASES AND VARIATIONS THEREOF

Written leases and the revision of certain leases

4.—(1) Where in respect of the tenancy of an agricultural holding—
(a) there is not in force a lease in writing; or
(b) there is in force a lease in writing, being either—
      (i) a lease entered into on or after November 1, 1948, or
      (ii) a lease entered into before that date, the stipulated period of which has expired and which is being continued in force by tacit relocation,
    but such lease contains no provision for one or more of the matters specified in Schedule 1 to this Act or contains a provision inconsistent with that Schedule or with section 5 of this Act,
either party may give notice in writing to the other requesting him to enter into a lease in writing containing, as the case may be, provision for all of the matters specified in Schedule 1 to this Act, or a provision which is consistent with that Schedule or with section 5 of this Act; and if within the period of 6 months after the giving of such notice no such lease has been concluded, the terms of the tenancy shall be referred to arbitration.

(2) On a reference under subsection (1) above, the arbiter shall by his award specify the terms of the existing tenancy and, in so far as those terms do not make provision for all the matters specified in Schedule 1 to this Act or make provision inconsistent with that Schedule or with section 5 of this Act, make such provision for those matters as appears to the arbiter to be reasonable.

(3) On a reference under subsection (1) above, the arbiter may include in his award any further provisions relating to the tenancy which may be agreed between the landlord and the tenant, and which are not inconsistent with this Act.

(4) The award of an arbiter under this section or section 5 of this Act shall have effect as if the terms and provisions specified and made therein were

contained in an agreement in writing between the landlord and the tenant, having effect as from the making of the award or from such later date as the award may specify.

DEFINITIONS
"agricultural holding": s.1(1).
"landlord": s.85(1).
"lease": s.85(1).
"tenant": s.1(1).

DERIVATIONS
Agricultural Holdings (Scotland) Act 1949, ss.4, 6(4).

GENERAL NOTE
See Gill, paras. 89–92.

Subs. (1)
This provision confers on a party to a tenancy the right to have a written lease in terms conforming to the statutory requirements as prescribed in Sched. 1 and s.5. Even if no formal lease exists, there may be informal writings meeting the requirements and binding on the parties by reason of their actings, in which case para. (a) of this subsection will not apply (*Grieve* v. *Barr*, 1954 S.L.T. 261). In practice, however, it is unlikely that the statutory requirements will be met except in a formal lease. The effect of para. (b) is that all current leases must conform to Sched. 1 but s.5 (see subs. (6)) applies only to leases entered into on or after November 1, 1948.

Subss. (2) and (3)
In the absence of agreement the arbiter cannot introduce in the lease any provision outwith the scope of the first Schedule.

Subs. (4)
Deferment of the effective date of the award is left entirely to the arbiter's discretion. The arbiter's power to vary the rent in respect of any provision in his award is dealt with in s.14, while s.46 deals with claims by a landlord or tenant for default in maintenance or repair of fixed equipment prior to transfer of liabilities in terms of the arbiter's award.

Fixed equipment and insurance premiums

5.—(1) When a lease of an agricultural holding to which this section applies is entered into, a record of the condition of the fixed equipment on the holding shall be made forthwith, and on being so made shall be deemed to form part of the lease; and section 8 of this Act shall apply to the making of such a record and to the cost thereof as it applies to a record made under that section.

(2) There shall be deemed to be incorporated in every lease of an agricultural holding to which this section applies—

(a) an undertaking by the landlord that, at the commencement of the tenancy or as soon as is reasonably practicable thereafter, he will put the fixed equipment on the holding into a thorough state of repair, and will provide such buildings and other fixed equipment as will enable an occupier reasonably skilled in husbandry to maintain efficient production as respects both—

(i) the kind of produce specified in the lease, or (failing such specification) in use to be produced on the holding, and

(ii) the quality and quantity thereof,

and that he will during the tenancy effect such replacement or renewal of the buildings or other fixed equipment as may be rendered necessary by natural decay or by fair wear and tear; and

(b) a provision that the liability of the tenant in relation to the maintenance of fixed equipment shall extend only to a liability to maintain the fixed equipment on the holding in as good a state of repair (natural decay and fair wear and tear excepted) as it was in—

(i) immediately after it was put in repair as aforesaid, or

(ii) in the case of equipment provided, improved, replaced or renewed during the tenancy, immediately after it was so provided, improved, replaced or renewed.

(3) Nothing in subsection (2) above shall prohibit any agreement made between the landlord and the tenant after the lease has been entered into whereby one party undertakes to execute on behalf of the other, whether wholly at his own expense or wholly or partly at the expense of the other, any work which the other party is required to execute in order to fulfil his obligations under the lease.

(4) Any provision in a lease to which this section applies requiring the tenant to pay the whole or any part of the premium due under a fire insurance policy over any fixed equipment on the holding shall be null and void.

(5) Any question arising as to the liability of a landlord or tenant under this section shall be determined by arbitration.

(6) This section applies to any lease of an agricultural holding entered into on or after November 1, 1948.

DEFINITIONS

"agricultural holding": s.1(1).
"fixed equipment": s.85(1).
"landlord": s.85(1).
"lease": s.85(1).
"produce": s.85(1).
"tenant": s.85(1).

DERIVATIONS

Agricultural Holdings (Scotland) Act 1949, s.5.

GENERAL NOTE

See Gill, paras. 119–129, 136.

Subs. (1)

The expense of making a record, along with the absence of a penalty for failure to comply with this requirement, has had the result that the requirement is rarely met, although the existence of a record can be important in relation to the undertakings as to the condition of fixed equipment implied in all leases entered into after November 1, 1948 in terms of subs. (2). Where the record is being made, the provisions of s.8(3)(4)(6)–(9) will apply.

Subs. (2)(a)

These provisions impose on the landlord contractual obligations *ad factum praestandum*, breach of which will render him liable to the tenant in damages. *Mora* may not be fatal to a tenant's claim (see *Secretary of State for Scotland* v. *Sinclair*, 1960 S.L.C.R. 10) but it may be affected by negative prescription. The obligation arising at the commencement of the tenancy must be complied with as soon thereafter as circumstances, including the existing state of the fixed equipment, permit. "A thorough state of repair" would seem to imply a higher standard than the phrase "good and sufficient tenantable order" or words to that effect as sometimes used in leases and other contexts. The obligation for repair or renewal is a continuing one subsisting throughout the period of the lease and any extension thereof by tacit relocation. "Fair wear and tear" is construed in accordance with established common-law principles. The landlord's obligations are, however, limited to what is required for the purposes of the lease and the type of farming for which it was granted (*Taylor* v. *Burnett's Trustees*, 1966 S.L.C.R., p. 139. See also *Spencer-Nairn* v. *I.R.C.*, 1985 S.L.T. (Lands Ct.) 46). Again, it is requirements of a hypothetical occupier as a reasonably competent farmer which have to be fulfilled and not those of the particular tenant in possession.

The non-application of these provisions to pre-1948 leases (see subs. (6)) means that under these leases, unless they provide otherwise, the landlord cannot be forced to undertake renewal or replacement of fixed equipment worn out by natural decay or fair wear and tear. In such cases the rules of the common law determine the extent of the landlord's obligation.

Subs. (2)(b)

These provisions, unlike those affecting the landlord, do not depart from the rules of the common law. As the counterpart of the landlord's obligations as regards the fixed equipment the tenant's obligations will not be enforceable while the landlord is in default (*Austin* v. *Gibson*, 1979 S.L.T. (Land Ct.) 12). Prima facie the landlord's claim for a breach by the tenant will be the cost of restoring the items affected to the required condition (*Duke of Portland* v. *Wood's Trustees*, 1927 S.C.(H.L.)1).

Subs. (3)
This is the authority for the post-lease agreement very frequently adopted in the creation of a new tenancy to overcome the incompetence of contracting out of the section's provisions and impose on the tenant a full repairing liability. It is important to ensure that the lease has been executed by both parties before they sign the post-lease agreement. Execution of the two documents on the same day may make the effectiveness of the post-lease agreement a matter of proof, should its effectiveness be called into question.

Subs. (4)
This subsection prohibits a practice whereby landlords in pre-1948 leases required their tenants to insure or pay the insurance premiums in respect of the fixed equipment. It would appear that this prohibition cannot be overcome by a provision in a post-lease agreement under subs. (3). Section 6 deals with the case of a pre-1948 lease with such a provision.

Subs. (5)
The arbiter's power to vary the rent in respect of any provision in his award is dealt with in s.14.

Subs. (6)
Among the important effects of the rules regulating leases which came into force on November 1, 1948 are matters mentioned in respect of subss. (2) and (4).
Note: In terms of s.25(4) of the Agriculture (Safety, Health and Welfare Provisions) Act 1956 as amended in terms of Sched. 11, para. 8, subss. (2), (3) and (5) of s.5 apply where a notice under s.3 of that Act requires any works in the nature of fixed equipment to be executed on an agricultural holding.

Sums recovered under fire insurance policy

6. Where the tenant of an agricultural holding is responsible for payment of the whole or part of the premium due under a fire insurance policy in the name of the landlord over any buildings or other subjects included in the lease of the holding and the landlord recovers any sum under such policy in respect of the destruction of, or damage to, the buildings or other subjects by fire, the landlord shall be bound, unless the tenant otherwise agrees, to expend such sum on the rebuilding, repair, or restoration of the buildings or subjects so destroyed or damaged in such manner as may be agreed or, failing agreement, as may be determined by the Secretary of State.

DEFINITIONS
"agricultural holdings": s.1(1).
"building": s.85(1).
"landlord": s.85(1).
"lease": s.85(1).
"tenant": s.85(1).

DERIVATION
Agricultural Holdings (Scotland) Act 1949, s.23.

GENERAL NOTE
See Gill, paras. 128 and 675.
See note to s.5(4). This matter comes within the administrative jurisdiction of the Secretary of State and so is outwith the scope of arbitration.

Freedom of cropping and disposal of produce

7.—(1) Subject to subsections (2) and (5) below, the tenant of an agricultural holding shall, notwithstanding any custom of the country or the provisions of any lease or of any agreement respecting the disposal of crops or the method of cropping of arable lands, have full right, without incurring any penalty, forfeiture or liability,—

(a) to dispose of the produce of the holding, other than manure produced thereon;

(b) to practise any system of cropping of the arable land on the holding.

(2) Subsection (1) above shall not have effect unless, before exercising his rights thereunder or as soon as is practicable after exercising them, the tenant makes suitable and adequate provision—

(a) in the case of an exercise of the right to dispose of crops, to return to the holding the full equivalent manurial value to the holding of all crops sold off or removed from the holding in contravention of any such custom, lease or agreement; and

(b) in the case of an exercise of the right to practise any system of cropping, to protect the holding from injury or deterioration.

(3) If the tenant of an agricultural holding exercises his rights under subsection (1) above so as to injure or deteriorate, or to be likely to injure or deteriorate, the holding, the landlord shall have the following remedies, but no other—

(a) should the case so require, he shall be entitled to obtain an interdict restraining the exercise of the tenant's rights under that subsection in that manner;

(b) in any case, on the tenant quitting the holding on the termination of the tenancy the landlord shall be entitled to recover damages for any injury to or deterioration of the holding attributable to the exercise by the tenant of his rights under that subsection.

(4) For the purposes of any proceedings for an interdict brought under subsection (3)(a) above, the question whether a tenant is exercising, or has exercised, his rights under subsection (1) above in such a manner as to injure or deteriorate, or to be likely to injure or deteriorate the holding, shall be determined by arbitration; and a certificate of the arbiter as to his determination of any such question shall, for the purposes of any proceedings (including an arbitration) brought under this section, be conclusive proof of the facts stated in the certificate.

(5) Subsection (1) above shall not apply—

(a) in the case of a tenancy from year to year, as respects the year before the tenant quits the holding or any period after he has received notice to quit or given notice of intention to quit which results in his quitting the holding; or

(b) in any other case, as respects the year before the expiry of the lease.

(6)—

(a) In this section "arable land" does not include land in grass which, by the terms of a lease, is to be retained in the same condition throughout the tenancy;

(b) the reference in paragraph (a) above to the terms of a lease shall, where the Secretary of State has directed under section 9 of the 1949 Act or an arbiter has directed under that section or under section 9 of this Act that the lease shall have effect subject to modifications, be construed as a reference to the terms of the lease as so modified.

DEFINITIONS
"agricultural holding": s.1(1).
"landlord": s.85(1).
"lease": s.85(1).
"produce": s.85(1).
"tenant": s.85(1).
"termination": s.85(1).

DERIVATION
Agricultural Holdings (Scotland) Act 1949, s.12.
Agriculture Act 1958, Sched. 1, Pt. II, para. 23.

General Note
    See Gill, pp. 152–161. (For the corresponding English provision see the Agricultural Holdings Act 1986, s.15).

Subs. (1)
    This provision contains the basic right of the agricultural tenant to act as he sees fit in the disposal of the produce of the holding (other than manure) and the cropping of the arable land (defined in subs. (6) as excluding land required by the lease to remain in grass). These rights are unaffected by any provisions in the lease or any custom which would prevent or restrict their exercise. The statutory provision, however, does not make such provision in leases illegal or inoperative but merely absolves the tenant, in certain defined circumstances and subject to certain safeguards, from complying with provisions inconsistent with his rights (see *Gore-Brown Henderson's Trustees* v. *Grenfell*, 1968 S.L.T. 237).

Subs. (2)
    The pre-conditions prescribed for the tenant's exercise of his rights under subs. (1) are that he return to the holding the full manurial value of crops sold off in contravention of his lease or local custom and that in practising any system of cropping he take steps to protect the holding from injury or deterioration.

Subs. (3)
    The landlord's remedies, should the tenant exercise his rights disregarding the requirements of subs. (2), are (a) interdict and (b) damages exigible when the tenant leaves. It is doubtful if the award of damages in this case is within the jurisdiction of an arbiter (see Gill, para. 161 and authorities there cited).

Subs. (4)
    Interdict proceedings have to be taken in the court but the question of whether the tenant's actions are injuring or liable to injure or deteriorate the holding has to be determined by arbitration, the arbiter's certificate being conclusive for the purposes of the interdict proceedings or the damages claim.

Subs. (5)
    While it is considered desirable that a farm tenant should have freedom of action in the matters referred to during the currency of his tenancy, it is right that a landlord should be able to prescribe the condition in which he will recover the holding on the tenant's departure. Hence it is provided that the tenant's freedoms under subs. (1) are not to apply during the final year of the tenancy in the case of a lease running on tacit relocation and during any period after the issue of notice to quit in any other case. It is suggested by Gill (para. 156) that it is now unnecessary legislatively to distinguish between the two cases with the same minimum period of notice of termination applying in all tenancies.

Subs. (6)
    Para. (b) should be read along with s.9, under which the terms of a lease as regards land to be retained in grass may be varied in the manner thus prescribed.

Record of condition, etc., of holding

8.—(1) The landlord or the tenant of an agricultural holding may, at any time during the tenancy, require the making of a record of the condition of the fixed equipment on, and of the cultivation of, the holding.
    (2) The tenant may, at any time during the tenancy, require the making of a record of—
    (a) existing improvements carried out by him or in respect of the carrying out of which he has, with the consent in writing of his landlord, paid compensation to an outgoing tenant;
    (b) any fixtures or buildings which, under section 18 of this Act, he is entitled to remove.
    (3) A record under this section shall be made by a person to be appointed by the Secretary of State, and shall be in such form as may be prescribed.
    (4) A record made under this section shall show any consideration or allowances which have been given by either party to the other.

(5) Subject to section 5 of this Act, a record may, if the landlord or the tenant so requires, be made under this section relating to a part only of the holding or to the fixed equipment only.

(6) Any question or difference between the landlord and the tenant arising out of the making of a record under this section shall, on the application of the landlord or the tenant, be referred to the Land Court for determination by them.

(7) The cost of making a record under this section shall, in default of agreement between the landlord and the tenant, be borne by them in equal shares.

(8) The remuneration of the person appointed by the Secretary of State to make a record under this section shall be such amount as the Secretary of State may fix, and any other expenses of and incidental to the making of the record shall be subject to taxation by the auditor of the sheriff court, and that taxation shall be subject to review by the sheriff.

(9) The remuneration of the person appointed by the Secretary of State to make a record under this section shall be recoverable by that person from either the landlord or the tenant, but any amount paid by either of those parties in respect of—

(a) that remuneration, or

(b) any other expenses of and incidental to the making of the record,

in excess of the share payable by him under subsection (7) above of the cost of making the record, shall be recoverable by him from the other party.

DEFINITIONS

"agricultural holdings": s.1(1).
"buildings": s.85(1).
"fixed equipment": s.85(1).
"landlord": s.85(1).
"prescribed": s.85(1).
"tenant": s.85(1).

DERIVATIONS

Agricultural Holdings (Scotland) Act 1949, s.17.

GENERAL NOTE

See Gill, pp. 132–139. (For the corresponding English provision see the Agricultural Holdings Act 1986, s.22).

Subs. (1)

This provision is wider than s.5(1) in so far as it results that a Record can be called for at any time under any lease irrespective of its date and may cover the state of cultivation as well as that of the fixed equipment. But a record made during the currency of a lease does not, like a record made in compliance with s.5(1), form part of the lease.

Subs. (2)

Para. (a). For the payment of compensation by an incoming tenant, see s.35.

Subs. (3)

The recorder is not functioning as an arbiter and need not be a member of the panel of arbiters. For the form of record see the Agriculture Records (Scotland) Regulations 1948 (S.I. 1948 No. 2817) as amended by the Agriculture Records (Scotland) Amendment Regulations 1979 (S.I. 1979 No. 799).

Subs. (4)

This provision would apply where, for example, the landlord had supplied materials for repair work the tenant was obliged to carry out or had paid for some part of an improvement effected by the tenant.

Subs. (5)

A record made in compliance with s.5(1) must deal with all fixed equipment on the holding.

Subs. (6)
Disputes in this matter are referred to the Land Court and not to an arbiter.

Subss. (6)–(9)
These administrative provisions, like the provisions of subss. (3) and (4), apply also to records made in compliance with s.5(1).

Arbitration as to permanent pasture

9.—(1) Where under the lease of an agricultural holding, whether entered into before or after the commencement of this Act, provision is made for the maintenance of specified land, or a specified proportion of the holding, as permanent pasture, the landlord or the tenant may, by notice in writing served on the other party, demand a reference to arbitration under this Act of the question whether it is expedient in order to secure the full and efficient farming of the holding that the amount of land required to be maintained as permanent pasture should be reduced.

(2) On a reference under subsection (1) above the arbiter may by his award direct that the lease shall have effect subject to such modifications of its provisions as to land which is to be maintained as permanent pasture or is to be treated as arable land, and as to cropping, as may be specified in the direction.

(3) If the arbiter gives a direction under subsection (2) above reducing the area of land which is to be maintained as permanent pasture, he may also by his award direct that the lease shall have effect as if it provided that on quitting the holding on the termination of the tenancy the tenant should leave—

(a) as permanent pasture, or
(b) as temporary pasture sown with seeds mixture of such kind as may be specified in that direction,

(in addition to the area of land required by the lease, as modified by the direction, to be maintained as permanent pasture) a specified area of land not exceeding the area by which the land required to be maintained as permanent pasture has been reduced by the direction under subsection (2) above.

DEFINITIONS
"agricultural holding": s.1(1).
"landlord": s.85(1).
"lease": s.85(1).
"tenant": s.85(1).
"termination of tenancy": s.85(1).

DERIVATIONS
Agricultural Holdings (Scotland) Act 1949, s.9.

GENERAL NOTE
See Gill, pp. 163–164. (For the corresponding English provision see the Agricultural Holdings Act 1986, s.14).

Subs. (1)
While these provisions apply to leases irrespective of their date, the requirement to maintain an area of permanent pasture has now become uncommon in leases. The jurisdiction in the matter formerly belonged to the Secretary of State but since 1958 it has come under arbitration.

In the case of *Secretary of State* v. *Maclean*, 1950 S.L.C.R. 33 the phrase "full and efficient use for agriculture" occurring in s.57 of the Agriculture (Scotland) Act 1948 (concerning compulsory acquisition to secure full and efficient use of land) was interpreted as meaning "use of land as a commercial unit, *i.e.* use of land in the normal course of good farming by an active intelligent farmer."

There are no statutory definitions of "pasture" or "permanent pasture." The statement in s.93(1) of the 1949 Act that "pasture includes meadow" has not been included in the interpretation provisions of s.85(1) of this Act.

Subss. (2) and (3)
    These provisions fall to be read along with the provisions of ss.51 and 53(2). As shown by
s.53(2), the parties may achieve the result of an arbitration under s.9 by agreement in writing
and exclude compensation for improvements, just as it is excluded by s.51 for anything done
under the arbiter's direction under s.9.

Power of landlord to enter on holding

10. The landlord of an agricultural holding or any person authorised by
him may at all reasonable times enter on the holding for any of the following
purposes—
    (a) viewing the state of the holding;
    (b) fulfilling the landlord's responsibilities to manage the holding in
        accordance with the rules of good estate management;
    (c) providing, improving, replacing or renewing fixed equipment on the
        holding otherwise than in fulfilment of such responsibilities.

Definitions
    "agricultural holdings": s.1(1).
    "fixed equipment": s.85(1).
    "good estate management": s.85(2) and Sched. 5 to the Agriculture (Scotland) Act 1948.
    "landlord": s.85(1).

Derivations
    Agricultural Holdings (Scotland) Act 1949, s.18.

General Note
    See Gill, pp. 143–144. (For the corresponding English provision see the Agricultural Hold-
ings Act 1986, s.23).
    It appears that the landlord may have a common-law right to enter the holding and again the
lease may contain provisions for entry, but this provision puts the matter beyond doubt.
    Para. (c) covers work for which the landlord is responsible at common law where his
obligation has not been written into the lease (s.4 and para. 5 of Sched. 1) or work for which he
is responsible in terms of special provisions in a lease, or again work which he is doing in making
an improvement within the terms of s.15(1).
    It is doubtful if a landlord entering the holding under these provisions is entitled to handle the
tenant's livestock (see *Luss Estates Co.* v. *Firkin Farm Co.*, 1985 S.L.T. (Land Ct.) 17).

Bequest of lease

11.—(1) Subject to subsections (2) to (8) below, the tenant of an agricultural holding may, by will or other testamentary writing, bequeath his lease
of the holding to his son-in-law or daughter-in-law or to any one of the
persons who would be, or would in any circumstances have been, entitled to
succeed to the estate on intestacy by virtue of the Succession (Scotland) Act
1964.
    (2) A person to whom the lease of a holding is so bequeathed (in this
section referred to as "the legatee") shall, if he accepts the bequest, give
notice of the bequest to the landlord of the holding within 21 days after the
death of the tenant, or, if he is prevented by some unavoidable cause from
giving such notice within that period, as soon as practicable thereafter.
    (3) The giving of a notice under subsection (2) above shall import accep-
tance of the lease and, unless the landlord gives a counter-notice under
subsection (4) below, the lease shall be binding on the landlord and on the
legatee, as landlord and tenant respectively, as from the date of the death of
the deceased tenant.
    (4) Where notice has been given under subsection (2) above, the landlord
may within one month thereafter give to the legatee a counter-notice
intimating that he objects to receiving him as tenant under the lease.
    (5) If the landlord gives a counter-notice under subsection (4) above, the
legatee may make application to the Land Court for an order declaring him

to be tenant under the lease as from the date of the death of the deceased tenant.

(6) If, on the hearing of such an application, any reasonable ground of objection stated by the landlord is established to the satisfaction of the Land Court, they shall declare the bequest to be null and void, but in any other case they shall make an order in terms of the application.

(7) Pending any proceedings under this section, the legatee, with the consent of the executor in whom the lease is vested under section 14 of the Succession (Scotland) Act 1964, shall, unless the Land Court on cause shown otherwise direct, have possession of the holding.

(8) If the legatee does not accept the bequest, or if the bequest is declared null and void under subsection (6) above, the right to the lease shall be treated as intestate estate of the deceased tenant in accordance with Part I of the Succession (Scotland) Act 1964.

DEFINITIONS
"lease": s.85(1).
"landlord": s.85(1).
"tenant": s.85(1).

DERIVATIONS
Agricultural Holdings (Scotland) Act 1949, s.20.
Succession (Scotland) Act 1964, s.31(1), Sched. 2, paras. 19, 20, 21.

GENERAL NOTE
See Gill, paras. 570–583.

Subs. (1)
It appears that a bequest in terms of this provision should be to a single individual (*Kennedy* v. *Johnstone*, 1956 S.C. 39) and again that a general bequest of estate or residue as opposed to specific bequest of the lease may not be an effective exercise of the statutory power of bequest (*Reid's Trustees* v. *Macpherson*, 1975 S.L.T. 101 at 109).

The category of possible legatees as here prescribed is wider than that of the persons to whom, on the tenant's intestacy *quoad* his lease, the executor may make over the lease under s.16 of the 1964 Act. But in practice this difference is of limited importance. In a tenancy constituted by a formal lease there will usually be an express exclusion of assignees resulting that the tenant has contracted out of his right to bequeath the tenancy (see *Kennedy* v. *Johnstone*, above) thus making a bequest ineffective unless the landlord has agreed to it in the tenant's lifetime or accepts the legatee after his death. Again, even if the power of bequest is exercisable, s.25 results that on the succession to the lease of anyone other than a near relative of the tenant (defined in Sched. 2, Pt. 3, para. 1 as his or her spouse or child, natural or adopted) the tenancy can be terminated by an incontestable notice to quit taking effect at the appropriate term. Such a successor does not have the extended security of tenure enjoyed by his predecessor in the tenancy.

The case of *Kennedy* v. *Johnstone* (above) which establishes that a tenant can contract out of his power of bequest of his tenancy has also been regarded as giving some support to the view that the transmissibility of the tenancy can be wholly renounced by the inclusion in the lease of an express exclusion of all successors. Such a provision, if effective, renders inapplicable, in the particular case, the provisions of s.12 *infra* and the various related provisions of the 1964 Act (see Gill Chaps. 4 and 5 and para. 585 and the article "Agricultural Tenancies; the Exclusion of Successors": 1988 33 J.L.S. 384).

Subs. (2)
Written notice is not specified and in one instance verbal notice by telephone was conceded by the landlord to be effective (*Irving* v. *Church of Scotland General Trustees*, 1960 S.L.C.R. 16). In practice, however, written notice by recorded delivery should be given to the person or persons ascertained to be the present owners of the property. There are reports of Land Court rulings on the question of "unavoidable course" as a reason for failure to give notice timeously (see *Mackinnon* v. *Martin*, 1958 S.L.C.R. 19 where the plea succeeded and *Wright* v. *Marquis of Lothian's Trustees*, 1952 S.L.C.R. 25 and *Thomson* v. *Lyall*, 1966 S.L.C.R. at p. 136 being cases in which it failed). It may be noted that "practicable" has been substituted for "possible" in the concluding phrase of this subsection but presumably it is considered that this variation in wording in a consolidating act leaves the meaning and effect of the provision unchanged. With

the Court of Session decision in *Garvie's Trustees* v. *Still*, 1972 S.L.T. 29 emphasising the limits of the Land Court's jurisdiction as resting entirely on statutory provision, it must now be accepted that the only functions of the Land Court under this section are to determine whether in terms of subs. (6) a reasonable ground of objection to the legatee as tenant has been stated by the landlord and to deal with the matter of interim possession under subs. (7). Neither the validity of the bequest nor the effectiveness of the notification to the landlord is within its jurisdiction (see Gill, paras. 605 and 667).

Subs. (3)

If notice to the landlord is duly given and not met by counter-notice under subs. (4) the legatee becomes tenant as from the date of the late tenant's death. If a legatee gives notice late and cannot show unavoidable cause for the delay he loses the right to the tenancy in a question with the landlord. But as the notice, although given late, implies his acceptance of the lease the tenancy interest comes to an end instead of becoming intestate estate available for transfer by the executor in terms of s.16 of the 1964 Act as referred to in s.12(1) (*Coats* v. *Logan*, 1985 S.L.T. 221, O.H.T.). As the terms of s.16(2) of the 1964 Act stand, this result cannot be avoided by the legatee's subsequently renouncing the tenancy.

Subs. (4)

While written counter-notice is not specified, counter-notice in writing should in practice be given by recorded delivery.

Subs. (5)

No time limit is prescribed for the tenant making application to the Land Court. It has been suggested that should the tenant's application be long delayed the landlord may take the initiative in bringing the matter before the court. There being, however, no statutory warrant for this course, any action by the landlord should be taken in the Sheriff Court. Pending the Land Court's decision whether the landlord has reasonable ground of objection to the legatee, the tenancy interest remains vested in the tenant's executor by Confirmation in terms of s.14(1) of the 1964 Act. If, however, the landlord's objection is rejected, the legatee becomes tenant as from the date of the tenant's death.

Subs. (6)

The grounds of objection must be personal to the legatee, the landlord not being entitled to found on considerations such as his need for vacant possession of the land or his ability to improve its standard of husbandry (*Fraser* v. *Murray's Trustees*, 1954 S.L.C.R. 10). On the other hand, it has been recognised that the landlord is entitled to have a tenant of reputable character with the necessary agricultural knowledge or skill and adequate financial resources to farm the particular holding. Alcoholism or convictions for serious crimes but not conviction for some minor offence would be regarded as a reasonable objection (*Luss Estate Co.* v. *Campbell*, 1973 S.L.C.R. App. 96). Again youth or inexperience will not disqualify a legatee who is in a position to get the necessary advice and assistance (see *Macrae* v. *Macdonald*, 1986 S.L.C.R. 69 (D.C.) and *Dunsinnon Estate Trustees* v. *Alexander*, 1978 S.L.C.R. App. 146). However, his performance in farming elsewhere, or on the farm itself, if he has had interim possession under subs. (7), will be relevant (see *Dunsinnon Estate Trustees* v. *Alexander*). His financial resources will not be regarded as inadequate because they are derived, in part, at least, from bank loans or similar sources (*Reid* v. *Duffus Estate*, 1955 S.L.C.R. 13).

Subs. (7)

The vesting of the lease in the executor, whose consent to interim possession is required, assumes that the executor has confirmed to the tenancy interest as part of the late tenant's estate. While the executor's consent would not normally be withheld, the landlord may be able to show cause why interim possession should be refused (see Gill, para. 579).

Subs. (8)

The provisions of the 1964 Act directly relevant are those of s.16 under which the executor, except with the landlord's consent, can dispose of the lease only to someone entitled to succeed to the late tenant's estate or part thereof or to claim legal rights or prior rights, therefrom. This represents a more limited class than that of the parties qualified to receive a bequest of the lease where that is permissible. Again, however, it is important from the point of view of security of tenure that the beneficiary selected to acquire the lease should if possible be a near relative as mentioned in connection with subs. (1).

It should be noted here that s.16(8) of the 1964 Act, as amended in terms of para. 24(c) of Sched. 11, makes it clear that when there is a valid bequest of a lease, vesting in the executor under s.14 of that Act, does not prevent the operation, in relation to the legatee, of subss. (2)–(8) of this section.

Right of landlord to object to acquirer of lease

12.—(1) A person to whom the lease of an agricultural holding is transferred under section 16 of the Succession (Scotland) Act 1964 (referred to in this section as "the acquirer") shall give notice of the acquisition to the landlord of the holding within 21 days after the date of the acquisition, or, if he is prevented by some unavoidable cause from giving such notice within that period, as soon as is practicable thereafter and, unless the landlord gives a counter-notice under subsection (2) below, the lease shall be binding on the landlord and on the acquirer, as landlord and tenant respectively, as from the date of the acquisition.

(2) Within one month after receipt of a notice given under subsection (1) above the landlord may give a counter-notice to the acquirer intimating that the landlord objects to receive him as tenant under the lease; and not before the expiry of one month from the giving of the counter-notice the landlord may make application to the Land Court for an order terminating the lease.

(3) On an application under subsection (2) above, the Land Court shall, if they are satisfied that the landlord has established a reasonable ground of objection, make an order terminating the lease, to take effect as from such term of Whitsunday or Martinmas as they may specify.

(4) Pending any proceedings under this section, the acquirer, with the consent of the executor in whom the lease is vested under section 14 of the Succession (Scotland) Act 1964 shall, unless the Land Court on cause shown otherwise direct, have possession of the holding.

(5) Termination of the lease under this section shall be treated, for the purposes of Parts IV and V of this Act (compensation), as termination of the acquirer's tenancy of the holding; but nothing in this section shall entitle him to compensation for disturbance.

DEFINITIONS
"agricultural holdings": s.1(1).
"landlord": s.85(1).
"lease": s.85(1).
"tenant": s.85(1).
"termination of tenancy": s.85(1).

DERIVATIONS
Agricultural Holdings (Scotland) Act 1949, s.21.
Successions Act (Scotland) Act 1964, Sched. 2, para. 22.

GENERAL NOTE
See Gill, Chap. 34.

Subss. (1) and (2)
The substantive provisions of the 1964 Act concerning intestate succession to a tenancy interest are fully explained in the text referred to. This subsection, proceeding on the same lines as the corresponding provisions in s.11, prescribes the steps to be taken by the acquirer, as the intestate successor is called, to intimate his claim to the lease to the landlord and, subject to the landlord's right of objection, to become tenant as from the date of his acquisition.

It should be noted that in contrast with the situation where the lease is effectively bequeathed, the successor's tenure of the tenancy runs not from the date of the late tenant's death but from the date of the successor's acquisition. Again the acquisition will have to be effected by some document of transfer from an executor who has confirmed to the tenant interest. There is no automatic divestiture of the executor such as takes place in the case of a bequest. It is doubtful whether the provisions of s.15(2) of the 1964 Act for the transfer of heritable property to a successor by docket on the confirmation or certificate of confirmation apply to leases but the terms of Sched. 1 to that Act could readily be adapted to provide a simple form of transfer. Differing from the position where a legatee is subject to objection by the landlord, the landlord objecting to an acquirer is authorised, not less than a month after giving counter-notice, to apply to the Land Court for an order terminating the lease.

Subs. (3)

The same considerations as apply under s.11(6) will influence the court in deciding whether or not the landlord has a reasonable ground of objection to the acquirer. A decision in the affirmative, however, results in an order terminating the tenancy, the executor having no further power of disposal. The Term and Quarter Days (Scotland) Act 1990, s.1(1)(a) and (2)(a), now defines "Whitsunday" and "Martinmas" as meaning May 28 and November 28 respectively for the purposes of any enactment or rule of law. Normally the court's order will take effect at the next term day but there would appear to be a discretion to defer its effect to a later term if circumstances justify this course.

Subs. (4)

This provides (as does s.11(7) in the case of a legatee) for interim possession by the acquirer pending proceedings. The reference to the lease as being vested in the executor seems at first sight, at least, inconsistent with the fact that a transfer of the lease to the acquirer will have been granted by the executor and intimated to the landlord, whose objection, if successful, has the result that the executor has no further concern with or interest in the tenancy. It appears, however, that the transfer to the acquirer must be regarded as subject to a suspensive condition, purified only if the landlord fails timeously to object to the acquirer as tenant, or having objected, is unsuccessful in the Land Court proceedings.

Subs. (5)

While the acquirer to whom the landlord successfully objects never attains the status of tenant, he is treated for certain purposes, such as compensation for improvements, as a tenant going out on the termination of the lease. (As to the different position of an unsuccessful legatee see Gill, para. 604.) The acquirer, however, is not entitled to compensation for disturbance, which, as a general rule, is payable only when a holding is vacated in compliance with a notice to quit from the landlord (see s.43).

Variation of rent

Variation of rent

13.—(1) Subject to subsection (8) below, the landlord or the tenant of an agricultural holding may, whether the tenancy was created before or after the commencement of this Act, by notice in writing served on the other party, demand a reference to arbitration of the question what rent should be payable in respect of the holding as from the next day after the date of the notice on which the tenancy could have been terminated by notice to quit (or notice of intention to quit) given on that date, and the matter shall be referred accordingly.

(2) On a reference under subsection (1) above, the arbiter shall determine, in accordance with subsections (3) to (7) below the rent properly payable in respect of the holding as from the "next day" mentioned in subsection (1) above.

(3) For the purposes of this section the rent properly payable in respect of a holding shall normally be the rent at which, having regard to the terms of the tenancy (other than those relating to rent), the holding might reasonably be expected to be let in the open market by a willing landlord to a willing tenant, there being disregarded (in addition to the matters referred to in subsection (5) below) any effect on rent of the fact that the tenant is in occupation of the holding.

(4) Where the evidence available to the arbiter is in his opinion insufficient to enable him to determine the rent properly payable or he is of the view that the open market for rents of comparable subjects in the surrounding area is distorted by scarcity of lets or by other factors, the rent properly payable for the purposes of this section shall be the rent which he would expect to be paid, in a market which was not affected by such distortion, having particular regard to the following—

(a) information about open market rents of comparable subjects outside the surrounding area;

(b) the entire range of offers made as regards any lease of subjects which are comparable after regard is had to the terms of that lease;

(c) sitting tenants' rents fixed by agreement for subjects in the surrounding area which are comparable after regard is had to any element attributable to goodwill between landlord and tenant or to similar considerations; and

(d) the current economic conditions in the relevant sector of agriculture.

(5) The arbiter shall not take into account any increase in the rental value of the holding which is due to improvements—

(a) so far as—

(i) they have been executed wholly or partly at the expense of the tenant (whether or not that expense has been or will be reimbursed by a grant out of moneys provided by Parliament) without equivalent allowance or benefit having been made or given by the landlord in consideration of their execution; and

(ii) they have not been executed under an obligation imposed on the tenant by the terms of his lease;

(b) which have been executed by the landlord, in so far as the landlord has received or will receive grants out of moneys provided by Parliament in respect of the execution thereof,

nor fix the rent at a higher amount than would have been properly payable if those improvements had not been so executed.

(6) The continuous adoption by the tenant of a standard of farming or a system of farming more beneficial to the holding than the standard or system required by the lease or, in so far as no system of farming is so required, than the system of farming normally practised on comparable holdings in the district, shall be deemed, for the purposes of subsection (5) above, to be an improvement executed at his expense.

(7) The arbiter shall not fix the rent at a lower amount by reason of any dilapidation or deterioration of, or damage to, fixed equipment or land caused or permitted by the tenant.

(8) Subject to subsection (9) below, a reference to arbitration under subsection (1) above shall not be demanded in circumstances which are such that any increase or reduction of rent made in consequence thereof would take effect as from a date earlier than the expiry of 3 years from the latest in time of the following—

(a) the commencement of the tenancy;

(b) the date as from which there took effect a previous variation of rent (under this section or otherwise);

(c) the date as from which there took effect a previous direction under this section that the rent should continue unchanged.

(9) There shall be disregarded for the purposes of subsection (8) above—

(a) a variation of rent under section 14 of this Act;

(b) an increase of rent under section 15(1) of this Act;

(c) a reduction of rent under section 31 of this Act.

DEFINITIONS

"agricultural holdings": s.1(1).
"improvement": s.85(1).
"landlord": s.85(1).
"lease": s.85(1).
"notice of intention to quit": s.21(2).
"notice to quit": s.21(2).
"tenant": s.85(1).

DERIVATIONS

Agricultural Holdings (Amendment) (Scotland) Act 1983, s.2.
Agricultural Holdings (Scotland) Act 1949, s.7.

GENERAL NOTE
See Gill, paras. 198–220a. (For the corresponding English provision see the Agricultural Holdings Act 1986, s.12 and Sched. 2).

Subss. (1) and (2)
Security of tenure for the tenant resulting in a tenancy's being able to continue indefinitely beyond its prescribed duration arrangements are necessary to keep rents in line with changing conditions. This is achieved by enabling either party to serve notice on the other, demanding arbitration as to the rent which should be payable as from the next day after the date on which the tenancy could have been terminated on due notice being given. In effect, therefore, a rent review is obtainable on the same period of notice as is required in terms of s.21(3) for termination of the tenancy, *i.e.* not less than one year and not more than two years. It follows that unless there is provision in the lease for a break, the rent cannot be varied during the prescribed duration of the tenancy, but only as from its expiry or subsequently as from the appropriate term where the tenancy is continuing on tacit relocation. While the matter is dealt with in subs. (8), it may be noted here that the rent of a holding cannot be reviewed under the provisions of this section more frequently than at intervals of three years.

Subs. (3)
This subsection contains the basic directions for the determination of the rent by the arbiter. Under the 1949 Act as originally framed the arbiter had a wide discretion and could take into account such considerations as the "sitting tenant" factor or the tenant's personal circumstances (see, *e.g. Guthe* v. *Broatch*, 1956 S.C. 132). The basis of assessment was more akin to a fair rent as applying under crofting legislation than to the market rent as introduced by amendments made by the 1958 Act. An exposition of the operation of the open market basis for determining a rent is to be found in certain decisions of the Land Court functioning in place of the arbiter under provisions now contained in s.60(2) (see *Secretary of State* v. *Young*, 1960 S.L.C.R. 31 and *Crown Estate Commissioners* v. *Gunn*, 1961 S.L.C.R. 173). As this subsection indicates, account has to be taken of the terms of the lease other than rent. Features such as a full repairing obligation on the tenant, a requirement to reside on the holding, a prohibition on letting grazings or a requirement to maintain a bound sheep stock could affect the rent a hypothetical tenant would be prepared to pay (see, *e.g. Secretary of State* v. *Davidson*, 1969 S.L.T. (Land Ct.) 7, *Strathclyde R.C.* v. *Arneil*, 1987 S.L.C.R. 44 and *British Alcan Aluminium Co.* v. *Shaw*, 1987 S.L.C.R. 1). Difficulty, however, has in many cases been experienced in arriving at the rent appropriate for a particular holding, there being in some districts at least few lets of comparable farms being negotiated and increasing competition for any available tenancies. Thus rents tended to be fixed on the basis of a hypothetical open market unfairly distorted in favour of the landlords (see *Kilmarnock Estates* v. *Tenants*, 1977 S.L.C.R. App. 141 and *Witham* v. *Stockdale*, 1981 S.L.T. (Land Ct.) 27). To remedy, or at least improve, the situation in this respect, the 1983 Act introduced the provisions now contained in subs. (4).
In a recent case the Land Court decided that parties to an agricultural lease cannot contract out of the statutory provisions for review of rent which are based on the open market criterion discounted for scarcity and intended to achieve a degree of consistency in farm renting. Accordingly they held to be invalid and ineffective a post-lease agreement requiring the rent of the holding to be reviewed annually by reference to the retail price index (*Moll* v. *Macgregor*, 1990 S.L.T. (Land Ct.) 59: also reported *sub nom. Wallace* v. *Moll*, 1989 S.L.C.R. 21.) In that case the lease was running on tacit relocation. In an earlier case of *Duncan* v. *Anderson*, 1985 S.L.C.R. 1 it was indicated, at p. 14, that provisions superseding the statutory provisions could be enforceable during the currency of the lease. There are, however, indications in the court's decision in the case of *Moll* (see p. 66 of the S.L.T. Report) that that view is no longer held.

Subs. (4)
This provision applies where the arbiter considers he has insufficient evidence to determine a rent or that the open market for rents of comparable subjects in the district on which he would normally base his decision is distorted by scarcity of lets or other factors. The arbiter is directed in such circumstances to fix a rent which he would expect to be paid in a market unaffected by distortion having regard to certain factors listed. Of these factors the first, being information about open market rents of comparable subjects in other districts, is useful where local conditions are not too dissimilar. Secondly, where there is evidence of a recent let of a comparable subject, the arbiter should consider not merely the rent offered by the successful applicant for the tenancy but also the whole range of offers, as the successful offer may involve an element of premium which should be disregarded. The terms of the respective leases must of

course be kept in view. Thirdly, transactions with sitting tenants are to be relevant provided that special factors such as mutual goodwill can be eliminated. In practice there are likely to be more of these transactions taking place than there will be new lets. Finally, the current economic condition in the relevant section of agriculture should be considered. The matters referred to in the subsection are, of course, not exhaustive of the factors or elements which may enter into the arbiter's determination of an appropriate rent for a holding. By way of precedents in law, and in some cases also as comparables in relation to the holding under consideration, arbiters will find guidance in the reports of Land Court decisions. Some of these will have arisen under the court's appellate jurisdiction in rent cases introduced by the 1983 Act and now provided for by s.61(2) and Sched. 7, para. 22. In other cases, particularly those decided before the 1983 Provisions took effect, the court will have been functioning as tribunal of first instance where parties have invoked the provisions of s.60(2) to refer their dispute to the Land Court instead of to an arbiter. Among recent Land Court cases which illustrate the application and working of the provisions of this subsection and related provisions are the following: *Earl of Seafield* v. *Stewart*, 1985 S.L.T. (Land Ct.) 35; *Kinnaird Trust* v. *Boyne*, 1985 S.L.C.R. 19; *Aberdeen Endowments Trust* v. *Will*, 1985 S.L.T. (Land Ct.) 23; *Buccleuch Estates* v. *Kennedy*, 1986 S.L.C.R. App. 1; *British Alcan Aluminium Co.* v. *Shaw*, 1987 S.L.C.R. 1; *Shand* v. *Christie's Trs.*, 1987 S.L.C.R. 29; *Towns* v. *Anderson*, 1989 S.L.T. (Land Ct.) 17.

Where the rent review has been undertaken by an arbiter appointed by the Secretary of State as opposed to one nominated by agreement of the parties (see Sched. 7, para. 1) the arbiter's award, which must disclose his findings in fact and the reasons for his decision, has, since the passing of the 1983 Act, been required to be made available to the Secretary of State as well as to the parties (see Sched. 7, para. 10) and a register of such awards can be seen at the Scottish Record Office. This arrangement was introduced with a view to achieving greater consistency in awards in rent arbitrations and must, as time goes on, provide an increasingly valuable source of information and guidance for arbiters undertaking rent reviews as well as for parties and their advisers involved in review proceedings.

Subs. (5)

While the application of this provision is not restricted to improvements for which the tenant on his outgoing can claim compensation under Pt. IV of this Act (*Towns* v. *Anderson*, 1989 S.L.T. (Land Ct.) 17), it does not apply to improvements made by the tenant or his predecessor under a previous lease (*Kilmarnock Estates* v. *Barr*, 1969 S.L.T. (Land Ct.) 10).

Where a rent is being reviewed on a holding where there are improvements affected by these provisions, the approved course appears to be to assess the rental value on the assumption that none of these improvements existed (*Mackenzie* v. *Bocardo S.A.*, 1986 S.L.C.R. 53, p. 64).

There are certain provisions in other Acts about matters which the arbiter is to disregard in assessing the rent of a holding. Under s.16 of the Agriculture Act 1986, as amended in terms of para. 44 of Sched. 11, the tenant is protected from being rented on a milk quota which he himself had transferred on to the holding (for an explanation of the arrangements applying according to circumstances see Gill, para. 207).

Under the Housing (Scotland) Act 1987, ss.246 and 256(4), an assessment of the rent during the period in which grant conditions apply should disregard so much of the value of the house or of any improvement works as is attributable to the grant. Again, the arbiter is directed by s.14A(1) of the Open Cast Coal Act 1958, as amended in terms of para. 11 of Sched. 11, to disregard any increase or diminution of rental value attributable to occupation of the holding or any part of it by the British Coal Corporation.

Subs. (6)

The tenant's claim for what is popularly known as High Farming is dealt with in s.44. It is not often that the conditions of that section are met but when this happens it is appropriate that the resulting improvement for which the tenant is responsible should not be reflected in his liability for rent.

Subs. (7)

Where the tenant has held successive leases the only dilapidations, *etc.* relevant to this provision will be those occurring during the current lease (*Kilmarnock Estates* v. *Barr*, 1969 S.L.T. (Land Ct.) 10), which the arbiter should ignore in assessing the rental value of the holding.

Subs. (8)

Before the passing of the 1983 Act the application of the statutory machinery for rent reviews was on a quinquennial basis. The 1983 Act introduced a triennial basis, which should result in rents being kept more closely in line with varying market trends and make it easier for an arbiter to arrive, as he should endeavour to do, at a rent which reflects the fact that it is to remain in force till the time for another review arrives.

As regards para. (a), the better view appears to be that the reference is to the commencement of the current lease and not to that of any previous lease between the same parties.

One effect of para. (b) is that if parties agree a revision of a rent without resorting to arbitration, the statutory machinery cannot be invoked so as to take effect less than three years after the agreed rent became operative.

Para. (c) shows that an unsuccessful attempt to have the rent varied by the statutory machinery has the result that three years must elapse before a variation can be effected in that way. It is perhaps not clear whether an agreement by the parties that the rent should remain unchanged would have the same effect. It had been indicated that the availability of the statutory machinery at intervals, as prescribed, does not prevent parties agreeing to an earlier review of the rent (*Boyd* v. *MacDonald*, 1958 S.L.C.R. 10 at p. 12) but in *Moll* v. *Macgregor* (*above*) at p. 66, the Land Court appears to have taken the view that an agreement in the lease or other document to vary the frequency of rent reviews would be unenforceable. In the past the general practice in lets for a term of years has been to make provision for breaks coinciding with the quinquennial, or as it is now, triennial availability of the statutory machinery.

Subs. (9)

In each of the cases referred to, what is taking place is not a review of the rent as a whole, which occurs when the statutory machinery is invoked, but an adjustment to take account of some change affecting the holding or the terms on which it is let.

Arbitrations under sections 4 and 5

14. Where it appears to an arbiter—

(a) on a reference under section 4 of this Act that, by reason of any provision which he is required by that section to include in his award, or

(b) on a reference under section 5 of this Act that, by reason of any provision included in his award,

it is equitable that the rent of the holding should be varied, he may vary the rent accordingly.

DEFINITIONS

"holding": s.1(1).

DERIVATIONS

Agricultural Holdings (Scotland) Act 1949, s.6(3).

GENERAL NOTE

See Gill, paras. 127 and 221. (For the corresponding English provision see the Agricultural Holdings Act 1986, s.8(4)).

Para. (a)

It would appear that it is only a provision which the arbiter is required to include in his award that can justify a variation and that a variation in respect of some other provision included with the agreement of the parties in terms of s.4(3) is not competent.

Increase of rent for certain improvements by landlord

15.—(1) Where the landlord of an agricultural holding has, whether before or after the commencement of this Act, carried out on the holding an improvement (whether or not one for the carrying out of which compensation is provided for under Part IV of this Act)—

(a) at the request of, or in agreement with, the tenant,

(b) in pursuance of an undertaking given by the landlord under section 39(3) of this Act, or

(c) in compliance with a direction given by the Secretary of State under powers conferred on him by or under any enactment,

subject to subsections (2) and (3) below, the rent of the holding shall, if the landlord by notice in writing served on the tenant within 6 months from the completion of the improvement so requires, be increased as from the completion of the improvement by an amount equal to the increase in the rental value of the holding attributable to the carrying out of the improvement.

(2) Where any grant has been made to the landlord out of moneys provided by Parliament, in respect of an improvement to which subsection (1) above applies, the increase in rent provided for by that subsection shall be reduced proportionately.

(3) Any question arising between the landlord and the tenant in the application of this section shall be determined by arbitration.

DEFINITIONS
"agricultural holdings": s.1(1).
"improvements": s.85(1).
"landlord": s.85(1).
"tenant": s.85(1).

DERIVATIONS
Agricultural Holdings (Scotland) Act 1949, s.13.

GENERAL NOTE
See Gill, paras. 224–227. (For the corresponding English provision see the Agricultural Holdings Act 1986, s.13).

Subs. (1)
The improvements covered by this provision are not restricted to improvements for which, if the tenant had made them, he could claim compensation at his outgoing. At least where there is agreement between the parties as contemplated in para. (a), anything enhancing the rental value of the holding will qualify for a rent increase.

In terms of s.25(5) of the Agriculture (Safety, Health and Welfare Provisions) Act 1956, works executed in compliance with that Act are deemed landlord's improvements for this purpose.

Para. (b) refers to the situation provided for in s.39 where the landlord elects to carry out himself an improvement which the tenant was proposing to make.

Subs. (2)
Another ground for reduction or abatement of the increase of rent can arise where the improvement takes the form of a livestock-rearing land improvement scheme under the Hill Farming Act 1946 as amended by the 1949 Act. In terms of s.7(3) of the 1946 Act the Secretary of State, if reducing the grant on the ground that the work has been badly done, may direct that the increase of rent be restricted accordingly, with retrospective effect if an increase in rent has already taken effect.

In terms of the Open Cast Coal Act 1958, s.14A(1) and (9), as amended in terms of the Housing and Planning Act 1986, Sched. A, para. 5 and in terms of para. 12 of Sched. 11, the landlord's right to claim an increase in rent in respect of an improvement is not to be prejudiced by the effect of any open-cast coal operations taking place.

Termination of tenancy

Leases not terminated by variation of terms, etc.

16. The lease of an agricultural holding shall not be brought to an end, and accordingly neither party shall be entitled to bring proceedings to terminate the lease or, except with the consent of the other party, to treat it as at an end, by reason only that any new term has been added to the lease or that any terms of the lease (including the rent payable) have been varied or revised in pursuance of this Act.

DEFINITIONS
"agricultural holding": s.1(1).
"lease": s.85(1).

DERIVATIONS
Agricultural Holdings (Scotland) Act 1949, s.10.

    See Gill, paras. 99–101.
    At common law the terms of a lease may be so altered by agreement of the parties that a new
tenancy contract is regarded as having been created, a result which can be significant in relation
to statutory provisions the application of which is dependent on the date when a lease was
entered into (see, *e.g.* s.5 and ss.68–70). Cases illustrating the point are *Tufnell* v. *Nether
Whitehaugh Co.*, 1977 S.L.T. (Land Ct.) 14 and *Mackie* v. *Gardner*, 1973 S.L.T. (Land Ct.) 11.
The intention of the section appears to be to make it clear that variation in the terms of leases
made in pursuance of provisions of the Act does not result in the creation of a new tenancy
contract.
    Differing from s.10 of the 1949 Act which it replaces, the section refers to variation or
revision "in pursuance of this Act" as contrasted with "in pursuance of any of the foregoing
provisions of this Act in that behalf," as the 1949 provision was worded. It would appear,
however, that this difference has no practical significance, the only relevant provisions being in
ss.2(1), 4, 5(2) and (3), 9, 13, 14 and 15, all of which replace provisions contained within the first
nine sections of the 1949 Act.

Prohibition of removal of manure, etc., after notice to quit, etc.

17. Where, in respect of an agricultural holding, notice to quit is given by
the landlord or notice of intention to quit is given by the tenant, the tenant
shall not, subject to any agreement to the contrary, at any time after the date
of the notice, sell or remove from the holding any manure or compost, or any
hay, straw or roots grown in the last year of the tenancy, unless and until he
has given the landlord or the incoming tenant a reasonable opportunity of
agreeing to purchase them on the termination of the tenancy at their fair
market value, or at such other value as is provided by the lease.

DEFINITIONS
    "agricultural holding": s.1(1).
    "landlord": s.85(1).
    "notice of intention to quit": s.85(1).
    "notice to quit": s.85(1).
    "tenant": s.85(1).
    "termination of tenancy": s.85(1).

DERIVATIONS
    Agricultural Holdings (Scotland) Act 1949, s.13.

GENERAL NOTE
    See Gill, paras. 440–445.
    As the wording of the section shows, contracting out is permissible, with the result that the
terms of the lease may supersede those of the section. It is suggested by Gill (*cf.* Connell's
Agricultural Holdings (Scotland) Acts (6th ed.) p. 122) that the words "the last year" be
interpreted to mean the last calendar year of the tenant's agricultural operations, being the only
basis on which, in the case of a Whitsunday outgoing, the separation of the tenant's last crop
could be covered. On what constitutes "a reasonable opportunity," see *Barbour* v. *McDowall*,
1914 S.C. 844. The opportunity may be given either to the landlord or to the incoming tenant; it
is not necessary that both should have it.
    If the lease makes no provision for the value at which the items specified in the section are to
be taken over, then, failing agreement, the matter will have to be dealt with by an arbitration
under the Act if it is the landlord who is taking over. If, however, an incoming tenant is
acquiring the goods, the arbitration provisions of the Act do not apply and any dispute as to
value will have to be settled by a private remit to a valuer if it is not to involve litigation. The fair
market value, being what the tenant could obtain for the items in question were he free to
remove them, may be greater than their value for consumption on the holding (see *Williamson*
v. *Stewart*, 1912 S.C. 235). If the lease provides for a take-over at valuation the arbitration will
be a non-statutory one even if the landlord is the party taking over (s.61(7)).

Tenant's right to remove fixtures and buildings

18.—(1) Subject to subsections (2) to (4) below, and to section 40(4)(a) of
this Act—

   (a) any engine, machinery, fencing or other fixture affixed to an agricultural holding by the tenant thereof; and

   (b) any building (other than one in respect of which the tenant is entitled to compensation under this Act or otherwise) erected by him on the holding,

not being a fixture affixed or a building erected in pursuance of some obligation in that behalf, or instead of some fixture or building belonging to the landlord, shall be removable by the tenant at any time during the continuance of the tenancy or before the expiry of 6 months, or such longer period as may be agreed, after the termination of the tenancy and shall remain his property so long as he may remove it by virtue of this subsection.

(2) The right conferred by subsection (1) above shall not be exercisable in relation to a fixture or building unless the tenant—

   (a) has paid all rent owing by him and has performed or satisfied all his other obligations to the landlord in respect of the holding; and

   (b) has, at least one month before whichever is the earlier of the exercise of the right and the termination of the tenancy, given to the landlord notice in writing of his intention to remove the fixture or building.

(3) If, before the expiry of the period of notice specified in subsection (2)(b) above, the landlord gives to the tenant a counter-notice in writing electing to purchase a fixture or building comprised in the notice, subsection (1) above shall cease to apply to that fixture or building, but the landlord shall be liable to pay to the tenant the fair value thereof to an incoming tenant of the holding.

(4) In the removal of a fixture or building by virtue of subsection (1) above, the tenant shall not do to any other building or other part of the holding any avoidable damage, and immediately after the removal shall make good all damage so occasioned.

DEFINITIONS
"agricultural holdings": s.1(1).
"building": s.85(1).
"landlord": s.85(1).
"tenant": s.85(1).
"termination of tenancy": s.85(1).

DERIVATIONS
Agricultural Holdings (Scotland) Act 1949, s.14.

GENERAL NOTE
   See Gill, Chap. 9. (For the corresponding English provision see the Agricultural Holdings Act 1986, s.10).

Subs. (1)
   Contracting out of these provisions is permissible (see *Premier Dairies* v. *Garlick* [1920] 2 Ch. 17), but, when operative, the provisions supersede the rules of common law applying to a tenant's trade fixtures. The fixtures or buildings which the tenant is given a statutory right to remove must be additional to anything provided by the landlord at the start of the tenancy and must be affixed or erected by the tenant without obligation. The term "building" appears to be used in a wide general sense and "fixtures" is not restricted to those having an agricultural purpose. The tenant's right of removal does not apply to any building for which he will be entitled to compensation at his outgoing. It could, however, apply if the tenant has carried out during the tenancy an improvement in the form of a building without giving the landlord due notice and so is not entitled to compensation (see s.38).

Subs. (2), para. (b)
   This provision takes account of the fact that the right of removal is exercisable at any time during the tenancy and not merely at or after its termination.

Subs. (3)
   The fair value to an incoming tenant, who may be hypothetical, may be less than the outgoing

tenant could obtain for the items if free to remove them. Failing agreement, the value will fall to be determined by arbitration under the Act.

Subs. (4)

At common law the prospect of damage to the heritable property being caused by the removal of a fixture could exclude the tenant's right of removal, but this provision contemplates damage being done and made good.

Payment for implements, etc., sold on quitting holding

19.—(1) Where a tenant of an agricultural holding has entered into an agreement or it is a term of the lease of the holding that the tenant will on quitting the holding, sell to the landlord or to the incoming tenant any implements of husbandry, fixtures, farm produce or farm stock on or used in connection with the holding, notwithstanding anything in the agreement or lease to the contrary, it shall be deemed to be a term of the agreement or of the lease, as the case may be, that the property in the goods shall not pass to the buyer until the price is paid and that payment of the price shall be made within one month after the tenant has quitted the holding or, if the price of the goods is to be ascertained by a valuation, within one month after the delivery of the award in the valuation.

(2) Where payment of the price is not made within one month as aforesaid the outgoing tenant shall be entitled to sell or remove the goods and to receive from the landlord or the incoming tenant, as the case may be, by whom the price was payable, compensation of an amount equal to any loss or expense unavoidably incurred by the outgoing tenant upon or in connection with such sale or removal, together with any expenses reasonably incurred by him in the preparation of his claim for compensation.

(3) Any question arising as to the amount of compensation payable under subsection (2) above shall be determined by arbitration.

DEFINITIONS
  "landlord": s.85(1).
  "lease": s.85(1).
  "produce": s.85(1).
  "tenant": s.85(1).

DERIVATIONS
  Agricultural Holdings (Scotland) Act 1949, s.22.

GENERAL NOTE
  See Gill, paras. 445 and 470.

Subs. (1)

Contracting out is prohibited. The lease or agreement will usually specify whether the sale is to be to the landlord or to the incoming tenant. In the absence of such specification the outgoing tenant has the choice and may elect to deal with the landlord as the party with the more permanent interest.

Subs. (2)

It is indicated in Connell (*op.cit.* p. 133) that there are difficulties in applying this provision in the case of sheep stocks bound to the ground.

Subs. (3)

Arbitration under this Act will apply if the landlord is involved but otherwise it would appear that the arbitration will be at common law.

Removal, of tenant for non-payment of rent

20.—(1) When 6 months' rent of an agricultural holding is due and unpaid, the landlord shall be entitled to raise an action of removing in the sheriff court against the tenant, concluding for his removal from the holding at the term of Whitsunday or Martinmas next ensuing after the action is raised.

(2) In an action raised under subsection (1) above, the sheriff may, unless the arrears of rent then due are paid or caution is found to his satisfaction for them, and for one year's rent further, decern the tenant to remove, and may eject him at the said term in like manner as if the lease were determined and the tenant had been legally warned to remove.

(3) A tenant of a holding removed under this section shall have the rights of an outgoing tenant to which he would have been entitled if his tenancy had terminated by operation of notice to quit or notice of intention to quit at the term when he is removed.

(4) Section 5 of chapter XV of Book L of the Codifying Act of Sederunt of June 14, 1913, anent removings, shall not apply in any case where the procedure under this section is competent.

DEFINITIONS
"agricultural holdings": s.1(1).
"landlord": s.85(1).
"notice of intention to quit": s.21(2).
"notice to quit": s.21(2).
"tenant": s.85(1).

DERIVATIONS
Agricultural Holdings (Scotland) Act 1949, s.19.

GENERAL NOTE
See Gill, paras. 272–273.

Subs. (1)
Under the Term and Quarter Days (Scotland) Act 1990, s.1(1)(a), (2)(a) the terms Whitsunday and Martinmas signify May 28 and November 28 respectively. If, as the wording of this subsection appears to indicate, a decree, when granted, must specify removal at the term specified in the crave, there may be practical difficulties if that term is reached before decree is granted.

Subs. (2)
The fact that the tenant can retain possession by paying or finding caution for the arrears at any time up to the granting of decree (see *Fletcher* v. *Fletcher*, 1932 S.L.T. (Sh. Ct.) 10 and *Westwood* v. *Keay* (1950) 66 Sh.Ct.Rep. 147) has the result that in practice the legal irritancy represented by this section is not often invoked. Where there is a lease it will usually contain a conventional irritancy which cannot be purged, or, again, the date on which the tenancy can be terminated by notice to quit may make it convenient for the landlord to proceed under s.22(2)(d).

Subs. (3)
It appears that the tenant removed under this section will be entitled to make his common-law waygoing claims as implied or expressed in the terms of the lease including compensation for improvements, provided that the statutory requirements are fulfilled. Gill (para. 272) indicates that compensation for disturbance will not be payable looking to the wording of the relevant section, now s.43(1). That view is expressed with reference to s.19 of the 1949 Act, which speaks of the tenancy terminating naturally at the appropriate term. As now worded, the subsection envisages the tenancy as terminating by the operation of notice to quit *or* notice of intention to quit. Compensation for disturbance would not be payable in the case of termination by notice of intention to quit but under s.43 is normally due where the tenant goes out in compliance with a notice to quit. Again, entitlement to compensation for disturbance may entail entitlement to an additional payment in terms of s.54.

Subs. (4)
The statutory provision now in force has superseded, in relation to rent arrears, a legal irritancy under the Act of Sederunt referred to. This applies where the tenant under an agricultural lease is one year in arrear with his rent or has deserted the holding, but is never used in present day practice.

PART III

NOTICE TO QUIT AND NOTICE OF INTENTION TO QUIT

Notice to quit and notice of intention to quit

21.—(1) Subject to section 20 of this Act and to subsections (6) and (7) below a tenancy of an agricultural holding shall not come to an end except by operation of a notice which complies with this subsection notwithstanding any agreement or any provision in the lease to the contrary.

(2) In this Act, a notice which complies with subsection (1) above is referred to as a "notice to quit" if it is given by the landlord to the tenant and as a "notice of intention to quit" if it is given by the tenant to the landlord.

(3) A notice complies with subsection (1) above if—

(a) it is in writing;

(b) it is a notice of intention to bring the tenancy to an end;

(c) where the notice is to take effect at the termination of the stipulated endurance of the lease, it is given not less than one year nor more than 2 years before that date;

(d) in the case of a lease continued in force by tacit relocation, it gives not less than one year nor more than 2 years' notice.

(4) The provisions of the Sheriff Courts (Scotland) Act 1907 relating to removings shall, in the case of an agricultural holding, have effect subject to this section.

(5) Notice to quit shall be given either—

(a) in the same manner as notice of removal under section 6 of the Removal Terms (Scotland) Act 1886; or

(b) in the form and manner prescribed by the Sheriff Courts (Scotland) Act 1907,

and such notice shall come in place of the notice required by the said Act of 1907.

(6) Nothing in this section shall affect the right of the landlord of an agricultural holding to remove a tenant whose estate has been sequestrated under the Bankruptcy (Scotland) Act 1985 or the Bankruptcy (Scotland) Act 1913, or who by failure to pay rent or otherwise has incurred irritancy of his lease or other liability to be removed.

(7) This section shall not apply—

(a) to a notice given in pursuance of a stipulation in a lease entitling the landlord to resume land for building, planting, feuing or other purposes (not being agricultural purposes); or

(b) in relation to subjects let under a lease for any period less than a year, not being a lease which by virtue of section 2 of this Act takes effect as a lease from year to year.

DEFINITIONS

"agricultural holding": s.1(1).

"agriculture": s.85(1).

"landlord": s.85(1).

"lease": s.85(1).

"tenant": s.85(1).

DERIVATIONS

Agricultural Holdings (Scotland) Act 1949, s.24.

Agriculture Act 1958, Sched. 1, Pt. II, para. 34.

GENERAL NOTE

See Gill, paras. 234–241 (resumption), 271 and 274–282 (irritancy), 283–306. (For the corresponding English provision see the Agricultural Holdings Act 1986, s.25).

Subs. (1)

This provision should be read along with s.3 concerning the continuation of leases by tacit relocation. The concluding words of this subsection make it clear that contracting out of its provisions is not permissible. "Agreement" as used in the corresponding provision, s.24(1) of the 1949 Act, has been construed as applying not only to an agreement made before the lease was entered into and to any agreement incorporated in the lease, but also to any agreement the parties may make during the currency of the tenancy. Thus in *Morrison's Executors* v. *Rendall*, 1986 S.L.T. 227 it was held that an agreement to terminate a lease otherwise than by statutory notice was invalid irrespective of when it was made as being an attempt to contract out of s.24(1) of the 1949 Act. It appears, however, that unilateral renunciation by the tenant may be effective to terminate a tenancy without statutory notice being given (see Gill, para. 250).

Subs. (2)

While in terms of subs. (5) notice to quit must conform to certain requirements in the matter of content and service, these do not apply to a notice of intention to quit. Any document making clear the tenant's intention to terminate the tenancy giving the requisite period of notice and served in conformity with the provisions of s.84 will suffice as a notice of intention to quit. The term "notice of intention to quit" appears to be an innovation in terminology but is more appropriate than the term "notice to quit" where the tenant is the party terminating the tenancy.

Subs. (3)

Notice must be given not less than one year and not more than two years before its effective date, being the date at which the contractual duration of the lease expires or at which there operates a provision for a break or an anniversary of the expiry date where tacit relocation is operating. Notice cannot be given before the commencement of the tenancy, *i.e.* before the contractual relationship of landlord and tenant has taken effect (*Lower* v. *Sorrell* [1963] 1 Q.B. 959).

Subs. (4)

The effect of this subsection is to amend, as regards the period of notice, the relevant provisions of the 1907 Act, being ss.34–38 and r.103 of the first Schedule as imported by s.39. In the case of *Milne* v. *The Earl of Seafield*, 1981 S.L.T. (Sh. Ct.) 37 a problem arose with the lease specifying a series of hand-over dates for different parts of the holding at the end of the tenancy. It was held that s.24(3) of the 1949 Act (which this subsection replaces) substituted the provisions of the 1949 Act for those of the 1907 Act not only in regard to the period of notice but also in regard to the terminus which the notice must specify, that being the termination of the lease and not, as under r.110 of the 1907 Act, the term of removal first in date if different from the date of termination.

Subs. (5)

Dealing with notices to quit, this subsection refers alternatively to s.6 of the Removal Terms (Scotland) Act 1886 and to the Sheriff Courts (Scotland) Act 1907. Section 6 of the 1886 Act provides for transmission by registered post of a notice of removal, the terms of which it does not specify. The first Schedule to the 1907 Act has been replaced by the Act of Sederunt (Ordinary Cause Rules Sheriff Court) 1983 (S.I. 1983 No. 747) as amended by the Act of Sederunt (Ordinary Cause Rules Amendment) 1983 (S.I. 1983 No. 1546). Rule 106 of the Schedule permits notice to be given by Messenger at Arms or Sheriff Officer or by registered letter. The Recorded Delivery Service Act 1962 makes recorded delivery equivalent to registered post. It has been held that any other method of giving notice to quit is ineffective even if receipt is acknowledged or could be proved. That was the view taken in the case of the *Department of Agriculture* v. *Goodfellow*, 1931 S.C. 556 where ordinary post had been used but that case was decided when the Agricultural Holdings (Scotland) Act 1923 which did not contain provisions for the service of notices, etc. as included in s.90(1) of the 1949 Act and now in s.84(1) was in force. Whatever method of service is adopted, the notice must as required by Rule 104 conform as nearly as possible to Form L (formerly H), in the Schedule. Form L has three essential elements; the subjects let, the lease or other tenancy contract, and the date of ish. The omission of any of these is fatal. Any description sufficient to identify the subjects and not in any way misleading will suffice (*Scott* v. *Livingstone*, 1919 S.C. 1). The lease must be referred to in terms which will identify it (*Rae* v. *Davidson*, 1954 S.C. 361, *Taylor* v. *Brick*, 1982 S.L.T. 25) and this may present difficulties in verbal or informal lettings where no formal lease has been entered into. The lease has to be specified as "the warrant upon which the notice is based" (*Watters* v. *Hunter*, 1927 S.C. 310 at p. 315). Where no lease exists, however, some indication of the basis of the tenancy may suffice (see *Watters* v. *Hunter*, above and *Gemmell* v. *Andrew*, 1975 S.L.T. (Land Ct.) 5). Finally, the notice must specify the ish, which, as explained with reference to subs. (3), is the date of termination of the lease and not any other date on which part of the subjects has to be vacated. Again, there may be difficulty if there is no formal lease or only some tenancy document not specifying the duration of the let. If a date of entry is specified, an ish on the anniversary of that date may be inferred (see *Morrison's Executors* v. *Rendall*, 1989 S.L.T. (Land Ct.) 89) but if neither entry nor ish is specified the date of the latter will be a matter of proof. (For a discussion of these questions with full citation of authorities see Gill (paras. 300–305)).

Subs. (6)

This subsection preserves for the landlord, as an exception to the requirements for a notice to quit, the right to operate a conventional irritancy contained in the lease in the event of a breach by the tenant of a condition to which the irritancy applies. It is pointed out by Gill, para. 271 that in referring to the tenant's bankruptcy in this context the Act is amplifying the common law under which sequestration alone is not a ground of legal irritancy and can justify removal of the tenant only if it is the subject of a conventional irritancy. In practice, irritancy clauses tend to be framed in broad general terms covering any form of default by the tenant and in many cases listing his bankruptcy as a ground for irritancy. The significant difference between the conventional irritancy and the legal irritancy as provided for in s.20 is that the conventional irritancy, once incurred, cannot be purged (*McDouall's Trs.* v. *McLeod*, 1949 S.C. 593 and *Dorchester Studios (Glasgow)* v. *Stone*, 1975 S.C. (H.L.) 56). This, however, applies only to irritancies which are in their terms materially different from the legal irritancy which would operate by implication (*British Rail Pension Trustee Co.* v. *Wilson*, 1989 S.L.T. 340 (O.H.)). A conventional irritancy will normally provide for the lease terminating and the tenant vacating the holding immediately on its occurrence. This does not, however, permit the landlord to reclaim possession of the holding *brevi manu*. If the tenant remains in possession after being notified that an irritancy has been incurred there will need to be an action of declarator of the irritancy with a conclusion for the tenant's removal and a defence by the tenant will usually result in the action being sisted for the issues to be examined in a statutory arbitration. Unless his right to do so is excluded in terms of the lease, the tenant, on the principle of mutuality, may base a defence on some failure by the landlord to fulfil his obligations under the lease (*MacNab* v. *Willison*, 1960 S.L.T. (Notes) 25). A tenant going out in terms of a conventional irritancy will forfeit all his statutory waygoing claims and, if the terms of the lease so provide, will even be deprived of the right to reap a crop which is growing when he leaves (*Chalmers Tr.* v. *Dick's Tr.*, 1909 S.C. 761).

Subs. (7)

Para. (a). Most formal leases give the landlord power to resume parts of the holding for purposes such as building and feuing. Provided that the resumption is not for an agricultural purpose it is exempted from the requirements of a notice to quit. While some leases purport to sanction resumption without any prior notice, it appears to be established that sufficient notice must be given to enable the tenant to make, in respect of the land resumed, such outgoing claims as have to be notifed to the landlord before the land is vacated. This applies to claims arising under ss.18 (removal of fixtures and buildings), 43(4)(b) (compensation for disturbance), and 44 (High Farming), where in each case a month's notice has to be given. To allow time for preparation of the claim it is considered that the landlord should be required to give at least two months' notice of the intended resumption and although Scottish authority on the matter is lacking it appears that any provision in the lease for a period of notice insufficient to enable the tenant, if so advised, to make these claims is invalid (*Disraeli's Agreement* [1939] Ch. 382; *Coates* v. *Diment* [1957] 1 All E.R. 890). As the wording of the subsections shows, the resumption, to qualify for exemption from the notice to quit requirements, must be for a non-agricultural purpose and in the event of dispute on this point a proof will be necessary (see *Sykes* v. *Edgar*, 1974 S.L.T. (Land Ct.) 4). It is of course essential that the resumption proposed falls within the terms of the relevant clause in the lease but in any event resumption will not be permitted if it appears contrary to good faith, or, as it is sometimes put, constitutes a fraud on the lease, *e.g.* in leaving the tenant with a holding which is not a viable agricultural unit (see *Trotter* v. *Torrance*, 1891 18R 848; *Admiralty* v. *Burns*, 1910 S.C. 531; *Turner* v. *Wilson*, 1954 S.C. 296; *Glencruilten Trs.* v. *Love*, 1966 S.L.T. (Land Ct.) 5; *Fotheringham* v. *Fotheringham*, 1987 S.L.T. (Land Ct.) 10; *Thomson* v. *Murray*, 1990 S.L.T. (Land Ct.) 45).

It has been held that the principle of mutuality in a lease does not prevent a landlord exercising a right of resumption because he is in default in his obligations under the lease (*Edmonstone* v. *Lamont*, 1975 S.L.T. (Sh. Ct.) 57).

The compensation and other rights of a tenant part of whose holding is resumed are dealt with in ss.49(1)(b) and (2), 54(1) and (2) and 58.

Para. (*b*). This exempts from the requirements of notices to quit and notices of intention to quit short lets sanctioned by the Secretary of State and the two categories of short-term lets covered by s.2(2).

Restrictions on operation of notices to quit

22.—(1) Where not later than one month from the giving of a notice to quit an agricultural holding (or, in a case where section 23(3) of this Act applies, within the extended period therein mentioned) the tenant serves on the landlord a counter-notice in writing requiring that this subsection shall apply to the notice to quit, subject to subsection (2) below and to section 25 of this Act, the notice to quit shall not have effect unless the Land Court consent to the operation thereof.

(2) Subsection (1) above shall not apply where—

(a) the notice to quit relates to land being permanent pasture which the landlord has been in the habit of letting annually for seasonal grazing or of keeping in his own occupation and which has been let to the tenant for a definite and limited period for cultivation as arable land on the condition that he shall, along with the last or waygoing crop, sow permanent grass seeds;

(b) the notice to quit is given on the ground that the land is required for use, other than agriculture, for which permission has been granted on an application made under the enactments relating to town and country planning, or for which (otherwise than by virtue of any provision of those enactments) such permission is not required;

(c) the Land Court, on an application in that behalf made not more than 9 months before the giving of the notice to quit, were satisfied that the tenant was not fulfilling his responsibilities to farm the holding in accordance with the rules of good husbandry, and certified that they were so satisfied;

(d) at the date of the giving of the notice to quit the tenant had failed to comply with a demand in writing served on him by the landlord requiring him within 2 months from the service thereof to pay any rent due in respect of the holding, or within a reasonable time to remedy any breach by the tenant, which was capable of being remedied, of any term or condition of his tenancy which was not inconsistent with the fulfilment of his responsibilities to farm in accordance with the rules of good husbandry;

(e) at the date of the giving of the notice to quit the interest of the landlord in the holding had been materially prejudiced by a breach by the tenant, which was not capable of being remedied in reasonable time and at economic cost, of any term or condition of the tenancy which was not inconsistent with the fulfilment by the tenant of his responsibilities to farm in accordance with the rules of good husbandry;

(f) at the date of the giving of the notice to quit the tenant's apparent insolvency had been constituted in accordance with section 7 of the Bankruptcy (Scotland) Act 1985;

(g) section 25(1) of this Act applies, and the relevant notice complies with section 25(2)(a), (b) and (d) of this Act;

and, where any of paragraphs (a) to (f) above applies, the ground under the appropriate paragraph on which the notice to quit proceeds is stated in the notice.

DEFINITIONS

"agricultural holding": s.1(1).
"agriculture": s.85(1).
"landlord": s.85(1).
"notice to quit": s.21(2).
"rules of good husbandry": s.85(2); Agriculture (Scotland) Act 1948, Sched. 6.
"tenant": s.85(1).

DERIVATIONS
Agricultural Holdings (Scotland) Act 1949, s.25.
Agriculture Act 1958, s.3(1)(3), Sched. 1, Pt. II, para. 35.

GENERAL NOTE
See Gill, paras. 327–341, 354–357, 366–369. (For the corresponding English provision see the Agricultural Holdings Act 1986, s.26 and Sched. 3, amended in respect of Case B by the Agricultural Holdings (Amendment) Act 1990).

Subs. (1)
There is no prescribed form of counter-notice, but the notice given should disclose that this subsection is being invoked (*Luss Estate Co.* v. *Colquhoun*, 1982 S.L.C.R. 1). Examples of documents held ineffective as counter-notices are to be found in *Secretary of State* v. *Fraser*, 1954 S.L.C.R. 24; *Mountford* v. *Hodkinson* [1956] 1 W.L.R. 422 and *Taylor* v. *Brick*, 1990 S.L.T. 25. Service within the time allowed is essential (*Luss Estates Co.* v. *Colquhoun*, above).

Subs. (2)
Listed here are the various circumstances in which the consent of the Land Court to the operation of a notice to quit is not required.
Para. (a). The land must be permanent pasture which the landlord has been letting as such for seasonal grazing or retaining for his own use. The requirement of "a definite and limited period" means that a lease from year to year does not qualify but there is no maximum period (see *Roberts* v. *Simpson* (1954) 70 Sh.Ct.Rep. 159 and *Stirrat* v. *Whyte*, 1968 S.L.T. 157, *per* Lord Cameron at p. 163). The statutory wording should be closely followed in drafting the lease. If the lease is allowed to continue on tacit relocation the landlord cannot invoke this provision to enable him to operate a notice to quit without Land Court consent.
Para. (b). The land must be required at the date of the notice (*Paddock Investments* v. *Long* [1975] 236 E.G. 803; *Jones* v. *Gates* [1954] 1 W.L.R. 222) but not necessarily by the landlord (*Rugby Joint Water Board* v. *Shaw Fox*; *Rugby Joint Water Board* v. *Foottit* [1973] A.C. 202). Planning permission for a non-agricultural use must already have been applied for and granted unless the proposed use is permissible irrespective of the Planning Acts, *e.g.* where it is not a development or is to be undertaken by the Crown. Where the authority for the proposed use is a development order, special or general, an application for Land Court consent founding on s.24(1)(e) will be the appropriate course. While an outline planning permission is sufficient for the purposes of this paragraph (*Paddock Investments* v. *Lang*, above; *Dow Agrochemicals* v. *Lane (E.A.) (North Lynn)* [1965] 192 E.G. 737) it appears to depend on the circumstances whether permission not covering the entire holding will suffice. As to specialities in applications for planning consent affecting agricultural holdings, see Gill, paras. 332–333).
Para. (c). Section 26 contains the procedure for obtaining a Certificate of Bad Husbandry from the Land Court. This paragraph enables the landlord to use the Certificate as a means of operating a notice to quit without Land Court consent. The notice to quit has to be served not later than nine months after the application for the Certificate is made but cannot be served before the Certificate is obtained. As to the reasoning underlying the timing of these steps, see *Macnabb* v. *A. J. Anderson*, 1955 S.C. 38, *per* Lord Patrick at p. 44.
Para. (d). The rent demand must be explicit and must be accurate as regards the parties and the amount of the rent which must be already due. As a result of the Term and Quarter Days (Scotland) Act 1990, s.(1), rents payable half-yearly or quarterly will in future fall due on the 28th of the respective months unless the lease specifies otherwise. On the expiry of the two-month period (but not earlier), the landlord may issue a notice to quit founding on the paragraph (*Macnabb* v. *A. J. Anderson* above, at p. 45). Payment of the rent after the expiry of the two-month period, whether before or after the issue of the notice to quit, is of no effect. (*Stoneman* v. *Brown* [1973] 1 W.L.R. 459; *Price* v. *Romilly* [1960] 1 W.L.R. 1360 at p. 1361). If the rent demand is invalid in any respect the notice to quit will be ineffective, provided that the tenant has demanded arbitration in accordance with s.23(2).
The demand to remedy can apply to a breach of any of the conditions of tenancy implied in the case of an oral or informal let or expressed in a formal lease, always provided that the condition in question is consistent with the rules of good husbandry as statutorily defined. The demand must be in clear and unambiguous terms for it to form the ground of a notice to quit. It does not, like a demand for rent, have to specify a time for compliance, but any time limit it prescribes must be reasonable for the action required to be taken and where no time is specified in the demand the question of fact will be whether the interval between the demand and the notice to quit has been in the circumstances reasonable (see *Pentland* v. *Hart*, 1967 S.L.T.

(Land Ct.) 2 and *Nicholls Trs.* v. *Maclarty*, 1971 S.L.C.R. 85. The breach must be one which is capable of being remedied, in contrast with the situation provided for in para. (e) dealing with an irremediable breach.

It appears that default in payment of rent or in remedying a breach as contemplated in this paragraph cannot, like an irritancy legal or conventional, be met with the plea that the landlord is in default in some obligation affecting him (*Wilson Clarke* v. *Graham*, 1963 S.L.T. (Sh. Ct.) 2) except where, in the case of a demand to remedy, the landlord's default is in some way preventing the tenant from taking the necessary action (*Shepherd* v. *Lomas* [1963] 1 W.L.R. 962).

Demands to remedy relating to the maintenance and repair of fixed equipment are the subject of special provisions contained in ss.32 and 66.

Para. (*e*). Examples of irremediable breaches as referred to in this paragraph are felling of timber contrary to the terms of the lease and without the landlord's consent or the neglect to maintain buildings or other structures, so that they collapse or disintegrate. As under para. (d), the condition breached must be consistent with the rules of good husbandry.

While paras. (d) and (e) are mutually exclusive, instances of both categories of breach may be present at the same time on a holding, in which case the landlord, after the expiry of his demand to remedy the remediable breaches, may serve a notice to quit founded on both categories of breach, provided that it discriminates in its terms between the breaches coming under the respective paragraphs and contains the necessary statement in each case (*MacNab* v. *Anderson*, 1957 S.C. 213).

In a case coming under para. (e) (but not in one coming under para. (d)) the Succession (Scotland) Act 1964, s.16(6)(b) as amended in terms of Sched. 11, para. 24(b), gives the arbiter a discretion as regards making an order in favour of the landlord where the tenancy interest is held by an executor.

Para. (*f*). Under s.7 of the 1985 Act, apparent insolvency is constituted in various ways, are being the granting of a trust deed for creditors, but in cases falling within s.7(1)(c) of that Act the debtor can disprove his apparent insolvency by showing that at the material time he was able and willing to pay his debts as they fell due (*cf. Murray* v. *Nisbet*, 1967 S.L.T. (Land Ct.) 14, a case dealt with under s.5 of the now-repealed Bankruptcy (Scotland) Act 1913). Para. (f) applies even if the tenant was apparently insolvent when the tenancy commenced (*cf. Hart* v. *Cameron* (1935) 51 Sh.Ct.Rep. 166).

It may be noted here that the section concludes with a statement that where any of the paras. (a) to (f) applies, the ground under the appropriate paragraph on which the notice to quit proceeds is to be stated in the notice. This requirement should be complied with in explicit terms, reproducing, or at least closely following, the wording of the relevant paragraph.

Para. (*g*). This relates to a notice to quit complying with the basic requirement of such a notice (see s.25(2)(a), referring to s.21) given to a tenant who is a legatee or intestate successor of a former tenant (see s.25(1)) and specifying an effective date complying with s.25(2)(b), the successor tenant not being a near relative of his predecessor and having acquired right to the lease after August 1, 1958.

Since the coming into force of s.6 of the Agriculture Act 1958 on August 1, 1958, the security of tenure given to agricultural tenants has not extended to their successors other than those who qualify as near relatives under provisions introduced in 1968. Provided that a notice to quit is issued to a successor other than a near relative of the late tenant, having its effective date within the time limits prescribed in s.25(2)(b), Land Court consent to its operation is not required.

Under s.6(3) of the 1958 Act the notice to quit had to contain a statement that it was given under that subsection. This requirement was not included when the 1958 provision was replaced by the Agricultural Holdings (Amendment) (Scotland) Act 1983 and does not appear in the present Act. The omission seems unfortunate, but it is apparently assumed that a successor tenant, other than a near relative, who receives a notice to quit should appreciate from the timing of its effective date that it is being given by virtue of para. (g) of this section. See also Gill, 360.

Consent by Land Court or arbitration on notices to quit

23.—(1) An application by a landlord for the consent of the Land Court under section 22 of this Act to the operation of a notice to quit shall be made within one month after service on the landlord by the tenant of a counter-notice requiring that subsection (1) of that section shall apply to the notice to quit.

(2) A tenant who has been given a notice to quit in connection with which any question arises under section 22(2) of this Act shall, if he requires such question to be determined by arbitration under this Act, give notice to the

landlord to that effect within one month after the notice to quit has been served on him.

(3) Where the award of the arbiter in an arbitration required under subsection (2) above is such that section 22(1) of this Act would have applied to the notice to quit if a counter-notice had been served within the period provided for in that subsection, that period shall be extended up to the expiry of one month from the issue of the arbiter's award.

(4) Where such an arbitration as is referred to in subsection (2) above has been required by the tenant, or where an application has been made to the Land Court for their consent to the operation of a notice to quit, the operation of the notice to quit shall be suspended until the issue of the arbiter's award or of the decision of the Land Court, as the case may be.

(5) Where the decision of the Land Court giving their consent to the operation of a notice to quit, or the award of the arbiter in such an arbitration as is referred to in subsection (2) above, is issued at a date later than 6 months before the date on which the notice to quit is expressed to take effect, the Land Court, on application made to them in that behalf at any time not later than one month after the issue of the decision or award aforesaid, may postpone the operation of the notice to quit for a period not exceeding 12 months.

(6) If the tenant of an agricultural holding receives from the landlord notice to quit the holding or a part thereof and in consequence thereof gives to a sub-tenant notice to quit that holding or part, section 22(1) of this Act shall not apply to the notice given to the sub-tenant; but if the notice to quit given to the tenant by the landlord does not have effect, then the notice to quit given by the tenant to the sub-tenant shall not have effect.

(7) For the purposes of subsection (6) above, a notice to quit part of the holding which under section 30 of this Act is accepted by the tenant as notice to quit the entire holding shall be treated as a notice to quit the holding.

(8) Where notice is served on the tenant of an agricultural holding to quit the holding or a part thereof, being a holding or part which is subject to a sub-tenancy, and the tenant serves on the landlord a counter-notice in accordance with section 22(1) of this Act, the tenant shall also serve on the sub-tenant notice in writing that he has served such counter-notice on the landlord and the sub-tenant shall be entitled to be a party to any proceedings before the Land Court for their consent to the notice to quit.

DEFINITIONS
  "agricultural holdings": s.1(1).
  "landlord": s.85(1).
  "lease": s.85(1).
  "notice to quit": s.85(1).
  "tenant": s.85(1).

DERIVATIONS
  Agricultural Holdings (Scotland) Act 1949, s.27.
  Agriculture Act 1958, Sched. 1, Pt. II, para. 37.

GENERAL NOTE
  See Gill, paras. 49–52 (Sub-tenants), 320–326 (Tenants' response to quit notice), 362–365, 370–374 (Landlord's application to Land Court) and 410 (Postponement of operation of notice to quit).

Subs. (1)
  The time limit is strictly enforced and cannot be extended (*Still* v. *Reid*, 1957 S.L.C.R. 16; *Gemmell* v. *Hodge*, 1974 S.L.T. (Land Ct.) 2). The application is made on a form provided by the Land Court.

Subs. (2)
  When notice to quit is given on any of the grounds provided in paras. (a) to (f) of s.22(2) the

ground will be stated in the notice and the tenant, if disputing the relevant facts, must call for arbitration within a month of receiving the notice.

Subs. (3)

A counter-notice is incompetent and of no effect as an initial response to a s.22(2) notice to quit, but if the arbitration called for by the tenant results in a decision in his favour the notice becomes one to which s.22(1) applies. Accordingly the tenant is given a month from the arbiter's decision to serve a counter-notice. There has been some question as to whether a landlord can proceed on a notice referring to s.22(2) on the basis that s.22(1) applies to the notice without the notice having indicated that he is to claim that right should the arbiter decide against him, but the better view appears to be that he can do so (see Gill, para. 364). Accordingly, the tenant who has succeeded in an arbitration on a s.22(2) notice should exercise his right to serve a counter-notice unless he is satisfied that the landlord is not to proceed further on the notice to quit.

Subss. (4) and (5)

These subsections make provision for delay taking place in the issue of the Land Court decision or the arbiter's award. Initially the operation of the notice to quit is suspended pending the issue of the decision so that the tenant may have a fair opportunity to adjust his farming activities but the Land Court is given a discretion where the award or decision is issued less than six months before the effective date of the notice to quit to postpone the operation of the notice for not more than 12 months. The application for postponement must be made not later than a month after the issue of the decision or award but may be made before its issue (*Moffat* v. *Young*, 1975 S.L.C.R. App. 98) and the postponement may be granted after the operative date of the notice has passed (*Allan-Fraser's Trs.* v. *Macpherson* 1981 S.L.T. (Land Ct.) 17).

Subs. (6)

Only a limited measure of protection is given by the Act to sub-tenants, even where, contrary to the legal implication in agricultural tenancies, sub-letting is permitted by the lease or authorised by the landlord. This subsection has the result that if the tenant, having received a notice to quit from the landlord, gives notice to quit to the sub-tenant, the latter must comply with that notice, but if for any reason the landlord's notice does not take effect the sub-tenant can ignore the notice he received from the tenant. The vulnerability of the sub-tenant has sometimes been used in a device to avoid the tenant's security of tenure, a nominee of the landlord taking the tenancy and sub-letting to the party who is to farm the holding. Since the decision of the Court of Appeal in *Gisbourne* v. *Burton* [1988] 3 W.L.R. 921, treating the occupant of the farm, who was a sub-tenant of the landlord's wife, as the true tenant, this device seems likely to fall out of use.

Subs. (7)

This refers to the option given by s.30 to a tenant who has to comply with a notice to quit covering part only of the holding, to treat the notice as affecting the whole holding. If this option is exercised any sub-lets there may be are terminated.

Subs. (8)

It is clear that sub-tenants have a concern with any action the tenant may take to prevent the operation of a notice to quit issued by the landlord. Accordingly, sub-tenants have to be notified that a counter-notice has been served and they are entitled to be parties to the ensuing proceedings in the Land Court.

Consents for purposes of section 22

24.—(1) Subject to subsection (2) below and to section 25(3) of this Act, the Land Court shall consent under section 22 of this Act to the operation of a notice to quit an agricultural holding or part of an agricultural holding if, but only if, they are satisfied as to one or more of the following matters, being a matter or matters specified by the landlord in his application for their consent—

    (a) that the carrying out of the purpose for which the landlord proposes to terminate the tenancy is desirable in the interests of good husbandry as respects the land to which the notice relates, treated as a separate unit;

    (b) that the carrying out thereof is desirable in the interests of sound management of the estate of which that land consists or forms part;

(c) that the carrying out thereof is desirable for the purposes of agricultural research, education, experiment or demonstration, or for the
purposes of the enactments relating to allotments, smallholdings or
such holdings as are referred to in section 64 of the Agriculture
(Scotland) Act 1948;

(d) that greater hardship would be caused by withholding than by giving
consent to the operation of the notice;

(e) that the landlord proposes to terminate the tenancy for the purpose of
the land being used for a use, other than for agriculture, not falling
within section 22(2)(b) of this Act.

(2) Notwithstanding that they are satisfied as aforesaid, the Land Court
shall withhold consent to the operation of the notice to quit if in all the
circumstances it appears to them that a fair and reasonable landlord would
not insist on possession.

(3) Where the Land Court consent to the operation of a notice to quit they
may (subject to section 25(4) of this Act) impose such conditions as appear
to them requisite for securing that the land to which the notice relates will be
used for the purpose for which the landlord proposes to terminate the
tenancy.

(4) Where, on an application by the landlord in that behalf the Land Court
are satisfied that by reason of any change of circumstances or otherwise any
condition imposed under subsection (3) above ought to be varied or
revoked, they shall vary or revoke the condition accordingly.

DEFINITIONS
   "agricultural holding": s.1(1).
   "agriculture": s.85(1).
   "good estate management": s.85(2); Agriculture (Scotland) Act 1948, Sched. 5.
   "good husbandry": s.85(2); Agriculture (Scotland) Act 1948, Sched. 6.
   "landlord": s.85(1).
   "notice to quit": s.21(2).
   "tenant": s.85(1).

DERIVATIONS
   Agricultural Holdings (Scotland) Act 1949, s.26.
   Agricultural Holdings (Amendment) (Scotland) Act 1983, s.4(1).
   Agriculture Act 1958, s.3(2)(3) and Sched. 1, Pt. II, para. 36.

GENERAL NOTE
   See Gill, paras. 375–390. (For the corresponding English provision see the Agricultural
Holding Act 1986, s.27).

Subs. (1)
   This subsection sets out the five grounds on any one of which the Land Court may consent to
the operation of a notice to quit. The ground or grounds on which the landlord is to found have
to be specified in the application made by him under s.23(1) but in many cases the ground will
already have been disclosed in the notice to quit in compliance with s.55 in order to obtain
exemption from the additional payment to which outgoing tenants may be entitled in terms of
s.54. The onus is, of course, on the landlord to satisfy the court on at least one ground.
   Para. (*a*). Here the landlord must demonstrate that he has proposals for the use of the
holding as an agricultural unit by himself, or by a tenant of his selection, which will represent a
material improvement on the management of the holding as farmed by the tenant, particularly
in such respects as productive capacity or future fertility (*Clark* v. *Smith*, 1981 S.L.C.R. 84;
Prior v. *J. & A. Henderson*, 1984 S.L.T. (Land Ct.) 51). He is not required to prove that the
tenant is inefficient or has been guilty of bad husbandry but what he must show is that under his
proposed régime there will be a material improvement in the farming of the holding. In support
of the case he may adduce evidence of his own, or his prospective tenants, standard of farming
on some other farm.
   The concluding words of the paragraph, however, make it clear that in arriving at their
decision the court must consider the issue of good husbandry in relation to the holding itself
treated as a separate unit (*Clark* v. *Smith*, above) and not, as the landlord may envisage it, as

part of some larger unit produced by amalgamation (*Clark* v. *Smith*, above; *Austin* v. *Gibson*, 1979 S.L.T. (Land Ct.) 12).

Para. (*b*). It seems to be open to question whether there is any significant difference between sound estate management as referred to in this paragraph and the landlord's duty of good estate management as described in the Schedule to the 1948 Act. It appears that management in this context is referred to in a physical rather than in a financial sense (*National Coal Board* v. *Naylor* [1972] 1 W.L.R. 908). The important difference from the ground for consent in para. (a) is that this paragraph involves consideration of the management situation in relation to the rest of the landlord's estate where such exists (*Peace* v. *Peace*, 1984 S.L.T. (Land Ct.) 6 at p. 7; *cf. Leask* v. *Gairns*, 1981 S.L.T. (Land Ct.) 11) although the paragraph is capable of application where the estate comprises the holding alone (*National Coal Board* v. *Naylor*, above).

Para. (*c*). There appears to be no recent instance of this ground for consent being invoked. The report in the case of *Edinburgh University* v. *Craik*, 1954 S.C. 190 involving an application for consent under the corresponding provision in the 1949 Act deals only with questions of procedure arising under the statutory provisions then in force. The paragraph seems to envisage a consideration by the court of the relative desirability in the public interest of the use of the holding for agriculture on the one hand and its use for one or more of the purposes indicated on the other.

Para. (*d*). As the copious citation of authorities in Gill (paras. 384–389) indicates, hardship is the most frequently invoked ground of consent and indeed is often invoked by landlords, along with one or more of the other grounds listed. Here it is possible to mention only some of the main conclusions which can be drawn from the decided cases. The onus is, of course, on the landlord to demonstrate that he will suffer greater hardship than the tenant from an adverse decision. In most cases there will be elements of hardship on both sides and it is for the Land Court to decide whether the landlord has demonstrated the greater hardship. Two cases which were concerned not with the consent to operation of a notice to quit but with the intimation of hardship to be given in that notice to avoid the landlord's being liable to the tenant for reorganisation compensation in accordance with provisions now contained in ss.54 and 55, must be taken as confirming that the mere fact of being unable to recover possession does not constitute hardship to the landlord (see *Graham* v. *Lamont*, 1971 S.C. 170 and *Copeland* v. *McQuaker*, 1973 S.L.T. 186, particularly the opinion of Sheriff Principal Maxwell, Q.C. (whose decision was sustained on appeal) at p. 190). While hardship is normally related to individuals, it may be pled by a company, a firm or a body of trustees who are in the position of landlords. Again, while hardship is normally personal to the parties involved in the proceedings, the effect of the decision on other parties such as employees, if not too remotely related to the tenancy, may be taken into consideration. A landlord's hardship may be minimised by balancing considerations such as the financial liabilities he would incur on the termination of the tenancy in payment of outgoing claims or the taking over of a bound sheep stock, or again by the fact he has purchased the farm with a tenant in possession, of whose security of tenure he must be regarded as having been aware, or, again, if he has acquired a tenanted farm gratuitously as opposed to purchasing it on the market. Also, in some cases the landlord's plea of hardship may fail because he has means of mitigating it otherwise than by terminating the tenancy.

Para. (*e*). It is necessary to appreciate the distinction between this provision and the provision contained in s.22(2)(b). That provision applies where planning permission for a non-agricultural use has already been granted or is not required otherwise than by virtue of any provision in the Planning Act. This provision applies when the proposed non-agricultural use is one for which permission is not required by reason of a particular provision in the Planning Act, an example being afforestation (see the Town and Country Planning (Scotland) Act 1972, s.19(2)(e), and *Carnegie* v. *Davidson*, 1966 S.L.T. (Land Ct.) 3). The tenant receiving and desiring to resist a notice to quit given in terms of s.22(2)(b) must call for arbitration on the statement in the notice. On the other hand, when a landlord invokes s.24(1)(e) and receives counter-notice from the tenant, the Land Court's consent to the operation of the notice to quit is required although with the merits and practicability of the landlord's proposals not being relevant, defence by the tenant will be difficult unless based on subs. (2) (*Carnegie* v. *Davidson*, above). As will be seen from the provisions of s.55, this ground of consent differs from the other grounds of consent in s.24 in relation to the tenant's entitlement to the additional payment for which s.54 provides.

Subs. (2)

This subsection takes the place of a proviso in identical terms which qualified s.26(1) of the 1949 Act. While a tenant must give notice in his pleadings if he is found on this provision, the plea is frequently taken either along with another defence by the tenant or by itself. The number of reported instances of it succeeding is, however, limited. It would seem to be difficult to envisage it doing so where the court has found in the landlord's favour on hardship. Even a fair and reasonable landlord could hardly be expected to insist on possession when he had satisfied the court that he would have sustained the greater hardship from an adverse decision. There are, however, cases of the plea succeeding against landlords seeking the court's consent on grounds other than hardship, the court's discretion in the matter being unlimited and enabling it to consider hardship although that had not been in issue as a ground of the landlord's application. In *Carnegie* v. *Davidson*, above, where consent was sought for afforestation under the equivalent of s.24(1)(e), the court, holding that the success of the landlord's scheme was "problematic" and that the landlord had another area equally suitable for the purpose, applied the proviso, as it then was, in favour of the tenant who was farming efficiently. Again in *Altyre Estate Trs*. v. *McLay*, 1975 S.L.T. (Land Ct.) 12, where the landlord was held to have succeeded under the equivalent of s.24(1)(b) *i.e.* on grounds of sound estate management, the tenant, an efficient farmer who would have suffered substantial loss if dispossessed and who was willing to take on the other farm with which amalgamation was proposed, invoked the plea successfully. More recently, the plea succeeded in the case of *Trustees of the Main Calthorpe Settlement* v. *Calder*, 1988 S.L.T. (Land Ct.) 30, a case of a near relative successor tenant occupying other agricultural land, involving the equivalent of Case 3 of Sched. 2 as the ground for consent in terms of s.25. The tenancy had been in the family and the holding efficiently farmed for many years and its addition as proposed to the landlord's other land was considered likely to make only a marginal addition to the efficiency of the unit.

Subs. (3)

This provision, which entitles the Land Court to attach conditions to its consent so as to ensure that the landlord uses the holding for the purposes stated in his application, may be regarded as a means of testing the good faith and veracity of the landlord in seeking consent to the operation of his notice to quit. The qualification referring to s.25(4) takes account of the fact that in certain amalgamation proposals affecting successor tenants, attachment of conditions to the consent is mandatory. A question may be said to arise whether the power is confined to cases of consent given in respect of applications under paras. (a), (b), (c) or (e) of subs. (1) and does not apply where hardship is the ground on which consent is given. Hardship applications, however, will nearly always disclose the landlord's proposals for the holding and in a number of instances conditions have been attached to the consent accordingly (see, *e.g.* *Robertson* v. *Lindsay*, 1957 S.L.C.R. 3; *Shaw-Mackenzie* v. *Forbes* 1957 S.L.C.R. 34; *Graham* v. *Lamont*, 1970 S.L.T. (Land Ct.) 100). The sanction for breach of conditions imposed under this section is to be found in s.27.

Subs. (4)

This takes account of the fact that conditions as attached to consent may subsist for a substantial period, during which there may be a significant change in circumstances.

Termination of tenancies acquired by succession

25.—(1) This section applies where notice to quit is duly given to the tenant of an agricultural holding who acquired right to the lease of the holding—

(a) under section 16 of the Succession (Scotland) Act 1964; or

(b) as a legatee, under section 11 of this Act.

(2) Notice to quit is duly given to a tenant to whom this section applies if—

(a) it complies with section 21 of this Act; and

(b) it specifies as its effective date—

(i) where, when he acquired right to the lease, the unexpired period of the lease exceeded 2 years, the term of outgo stipulated in the lease;

(ii) where, when he acquired right to the lease, the unexpired period was 2 years or less, the term of outgo stipulated in the lease or the corresponding date in any subsequent year, being a date not less than one nor more than 3 years after the said acquisition;

(c) where he was a near relative of the deceased tenant from whom he acquired right, it specifies the Case set out in Schedule 2 to this Act under which it is given; and

(d) where he was not a near relative of the deceased tenant from whom he acquired right, he acquired right to the lease after August 1, 1958.

(3) Section 22(1) of this Act shall apply and section 24 of this Act shall not apply where subsection (2)(c) above applies and notice to quit is duly given in accordance with subsection (2)(a) to (c) above; and in such a case the Land Court shall consent to the operation of a notice duly given—

(a) where the holding was let before January 1, 1984, if they are satisfied that the circumstances are as specified in any Case set out in Part I of Schedule 2 to this Act;

(b) where the holding was let on or after that date and the notice specifies any of Cases 4, 5 or 7 in that Schedule, unless the tenant satisfies them that the circumstances are not as specified in that Case (provided that, for the purposes of Case 7, the tenant shall not be required to prove that he is not the owner of any land);

(c) where the holding was let on or after that date, if they are satisfied that the circumstances are as specified in Case 6 in that Schedule;

except that where any of Cases 1, 2, 3, 6 or 7 in that Schedule is specified, the Court shall withhold consent on that ground if it appears to them that a fair and reasonable landlord would not insist on possession.

(4) Where consent is given because the circumstances are as specified in Case 2 or 6 in Schedule 2 to this Act, the Land Court shall impose such conditions as appear to them necessary to secure that the holding to which the notice relates will, within 2 years after the termination of the tenancy, be amalgamated with the land specified in the notice; and section 27 of this Act shall, with any necessary modifications, apply to a condition imposed under this subsection as that section applies to a condition imposed under section 24 of this Act.

(5) Part III of Schedule 2 to this Act shall have effect for the purposes of interpretation of this section and that Schedule.

DEFINITIONS
"agricultural holding": s.1(1).
"amalgamation": Sched. 2, Pt. III.
"landlord": s.85(1).
"lease": s.85(1).
"near relative": Sched. 2, Pt. III.
"notice to quit": s.21(2).
"tenant": s.85(1).

DERIVATIONS
Agricultural Holdings (Scotland) Act 1949, s.26A.
Agricultural Holdings (Amendment) (Scotland) Act 1983, ss.3, 4(2).

GENERAL NOTE
See Gill, paras. 358–361, 363.

Subs. (1)
Section 22(2)(g) excludes from the requirement of Land Court consent to its operation a notice to quit to which this section applies, *i.e.* a notice given to a successor, testate or intestate, of a former tenant, which complies with the conditions of subs. (2)(a)(b) and (d).

Subs. (2)
Firstly, under para. (a) the notice to quit must comply with the requirements of s.21.
Secondly, under para. (b) the notice has to be given for an effective date within the time limits prescribed. Under the 1949 Act as it originally stood, a successor, testate or intestate, had the same security of tenure as his predecessor. The 1958 Act changed the position in this respect by permitting the landlord to terminate the tenancy of a successor provided that he did so within certain time limits, disregard of which put the successor in the same position as his predecessor. These time limits run from the successor's acquisition of the tenancy which for the legatee or testate successor will normally be the date of the former tenant's death but in the case of the intestate successor that of his acquisition from the executor. If the lease when acquired by the successor tenant has more than two years to run, it must be terminated at the date of its expiry. Where the unexpired period is shorter, termination may be at the date of expiry or the

corresponding date in any subsequent year not less than one nor more than three years after the acquisition.

Consistently with these requirements, the notice may be given for a break in the lease occurring not less than a year after the acquisition.

Thirdly, under para. (d) the recipient of the notice must have acquired a right to the lease after August 1, 1958, when the 1958 Act took effect, and must not be within the category of near relatives of the former tenant as defined for purposes of the Act in Sched. 2, Pt. III, para. 1. The remaining subsections are concerned with the position of the near relative successor who since the passing of the 1968 Act has had security of tenure like his predecessor, but subject to the qualification that his tenancy may be terminated on any one of a number of special grounds now set out in Sched. 2 to this Act, provided that the necessary action is taken by the landlord within the time limits specified in subs. (2)(b).

Subs. (3)

This prescribes the procedure applicable where notice to quit is given to a successor within the statutory category of a near relative of the late tenant. Differing in this respect from a notice to quit given to a successor outwith that category, this notice is affected by s.22(1) and so requires Land Court consent for its operation if counter-notice is served. Provided, however, that he complies with the time limits prescribed in subs. (2)(b), the grounds on which a landlord may apply for consent are not restricted to those specified in s.24(1) but include the additional grounds contained in Sched. 2 which apply only to tenancies held by near relative successors. To found on any of these grounds the landlord must give a notice to quit complying with s.25(2)(a) to (c), *i.e.* fulfilling (1) the basic requirements of s.21 for all notices to quit; (2) the requirements of s.25(2)(b) as regards its effective date; and (3) the requirement of s.25(2)(c) by specifying the Case set out in Sched. 2 under which it is given. Sched. 2 distinguishes between holdings according to whether they were or were not let before January 1, 1984, the 1983 Act having made changes effective from that date. The three Cases in Pt. I of the Schedule apply to pre-1984 tenancies and in these cases the onus of satisfying the court is on the landlord. The four Cases in Pt. II of the Schedule apply to tenancies originating from 1984 onwards. In Case 6 the onus rests on the landlord in the usual way. In Cases 4, 5 or 7, however, it is for the tenant to satisfy the court that the circumstances are not as specified in the Case founded on, but where Case 7 is invoked the tenant is not to be required to prove that he is not the owner of any land. Except where consent is sought under Case 4 or Case 5, it is in the court's discretion to withhold consent on the fair and reasonable landlord plea.

For details of the Cases and comments thereon, reference should be made to Sched. 2 and the annotations thereto.

Subs. (4)

Cases 2 and 6 in the Schedule each involve a proposal by the landlord to use the holding for amalgamation with certain other land within two years of the tenancy ending. In these cases it has been considered appropriate to make mandatory the attachment to the Land Court's consent of conditions which will secure that the amalgamation, as projected, takes place within that period.

Subs. (5)

Part III of Sched. 2 contains, *inter alia*, the definition of "near relative" as meaning a surviving spouse or child, natural or adopted, of the deceased tenant.

Certificates of bad husbandry

26.—(1) For the purposes of section 22(2)(c) of this Act, the landlord of an agricultural holding may apply to the Land Court for a certificate that the tenant is not fulfilling his responsibilities to farm in accordance with the rules of good husbandry, and the Land Court, if satisfied that the tenant is not fulfilling his said responsibilities, shall grant such a certificate.

(2) In determining whether to grant a certificate under this section, the Land Court shall disregard any practice adopted by the tenant in compliance with any obligation imposed on him by or accepted by him under section 31B of the Control of Pollution Act 1974.

DEFINITIONS

"agricultural holding": s.1(1).
"landlord": s.85(1).
"rules of good husbandry": s.85(2); Agriculture (Scotland) Act 1948, Sched. 6.
"tenant": s.85(1).

DERIVATIONS
Agricultural Holdings (Scotland) Act 1949, s.28.
Agriculture Act 1958, Sched. 1, Pt. II, para. 38.
Water Act 1989, Sched. 25, para. 12.

GENERAL NOTE
See Gill, paras. 107–114 and 169. (For the corresponding English provision see the Agricultural Holdings Act 1986, Sched. 3, Pt. II, para. 9).

Subs. (1)
The Certificate, if obtained, enables the landlord, in accordance with s.22(2)(c), to serve within the prescribed time limit of nine months a notice to quit for the operation of which Land Court consent is not required. In making his application for a Certificate, the landlord must specify the husbandry rules on the breach of which he is to found and he must adduce convincing evidence to discharge the onus of proof (see, *e.g. McGill* v. *Bichan*, 1982 S.L.C.R. 33 and *Austin* v. *Gibson*, 1977 S.L.T. (Land Ct.) 12). A proof is required even if the application is unopposed (*Buchanan* v. *Buchanan*, 1983 S.L.T. (Land Ct.) 31) and the court's inspection of the holding, which may have to take place more than once, is a crucial element (*Rae* v. *Pringle*, 1990 Borders R.N. 27). In a recently reported case (*Cambusmore Estate Trs.* v. *Little*, 1991 S.L.T. (Land Ct.) 33), the court, having found that a definite breach of r. 1 of the Rules of Good Husbandry (which requires, *inter alia*, a reasonable standard of efficient production to be maintained with the unit kept in a condition to enable such a standard to be attained in future) had occurred, granted the Certificate, holding that the words "other relevant circumstances" as used in that rule were restricted to circumstances relating to the unit itself and its production and did not include mitigating factors relating to the tenant's personal circumstances. A tenant's breach may, however, be excused if it has been materially contributed to by the landlord's breach of the rules of good estate management as contained in Sched. 5 to the 1948 Act (*Austin* v. *Gibson* and *Buchanan* v. *Buchanan*, above) but the fact that the landlord is entitled to remedy the tenant's breach of the lease at his own hand does not debar him from claiming a Certificate based on such a breach (*Halliday* v. *Ferguson*, 1961 S.C. 24).

Subs. (2)
This replaces the proviso added to s.28 of the 1949 Act by the Water Act 1989, s.190, and Sched. 25, para. 12. Section 31(B) of the Control of Pollution Act 1974, as amended in terms of Sched. 11, para. 39, contains special provisions operative in an area designated as a nitrate-sensitive area (see Gill, para. 169).

Penalty for breach of condition

27.—(1) Where, on giving consent under section 22 of this Act to the operation of a notice to quit an agricultural holding or part of an agricultural holding, the Land Court imposes a condition under section 24(3) of this Act, and it is proved, on an application to the Land Court on behalf of the Crown that the landlord—

(a) has failed to comply with the condition within the period allowed, or
(b) has acted in breach of the condition,

the Land Court may impose on the landlord a penalty of an amount not exceeding 2 years' rent of the holding at the rate at which rent was payable immediately before the termination of the tenancy, or, where the notice to quit related to a part only of the holding, of an amount not exceeding the proportion of the said 2 years' rent which it appears to the Land Court is attributable to that part.

(2) A penalty imposed under this section shall be a debt due to the Crown and shall, when recovered, be paid into the Consolidated Fund.

DEFINITIONS
"agricultural holdings": s.1(1).
"landlord": s.85(1).
"notice to quit": s.21(2).
"termination of tenancy": s.85(1).

DERIVATIONS
   Agricultural Holdings (Scotland) Act 1989, s.30.
   Agriculture Act 1958, Sched. 1, Pt. II, para. 40.

GENERAL NOTE
   See Gill, para. 411. (For the corresponding English provision see the Agricultural Holdings
Act 1986, s.27 (6)–(9)).

Subs. (1)
   This enables the Land Court, on an application on behalf of the Crown, to impose a penalty
for breach by a landlord of conditions attached by the court in giving consent to a notice to quit
in exercise of the power given them by s.24(3) or in compliance with the direction in s.25(4).

Subs. (2)
   The penalty, which will be recoverable by civil diligence, belongs to the Crown and it is not
available to compensate the tenant who may be deprived of his tenancy unjustly. It may be
questionable if, in practice, the maximum penalty of two years' rent represents a sufficient
deterrent. Before its amendment in 1958, s.30 of the 1949 Act empowered the Secretary of
State to take possession of the land affected by a breach.

Effect on notice to quit of sale of holding

   28.—(1) This section shall apply where a contract for the sale of the
landlord's interest in land which comprises or forms part of an agricultural
holding is made after the giving of a notice to quit and before its expiry.
   (2) Unless, within the period of 3 months ending with the date on which a
contract to which this section applies is made, the landlord and the tenant
have agreed in writing whether or not the notice to quit shall continue to
have effect—
   (a) the landlord shall—
             (i) within 14 days after the making of the contract; or
             (ii) before the expiry of the notice to quit,
        whichever is the earlier, give notice to the tenant of the making of the
        contract; and
   (b) the tenant may, before the expiry of the notice to quit and not later
        than one month after he has received notice under paragraph (a)
        above, give notice in writing to the landlord that he elects that the
        notice to quit shall continue to have effect.
   (3) Where this section applies, unless—
   (a) the landlord and tenant have agreed that the notice to quit shall
        continue to have effect;
   (b) the tenant has so elected, under subsection (2)(b) above; or
   (c) the landlord having failed to give notice of the making of the contract
        in accordance with subsection (2)(a) above, the tenant quits the
        holding in consequence of the notice to quit,
the notice to quit shall cease to have effect.
   (4) Where this section applies and there is an agreement between the
landlord and the tenant that the notice to quit shall continue to have effect,
the notice shall not be invalid by reason only that the agreement is
conditional.

DEFINITIONS
   "agricultural holdings": s.1(1).
   "landlord": s.85(1).
   "notice to quit": s.21(2).
   "tenant": s.85(1).

DERIVATIONS
   Agricultural Holdings (Scotland) Act 1949, s.31.

GENERAL NOTE
   See Gill, paras. 414–416.

Subs. (1)

As is indicated here, the section is concerned with the situation in which a landlord is seeking to sell the holding with entry and vacant possession at or after the termination of the current tenancy. The section originated in the Act of 1923 under which tenants had no security of tenure beyond the endurance of their leases, the intention apparently being to dissuade the landlord from terminating tenancies solely for the purpose of selling with vacant possession. With the security of tenure now enjoyed by tenants the provision would appear to be unnecessary. Its counterpart in England, s.30 of the Agricultural Holdings Act 1948, is no longer in force. Its continued existence in Scottish legislation, however, may be said to represent a trap for the unwary as it means that even when a notice to quit has been served and became unconditional as a result of the tenant not taking timeous action to oppose it, or again where his opposition has failed, the landlord cannot conclude an effective contract of sale till the operative date of the notice to quit arrives.

Subss. (2) and (3)

Subs. (2) indicates the action to be taken in the situation envisaged in subs. (1) and the way in which the difficulty can be overcome by agreement between the parties or by the tenant's election to let the notice to quit remain in force after receiving from the landlord the appropriate notice of the contract of sale. Subs. (3)(c) covers the situation where, with the landlord having failed to give notice to the tenant in accordance with subs. (2)(a), the tenant has gone out in compliance with the notice to quit. In these circumstances the notice to quit is to be regarded as effective, with the result that the tenant will be entitled to make the usual outgoing claims.

Subs. (4)

This provision enables a landlord to arrange with his tenant that the notice to quit will be effective if, but only if, the landlord is able, during the currency of the notice, to find a purchaser for the property. In accordance with subs. (2), however, the contract with the purchaser will have to be concluded not later than three months after the agreement between landlord and tenant.

Notice to quit part of holding to be valid in certain cases

29.—(1) A notice to quit part of an agricultural holding held on a tenancy from year to year shall not be invalid on the ground that it relates to part only of the holding if it is given—

(a) for the purpose of adjusting the boundaries between agricultural units or of amalgamating agricultural units or parts thereof, or

(b) with a view to the use of the land to which the notice relates for any of the purposes mentioned in subsection (2) below,

and the notice states that it is given for that purpose or with a view to such use, as the case may be.

(2) The purposes referred to in subsection (1)(b) above are—

(a) the erection of farm labourers' cottages or other houses with or without gardens;

(b) the provision of gardens for farm labourers' cottages or other houses;

(c) the provision of allotments;

(d) the provision of small holdings under the Small Landholders (Scotland) Acts 1886 to 1931, or of such holdings as are referred to in section 64 of the Agriculture (Scotland) Act 1948;

(e) the planting of trees;

(f) the opening or working of coal, ironstone, limestone, brickearth, or other minerals, or of a stone quarry, clay, sand, or gravel pit, or the construction of works or buildings to be used in connection therewith;

(g) the making of a watercourse or reservoir;

(h) the making of a road, railway, tramroad, siding, canal or basin, wharf, or pier, or work connected therewith.

DEFINITIONS

"agricultural holding": s.1(1).

"agricultural unit": s.85(1).

"notice to quit": s.21(2).

DERIVATIONS
  Agricultural Holdings (Scotland) Act 1949, s.32.

GENERAL NOTE
  See Gill, Chap. 20. (For the corresponding English provision see the Agricultural Holdings
Act 1986, s.31).

Subs. (1)
  A notice to quit part of the subjects of let is at common law invalid and but for some enabling
provision would be invalid under the Act as not relating to the whole subjects of let.
  The facilities given by the section are restricted to yearly lets, including lets running on tacit
relocation. They do not enable a tenancy to be broken during its currency. They are made
available in general terms for adjustments of boundaries and amalgamations affecting agricultural units and also for certain specific purposes as listed in subs. (2). The notice to quit must
state the purpose or intended use for which it is given.

Subs. (2)
  There is some doubt as to whether "other houses" in paras. (a) and (b) is restricted to houses
for purposes connected with agriculture. On the basis of an English decision in the case of
Paddock Investments v. *Lorg* [1975] 236 E.G. 803, Gill (at para. 418) considers that the
restriction applies. The opposite view, as taken in Connell's *Agricultural Holdings (Scotland)*
Act (6th ed.), p. 148), would make the section applicable to housing development generally and
might be expected to be used by landlords such as local authorities seeking building ground. In
practice, however, it appears that the section is not often invoked. While resumption clauses as
usually found in agricultural leases cannot be used for agricultural purposes, their use for any
other purpose has the advantage that the tenant cannot, as he can do under s.29, invoke the
procedure for contesting the operation of a notice to quit.
  In the case of *Hamilton* v. *Lorimer*, 1959 S.L.C.R. 7 the tenant appealed successfully to the
Land Court against sanction being given by the Secretary of State for the operation of a notice
to quit under s.32 of the 1949 Act.

Tenant's right to treat notice to quit part as notice to quit entire holding

  30. Where a notice to quit part of an agricultural holding is given to a
tenant, being a notice which is rendered valid by section 29 of this Act, and
the tenant within 28 days after—
  (a) the giving of the notice, or
  (b) where the operation of the notice depends on any proceedings under
      the foregoing provisions of this Act, the time when it is determined
      that the notice has effect,
whichever is later, gives to the landlord a counter-notice in writing that he
accepts the notice as a notice to quit the entire holding, to take effect at the
same time as the original notice, the notice to quit shall have effect
accordingly.

DEFINITIONS
  "agricultural holdings": s.1(1).
  "landlord": s.85(1).
  "notice to quit": s.21(2).
  "tenant": s.85(1).

DERIVATION
  Agricultural Holdings (Scotland) Act 1949, s.33.

GENERAL NOTE
  See Gill, para. 421. (For the corresponding English provision see the Agricultural Holdings
Act 1986, s.32).
  If the tenant who is to lose part of his holding by the operation of s.29 does not wish to
continue the tenancy of the holding as thus reduced, he can terminate the tenancy at the date at
which the notice to quit takes effect by serving a counter-notice on the landlord within 28 days
after he received notice to quit under s.29, or, if he has contested that notice, 28 days after the
Land Court's decision against him.
  For the effect of such action on the tenant's claim for compensation for disturbance, see
s.43(7).

Reduction of rent where tenant dispossessed of part of holding

31.—(1) Where—

(a) the tenancy of part of an agricultural holding terminates by reason of a notice to quit which is rendered valid by section 29 of this Act; or

(b) the landlord of an agricultural holding resumes possession of part of the holding in pursuance of a provision in that behalf contained in the lease,

the tenant shall be entitled to a reduction of rent of an amount, to be determined by arbitration, proportionate to that part of the holding, together with an amount in respect of any depreciation of the value to him of the residue of the holding caused by the severance or by the use to be made of the part severed.

(2) Where subsection (1)(b) above applies, the arbiter, in determining the amount of the reduction, shall take into account any benefit or relief allowed to the tenant under the lease in respect of the part whose possession is being resumed.

DEFINITIONS
"agricultural holding": s.1(1).
"landlord": s.85(1).
"lease": s.85(1).
"notice to quit": s.21(2).
"tenant": s.85(1).

DERIVATIONS
Agricultural Holdings (Scotland) Act 1949, s.34.

GENERAL NOTE
See Gill, paras. 228–233. (For the corresponding English provision see the Agricultural Holdings Act 1986, s.33).

Subs. (1)
When the size of the holding is reduced as a result of the operation of a notice to quit affecting part of the holding or the exercise of a power of resumption in the lease, the tenant is entitled to have the rent reduced. Three elements enter into the arbiter's calculation of this reduction. Firstly, the rental value of the land of which the tenant is dispossessed forms the basis of assessment of the reduction of rent proportionate to the part of the holding taken back, the basis of assessment being the rental value of the area of which the tenant is dispossessed rather than the average rental per hectare of the holding (*Hoile* v. *Sheriffs*, 1948 S.L.C.R. 24; *cf.* s.43(7)). Secondly, there is the severance element, which should be assessed on the lines applied in compensation for compulsory acquisition. Finally, there is the injurious affection element which will be assessed, as in a compulsory acquisition, reflecting any prejudice to the land retained in the holding likely to be caused by the intended use of the land taken back by the landlord.

Subs. (2)
If, as sometimes happens, the lease makes provision for compensation for the tenant's loss of part of the holding as a result of the exercise of a power of assumption and this provision is more favourable to the tenant than the provision in this section, the tenant is entitled to disregard the statutory provision and base his claim on the lease alone. The same applies to the tenant's outgoing claims under s.49.

Further restrictions on operation of certain notices to quit

32.—(1) Subsections (2) to (5) below shall apply where—

(a) notice to quit an agricultural holding or part of an agricultural holding is given to a tenant; and

(b) the notice includes a statement in accordance with section 22(2) of this Act and paragraph (d) thereof to the effect that it is given by reason of the tenant's failure to remedy a breach of a kind referred to in section 66(1) of this Act.

(2) If not later than one month from the giving of the notice to quit the tenant serves on the landlord a counter-notice in writing requiring that this subsection shall apply to the notice to quit, subject to subsection (3) below, the notice to quit shall not have effect (whether as a notice to which section 22(1) of this Act does or does not apply) unless the Land Court consent to the operation thereof.

(3) A counter-notice under subsection (2) above shall be of no effect if within one month after the giving of the notice to quit the tenant serves on the landlord an effective notice under section 23(2) of this Act requiring the validity of the reason stated in the notice to quit to be determined by arbitration.

(4) Where—

(a) the tenant has served on the landlord a notice of the kind referred to in subsection (3) above;

(b) the notice to quit would, apart from this subsection, have effect in consequence of the arbitration; and

(c) not later than one month from the date on which the arbiter's award is delivered to the tenant the tenant serves on the landlord a counter-notice in writing requiring that this subsection shall apply to the notice to quit;

the notice to quit shall not have effect (whether as a notice to which section 22(1) of this Act does or does not apply) unless the Land Court consent to the operation thereof.

(5) On an application made in that behalf by the landlord, the Land Court shall consent under subsection (2) or (4) above or (6) below to the operation of the notice to quit unless in all the circumstances it appears to them that a fair and reasonable landlord would not insist on possession.

(6) Where a notice to quit is given in accordance with section 66(3) of this Act in a case where the arbitration under that section followed an earlier notice to quit to which subsection (1) above applied, if the tenant serves on the landlord a counter-notice in writing within one month after the giving of the subsequent notice to quit (or, if the date specified in that notice for the termination of the tenancy is earlier, before that date), the notice to quit given under section 66(3) of this Act shall not have effect unless the Land Court consent to the operation thereof.

DEFINITIONS
"agricultural holding": s.1(1).
"landlord": s.85(1).
"notice to quit": s.21(2).
"tenant": s.85(1).
"termination of tenancy": s.85(1).

DERIVATIONS
Agriculture (Miscellaneous Provisions) Act 1976, s.14.

GENERAL NOTE
See Gill, paras. 342–353. (For the corresponding English provision see the Agricultural Holdings Act 1986, s.28).

Subs. (1)
As disclosed here the operative provisions of the section apply where a notice to quit in terms of s.22(2)(d) is given founding on the tenant's failure to comply with a demand to remedy a breach of a condition of his tenancy by doing any work of provision, repair, maintenance or replacement of fixed equipment, that being the kind of breach referred to in s.66(1).

Subs. (2)
Normally a notice to quit given in terms of s.22(2) does not require Land Court consent for its operation and so cannot be met with a counter-notice, but in the particular circumstances referred to in subs. (1), the tenant is empowered, by serving a counter-notice, to make Land Court consent necessary.

Subs. (3)

The counter-notice is, however, rendered ineffective if within the month following the service of the notice to quit the tenant takes the course open to him with any s.22(2) notice to quit by calling for arbitration on the reasons stated therein.

Subs. (4)

When the tenant, having duly called for arbitration, receives an adverse decision from the arbiter, he has a month to serve a counter-notice applying this subsection to the notice to quit and making the notice ineffective except with Land Court consent.

Subs. (5)

This subsection has the result, however, that the only ground on which the Land Court can refuse their consent is that in their view a fair and reasonable landlord would not insist on possession. Again, as pointed out by Gill (para. 349), the wording of this provision is significantly different from that of the proviso to s.26 of the 1949 Act (now replaced by s.24(2) of this Act), the use of the words "shall consent...unless" putting the onus on the tenant to demonstrate circumstances justifying the refusal of consent.

Subs. (6)

One of the possible consequences of the power conferred on arbiters by s.66 is that a landlord may have to serve a second notice to quit, the first one having been rendered inoperative by the time allowed by the arbiter for the tenant to comply with the demand to remedy. In these circumstances the Land Court, on application to them being made, will fix a new date for termination of the tenancy and the landlord can serve a second notice to quit in conformity with the provisions of s.66(3). The subsection under discussion here enables the tenant by counter-notice to make the operation of the second notice to quit subject to Land Court consent.

PART IV

COMPENSATION FOR IMPROVEMENTS

Improvements

33. In this Part the following are referred to as "improvements"—
   "1923 Act improvement" means an improvement carried out on an agricultural holding, being an improvement specified in Schedule 3 to this Act, and begun before July 31, 1931;
   "1931 Act improvement" means an improvement so carried out, being an improvement specified in Schedule 4 to this Act and begun on or after July 31, 1931 and before November 1, 1948;
   "old improvement" means a 1923 Act improvement or a 1931 Act improvement;
   "new improvement" means an improvement carried out on an agricultural holding, being an improvement specified in Schedule 5 to this Act begun on or after November 1, 1948.

DEFINITIONS
   "agricultural holding": s.1(1).

DERIVATIONS
Agricultural Holdings (Scotland) Act 1949, ss.36, 47.

GENERAL NOTE
   See Gill, para. 473.
   This classification of improvements is based on the principle that a tenant's rights to compensation for improvements depends on the law as it stood when he made the improvements and is unaffected by any changes in the law which may have taken place subsequently but before his outgoing. While claims for old improvements in the 1923 Act category must now be rare, the right to make such claims does not begin to prescribe until they are exigible. Thus, for example, the successor of the tenant who made the improvement may still be occupying a holding where there is an improvement of a lasting nature such as a building for which compensation on the basis of the 1923 Act will be payable at his outgoing.

Right to compensation for improvements

34.—(1) Subject to subsections (2) to (4), (7) and (8) below, and to sections 36 and 39 to 42 of this Act, a tenant of an agricultural holding shall be entitled, on quitting the holding at the termination of the tenancy, to compensation from the landlord in respect of improvements carried out by the tenant.

(2) A tenant whose lease was entered into before January 1, 1921 shall not be entitled to compensation under this section for an improvement which he was required to carry out by the terms of his tenancy.

(3) A tenant shall not be entitled to compensation under this section for an old improvement carried out on land which, at the time the improvement was begun, was not a holding within the meaning of the Agricultural Holdings (Scotland) Act 1923 as originally enacted, or land to which provisions of that Act relating to compensation for improvements and disturbance were applied by section 33 of that Act.

(4) Nothing in this section shall prejudice the right of a tenant to any compensation to which he is entitled—
   (a) in the case of an old improvement, under custom, agreement or otherwise;
   (b) in the case of a new improvement, under an agreement in writing between the landlord and the tenant;
in lieu of any compensation provided by this section.

(5) Where a tenant has remained in an agricultural holding during two or more tenancies, he shall not be deprived of his right to compensation under subsection (1) above by reason only that the improvements were not carried out during the tenancy on the termination of which he quits the holding.

(6) Subject to section 36(4) of this Act, a tenant shall be entitled to compensation under this section in respect of the 1931 Act improvement specified in paragraph 28 of Schedule 4 to this Act, or the new improvement specified in paragraph 32 of Schedule 5 to this Act (laying down of temporary pasture), notwithstanding that the laying down or the leaving at the termination of the tenancy of temporary pasture was in contravention of the terms of the lease or of any agreement made by the tenant respecting the method of cropping the arable lands; but, in ascertaining the amount of the compensation, the arbiter shall take into account any injury to or deterioration of the holding due to the contravention (except insofar as the landlord may have recovered damages therefor).

(7) Where under an agreement in writing entered into before January 1, 1921 a tenant is entitled to compensation which is fair and reasonable having regard to the circumstances existing at the time of the making of the agreement, for an old improvement specified in Part III of Schedule 3 to this Act or in Part III of Schedule 4 to this Act, such compensation shall, as respects that improvement, be substituted for compensation under subsection (1) above.

(8) Compensation shall not be payable under this Part of this Act in respect of repairs of the kind specified in paragraph 29 of Schedule 3 to this Act or in paragraph 29 of Schedule 4 to this Act unless, before beginning to execute any such repairs, the tenant gave to the landlord notice in writing under paragraph (29) of Schedule 1 to the Agricultural Holdings (Scotland) Act 1923, or under paragraph (30) of Schedule 1 to the Small Landholders and Agricultural Holdings (Scotland) Act 1931, of his intention to execute the repairs, together with particulars thereof, and the landlord failed to exercise the right conferred on him by the said paragraph (29) or, as the case may be, the said paragraph (30) to execute the repairs himself within a reasonable time after receiving the notice.

DEFINITIONS
   "agricultural holding": s.1(1).

"landlord": s.85(1).
"new improvement": s.33.
"old improvement": s.33.
"tenant": s.85(1).
"termination of tenancy": s.85(1).

DERIVATIONS
Agricultural Holdings (Scotland) Act 1949, ss.37, 41, 42, 43, 44(4), 45, 53, 54.

GENERAL NOTE
See Gill, paras. 471–496. (For the corresponding English provision see the Agricultural Holdings Act 1986, s.64 and Scheds. 7–9).

Subs. (1)
The scheme of this Part of the Act being to deal together with old and new improvements, this subsection replaces ss.37(1) and 48(1) of the 1949 Act. The tenant is entitled to compensation for improvements on quitting at the termination of the tenancy as defined in s.85(1) whether or not he leaves as a consequence of a notice to quit which under s.43 is normally essential for compensation for disturbance to be due.

Subs. (2)
The exclusion, as previously contained in provisos to ss.37(1) and 48(1) of the 1949 Act, applies irrespective of when the improvement has been carried out.

Subs. (3)
This replaces s.44(4) of the 1949 Act dealing with old improvements. As to rights of compensation in relation to non-statutory land, see Gill, para. 20.

Subs. (4)
This replaces s.37(2) of the 1949 Act for old improvements and s.48(2) for new improvements, being provisions for what is known as "substituted compensation," *i.e.* compensation for improvements claimed on a basis other than that of the relevant provisions of the Act. In the case of new improvements, para. (b) makes the only alternative basis agreement in writing between the parties but such an agreement need not be in probative form (see s.78). By contrast, para. (a), dealing with old improvements, contains a much wider basis for substituted compensation, referring as it does to "custom, agreement or otherwise." The last two words would seem to imply that verbal agreement, proved in any way, would suffice. As regards customary compensation, it may be noted here that there have not been included in this Act the provisions of s.100 of the 1949 Act, which in broad general terms preserved any rights derived from, *inter alia*, "any custom of the country." Section 85(4), however, replacing s.93(5) of the 1949 Act, provides for custom (apparently local or general) being taken into account in relation to the terms and provisions of leases or agreements relating to agricultural holdings. Customary compensation as arising under s.37(2) of the 1949 Act, is discussed in Connell (*op. cit.*, p. 156, note 6).
As noted under the reference to subs. (7), the general rule is that substituted compensation does not apply to improvements listed in Pt. III of the statutory Schedules.

Subs. (5)
This replaces ss.45 and 54 of the 1949 Act, which made identical provisions for old and new improvements. It is implied that the tenancies must have been continuous.

Subs. (6)
This replaces s.43 of the 1949 Act (old improvements) and s.53 (new improvements). The tenant's right to compensation for temporary pasture, even if laid down in contravention of the lease, is a consequence of his freedom of cropping in terms of s.7. In contrast with the laying down of permanent pasture, it does not require the prior consent of the landlord to qualify for compensation. Where there is injury or deterioration of the holding by reason of the contravention of the lease, the landlord may have recovered damages under s.7(3)(b).

Subs. (7)
This replaces s.42 of the 1949 Act. There must now be very few cases in which its provisions will apply, particularly as it relates only to the improvements of a temporary nature as appearing in Pt. III of the statutory Schedules. A commentary on certain aspects of the 1949 section is to be found in Connell (*op. cit.*, pp. 160/161).

It should be noted here that it is only in the circumstances of this subsection and in the special case of market gardens (see s.41(1)) that substituted compensation can apply to Pt. III improvements.

Subs. (8)

This replaces s.41 of the 1949 Act, excluding compensation for repairs to buildings as old improvements unless prior notice in writing was given to the landlord to conform to the provisions of the 1923 Act or those of the 1931 Act, as the case might be, and he failed to exercise, within a reasonable time, his right to execute the repairs himself.

Payment of compensation by incoming tenant

35.—(1) This section applies to compensation which is payable or has been paid to an outgoing tenant of an agricultural holding by the landlord under or in pursuance of this Act or the Agricultural Holdings (Scotland) Act 1923, the Small Landholders and Agricultural Holdings (Scotland) Act 1931, the Agriculture (Scotland) Act 1948 or the 1949 Act.

(2) Subject to subsection (3) below, any agreement made after November 1, 1948 between an incoming tenant and his landlord whereby the tenant undertakes to pay to the outgoing tenant or to refund to the landlord any compensation to which this section applies shall be null and void.

(3) Subsection (2) above shall not apply in the case of an improvement of a kind referred to in Part III of Schedule 5 to this Act, where the agreement is in writing and states a maximum amount which may be payable thereunder by the incoming tenant.

(4) Where, on entering into occupation of an agricultural holding, a tenant, with the consent in writing of the landlord pays to the outgoing tenant compensation to which this section applies—

(a) in respect of an old improvement, in pursuance of an agreement in writing made before November 1, 1948; or

(b) where subsection (3) above applies,

the incoming tenant shall be entitled, on quitting the holding, to claim compensation for the improvement or part in like manner, if at all, as the outgoing tenant would have been entitled if the outgoing tenant had remained tenant of the holding and quitted it at the time at which the tenant quits it.

(5) Where, in a case not falling within subsection (2) or (3) above, a tenant, on entering into occupation of an agricultural holding, paid to his landlord any amount in respect of the whole or part of a new improvement, he shall, subject to any agreement in writing between the landlord and the tenant, be entitled on quitting the holding to claim compensation in respect of the improvement or part in like manner, if at all, as he would have been entitled if he had been tenant of the holding at the time when the improvement was carried out and the improvement or part thereof had been carried out by him.

DEFINITIONS

"agricultural holding": s.1(1).
"improvement": ss.33, 85(1).
"landlord": s.85(1).
"new improvement": ss.33, 85(1).
"old improvement": ss.33, 85(1).
"tenant": s.85(1).

DERIVATIONS

Agricultural Holdings (Scotland) Act 1949, ss.11, 46, 55.

GENERAL NOTE

See Gill, paras. 475, 491. (For the corresponding English provision see the Agricultural Holding Act 1986, s.69(2)(3)).

Subs. (1)

The terms of this subsection indicate that the section is to apply to payment of compensation to an outgoing tenant, whether for new improvements or for 1923 or 1931 old improvements.

Subss. (2) and (3)

Subs. (2) replaces s.11(1) and (2) of the 1949 Act. It will be noted that the exception made by subs. (3) is restricted to new improvements of a temporary nature. It is, however, only agreements between landlords and incoming tenants which are affected by these provisions. They do not affect any agreements which may be made between incoming and outgoing tenants.

Subs. (4)

Subs. (4) replaces s.46 of the 1949 Act. Head (a) covers the first part of the 1949 section and deals with the case of a pre-November 1948 agreement for payment for an old improvement; head (b) covers the latter part of s.46 along with s.55(1) of the 1949 Act and thus applies to agreements entered into after November 1, 1948 for payment for old improvements or new improvements within the category of temporary improvements covered by the current or post-1948 Schedule. It will be noted that this Schedule is being applied here even although the improvements in question may be old improvements made before it came into force. This is the effect of the reference in s.46 of the 1949 Act to "an old improvement of the kind specified in Pt. III of the First Schedule to this Act": *cf.* subs. (3), referring to Pt. III of Sched. 5 to this Act. The practical effect as regards an agreement enfranchised by these provisions is that the tenant who has made payment for his predecessor's improvements will have a claim for these improvements in so far as they still have value at his outgoing.

Subs. (5)

This replaces s.55(2) of the 1949 Act, covering cases of agreement not within subss. (2) or (3) of the section. These subsections concern agreements involving an incoming tenant, a landlord and an outgoing tenant. There may, however, be no outgoing tenant, in which case the incoming tenant will simply be paying the landlord for a new improvement. Again, the improvement may be one outwith the category of temporary improvements referred to in subs. (3). In such cases, in the absence of agreement to the contrary, the tenant, having paid for the improvement, is entitled to claim for it at his outgoing in so far as it still has value.

Amount of compensation under this Part

36.—(1) Subject to subsections (2) to (4) below, the amount of any compensation payable to a tenant under this Part of this Act shall be such sum as fairly represents the value of the improvement to an incoming tenant.

(2) In the ascertainment of the amount of compensation payable in respect of an old improvement, there shall be taken into account any benefit which the landlord has given or allowed to the tenant (under the lease or otherwise) in consideration of the tenant carrying out the improvement.

(3) In the ascertainment of the amount of compensation payable under this section for a new improvement, there shall be taken into account—

   (a) any benefit which the landlord has agreed in writing to give the tenant in consideration of the tenant carrying out the improvement; and

   (b) any grant out of moneys provided by Parliament which has been or will be made to the tenant in respect of the improvement.

(4) In ascertaining the amount of any compensation payable under section 34(6) of this Act, the arbiter shall take into account any injury to or deterioration of the holding due to the contravention of the lease or agreement referred to in that subsection, except in so far as the landlord has recovered damages in respect of such injury or deterioration.

DEFINITIONS

"landlord": s.85(1).

"lease": s.85(1).

"new improvement": s.33.

"old improvement": s.33.

"tenant": s.85(1).

DERIVATIONS
    Agricultural Holding (Scotland) Act 1949, ss.38, 43, 44(1), 49, 53.

GENERAL NOTE
    See Gill, paras. 478, 479, 490. (For the corresponding English provision see the Agricultural
Holdings Act 1986, s.66).

Subs. (1)
    This replaces ss.38 (old improvements) and 49(1) (new improvements) of the 1949 Act, the
same basis of valuation applying in both cases. This basis applies whether or not there is an
incoming tenant and in any event falls to be applied disregarding any special needs of an
incoming tenant, should there be one, the true criterion being the value to a hypothetical tenant
continuing to use the holding as has been done. The value of the improvement should be
assessed as the addition it makes to the value of the holding as a whole (*Mackenzie* v.
McGillivray, 1921 S.C. 722). While the cost to the outgoing tenant of making the improvement
is of doubtful relevance, an appropriate basis of assessment may be the current or present-day
cost of providing the improvement, less some allowance for the age and condition of the item in
question.

Subs. (2)
    This deals with old improvements and replaces s.44(1)(a) of the 1949 Act. Differing in this
respect from the corresponding provision for new improvements (see subs. (3)) the benefit for
which deduction is to be made does not require to be documented in any way. It must, however,
be given voluntarily and not under obligation by the landlord. It will often have taken the form
of provision of material for work or a pecuniary contribution to its cost. In the absence of
express evidence it is for the landlord to prove its causal connection with the execution of the
improvement (*McQuater* v. *Ferguson*, 1911 S.C. 640; *Earl of Galloway* v. *McLelland*, 1915 S.C.
1062; *Mackenzie* v. *McGillivray*, above).
    The provisions of subs. (1)(b)(2)(3) and (5) of s.44 of the 1949 Act dealing with deductions
for manure sold off the holding, and Government grants for liming or for drainage works
carried out to implement Defence regulations, being apparently regarded as spent, have been
omitted.

Subs. (3)
    This deals with new improvements and replaces s.49(2) of the 1949 Act.
    Para. (a). The requirement of a written agreement would seem to eliminate some, at least, of
the questions which could arise in connection with an old improvement. Problems of valuation,
however, can arise in either case and it is suggested by Gill (para. 478) that the proportion of the
original cost represented by the benefit should be ascertained and that proportion of the current
value of the improvement should be deducted to arrive at the amount of compensation due.
    Para. (b). In the case of improvement grants for the provision or repair of housing accommo-
dation, deduction will be required only so long as the grant conditions remain in force (see
Housing (Scotland) Act 1987, ss.246 and 256 (as amended in terms of Sched. 11, para. 54)).

Subs. (4)
    See note to s.34(6), the content of which subsection, so far as replacing ss.43 and 53 of the
1949 Act, is being reported in this subsection.

Consents necessary for compensation for some improvements

    37.—(1) Compensation under this Part of this Act shall not be payable
for—
    (a) a 1923 Act improvement specified in Part I of Schedule 3 to this Act;
    (b) a 1931 Act improvement specified in Part I of Schedule 4 to this Act;
        or
    (c) a new improvement specified in Part I of Schedule 5 to this Act;
unless, before the improvement was carried out, the landlord consented to it
in writing (whether unconditionally or upon terms as to compensation or
otherwise agreed on between the parties).
    (2) Where such consent was given on terms agreed as to compensation,
the compensation payable under the agreement shall be substituted for
compensation under section 34 of this Act.

DEFINITIONS
  "1923 Act improvement": s.33.
  "1931 Act improvement": s.33.
  "landlord": s.85(1).
  "new improvement": s.33.

DERIVATIONS
  Agricultural Holdings (Scotland) Act 1949, ss.39, 50.

GENERAL NOTE
  See Gill, paras. 474, 481, 492. (For the corresponding English provision see the Agricultural
Holding Act 1986, s.67).

Subs. (1)
  This replaces ss.39(1) (old improvements) and 50(1) (new improvements) of the 1949 Act,
stating the rule that for permanent or major improvements listed in the first part of the
Schedules the landlord's prior written consent is necessary if the improvement is to qualify for
compensation at the tenant's outgoing. The terms on which consent is given, which can vary
widely, are exemplified by Gill (para. 481). It appears that an agreement excluding compensation is valid (*Turnbull* v. *Millar*, 1942 S.C. 521).

Subs. (2)
  This replaces ss.39(2) (old improvements) and 50(2) (new improvements) of the 1949 Act.
When substituted compensation has been agreed in this way, an arbiter will, in accordance with
Sched. 7, para. 13, make an award in terms of the agreement.

Notice required of certain improvements

38.—(1) Subject to subsections (2) to (6) below, compensation under this
Act shall not be payable for—
  (a) a 1923 Act improvement specified in Part II of Schedule 3 to this Act;
  (b) a 1931 Act improvement specified in Part II of Schedule 4 to this Act;
  (c) a new improvement specified in Part II of Schedule 5 to this Act;
unless the tenant gave notice to the landlord in accordance with subsection
(3) below of his intention to carry it out and of the manner in which he
proposed to do so.
  (2) Subsection (1) above shall not apply in the case of an improvement
mentioned in subsection (1)(a) or (b) above, if the parties agreed by the
lease or otherwise to dispense with the requirement for notice under subsection (3).
  (3) Notice shall be in accordance with this subsection if it is in writing
and—
  (a) in the case of an improvement mentioned in subsection (1)(a) above,
      it was notice under section 3 of the Agricultural Holdings (Scotland)
      Act 1923, given not more than 3 nor less than 2 months,
  (b) in the case of an improvement mentioned in subsection (1)(b) above,
      it was notice under the said section 3, given not more than 6 nor less
      than 3 months,
  (c) in the case of an improvement mentioned in subsection (1)(c) above,
      it was given not less than 3 months,
before the tenant began to carry out the improvement.
  (4) In the case of an improvement mentioned in subsection (1)(a) or (b)
above, compensation shall not be payable unless—
  (a) the parties agreed on the terms as to compensation or otherwise on
      which the improvement was to be carried out;
  (b) where no such agreement was made and the tenant did not withdraw
      the notice, the landlord failed to exercise his right under the said
      section 3 to carry out the improvement himself within a reasonable
      time; or
  (c) in the case of an improvement mentioned in subsection (1)(b) above,
      where the landlord gave notice of objection and the matter was

referred under section 28(2) of the Small Landholders and Agricultural Holdings (Scotland) Act 1931 for determination by the appropriate authority, that authority was satisfied that the improvement should be carried out and the improvement was carried out in accordance with any directions given by that authority as to the manner of so doing.

(5) If the parties agreed (either after notice was given under this section or by an agreement to dispense with it) on terms as to compensation, the compensation payable under the agreement shall be substituted for compensation under this Part of this Act.

(6) In subsection (4) above, "the appropriate authority" means—

(a) in relation to the period before September 4, 1939, the Department of Agriculture for Scotland;

(b) in relation to the period starting on that day, the Secretary of State.

DEFINITIONS
"1923 Act improvement": s.33.
"1931 Act improvement": s.33.
"improvement": s.85(1).
"landlord": s.85(1).
"lease": s.85(1).
"new improvement": s.85(1).
"tenant": s.85(1).

DERIVATIONS
Agricultural Holdings (Scotland) Act 1949, ss.40, 51.

GENERAL NOTE
See Gill, paras. 482–485, 494, 495. (For the corresponding English provision see the Agricultural Holdings Act 1986, s.68).

Subs. (1)
This replaces ss.40(1)(2) (old improvements) and 51(1) (new improvements) of the 1949 Act and applies the requirement of notice to the landlord before execution to all improvements appearing in Pt. II of the statutory schedules. The only 1923 Act improvement affected falls under the heading of Drainage (Sched. 3, para. 19).

Subs. (2)
This replaces the provisos to ss.40(1) (1923 Act improvements) and 40(2) (1931 Act improvements) of the 1949 Act whereby the parties may, by agreement, have dispensed with notice.

Subs. (3)
This provides for notice being given in writing and specifies the period applying in respect of each category of improvement as previously prescribed in ss.40(1)(2) and 51(1) of the 1949 Act.

Subs. (4)
This deals in paras. (a) and (b) with old improvements in both categories and replaces s.40(1)(b) and (2)(b) of the 1949 Act, restricting compensation to cases where, notice having been given and not withdrawn, the landlord failed to exercise his statutory right to carry out the improvements himself. Para. (c), replacing s.40(2)(c) of the 1949 Act dealing with 1931 Act improvements, refers to certain special provisions of that Act whereby objection by the landlord led to an appropriate authority (as now defined in subs. (6)) determining whether an improvement should be carried out and, if considered necessary, supervising its execution.

Subs. (5)
This replaces ss.40(3) (old improvements) and 51(2)(3) (new improvements) of the 1949 Act, enabling the parties, either after notice has been given or by an agreement dispensing with notice, to agree on "substituted compensation". It is not, however, clear that the right to compensation can be wholly eliminated, as appears to be the case with improvements requiring the landlord's consent in terms of s.37.

Subs. (6)
This defines "appropriate authority" for the purposes of subs. (4), taking account of a departmental reorganisation in 1939.

Compensation for Sch. 5, Pt. II, improvements conditional on approval of Land Court in certain cases

39.—(1) Subject to subsections (2) to (4) below, compensation under this Part of this Act shall not be payable in respect of a new improvement specified in Part II of Schedule 5 to this Act if, within one month after receiving notice under section 38(3) of this Act from the tenant of his intention to carry out the improvement, the landlord gives notice in writing to the tenant that he objects to the carrying out of the improvement or to the manner in which the tenant proposes to carry it out.

(2) Where notice of objection has been given under subsection (1) above, the tenant may apply to the Land Court for approval of the carrying out of the improvement, and on such application the Land Court may approve the carrying out of the improvement either—

(a) unconditionally, or

(b) upon such terms, as to reduction of the compensation which would otherwise be payable or as to other matters, as appears to them to be just,

or may withhold their approval.

(3) If, on an application under subsection (2) above, the Land Court grant their approval, the landlord may, within one month after receiving notice of the decision of the Land Court, serve notice in writing on the tenant undertaking to carry out the improvement himself.

(4) Where, on an application under subsection (2) above the Land Court grant their approval, then if either—

(a) no notice is served by the landlord under subsection (3) above, or

(b) such a notice is served but, on an application made by the tenant in that behalf, the Land Court determines that the landlord has failed to carry out the improvement within a reasonable time,

the tenant may carry out the improvement and shall be entitled to compensation under this Part of this Act in respect thereof as if notice of objection had not been given by the landlord, and any terms subject to which the approval was given shall have effect as if they were contained in an agreement in writing between the landlord and the tenant.

DEFINITIONS
   "improvement": s.85(1).
   "landlord": s.85(1).
   "tenant": s.85(1).

DERIVATION
   Agricultural Holdings (Scotland) Act 1949, s.52.
   Agriculture Act 1958, Sched. 1, Pt. II, para. 41.

GENERAL NOTE
   See Gill, paras. 485–487.

Subs. (1)
   Section 38(4) having dealt under reference to earlier legislation with the landlord's right to object to old improvements in Pt. II of the statutory schedules and so prevent them qualifying for compensation at the tenant's outgoing, this section provides the landlord with similar rights in respect of new improvements.

Subs. (2)
   Whereas with old improvements an objection maintained by the landlord resulted in a reference to a Government department or Minister, the Land Court has the jurisdiction when there is an objection to a proposed new improvement. While subs. (1) gives the landlord a month from receiving the tenant's notice to give notice of objection, no time limit is prescribed for the tenant's application to the court. The test to be applied by the court is whether the proposed improvement is reasonable and desirable on agricultural grounds for the efficient management of the holding. A landlord is not to have imposed on him a contingent liability to

pay compensation for an improvement which is inconsistent with the type of farming prescribed by the lease or is to be executed in a manner injurious to or out of keeping with other parts of the holding. The following cases, some of them involving the attachment of conditions to the approval, exemplify the Land Court's exercise of this jurisdiction: *Taylor* v. *Burnett's Trs.*, 1966 S.L.C.R. 139; *Fotheringham* v. *Fotheringham*, 1978 S.L.C.R. 144; *Hutchison* v. *Wolfe Murray*, 1980 S.L.C.R. 112; *Renwick* v. *Rodger*, 1988 S.L.T. (Land Ct.) 23; *Mackinnon* v. *Arran Estate Trust*, 1988 S.L.C.R. 32.

Subs. (3)
It will be to the landlord's advantage to carry out the improvement himself if he can do so at less cost than the tenant's proposal would entail. In so doing he will not only be extinguishing a contingent liability for outgoing compensation but also becoming entitled to claim an increase of rent under the provisions of s.15.

Subs. (4)
What is a reasonable time for the landlord to carry out the improvement must depend on the circumstances. It should be noted that where a landlord defaults and the tenant himself proceeds with the improvement, he will do so subject to any conditions the Land Court may have imposed in giving their approval.

PART V

OTHER PROVISIONS REGARDING COMPENSATION

Market gardens

Market gardens
40.—(1) This section applies to any agricultural holding which, by virtue of an agreement in writing made on or after January 1, 1898, is let or is to be treated as a market garden.
(2) This section also applies where—
(a) a holding was, on January 1, 1898 under a lease then current, in use or cultivation as a market garden with the knowledge of the landlord; and
(b) an improvement of a kind specified in Schedule 6 to this Act (other than such an alteration of a building as did not constitute an enlargement thereof) has been carried out on the holding; and
(c) the landlord did not, before the improvement was carried out, serve on the tenant a written notice dissenting from the carrying out of the improvement;
in relation to improvements whether carried out before or after January 1, 1898.
(3) In the application of Part IV of this Act to an agricultural holding to which this section applies, subject to subsections (5) and (7) below, the improvements specified in Schedule 6 to this Act shall be included in the improvements specified in Part III of each of Schedules 3, 4 and 5 to this Act.
(4) In the case of an agricultural holding to which this section applies—
(a) section 18 of this Act shall apply to every fixture or building affixed or erected by the tenant to or upon the holding or acquired by him since December 31, 1990 for the purposes of his trade or business as a market gardener;
(b) it shall be lawful for the tenant to remove all fruit trees and fruit bushes planted by him on the holding and not permanently set out, but if the tenant does not remove such fruit trees and fruit bushes before the termination of his tenancy they shall remain the property of the landlord and the tenant shall not be entitled to any compensation in respect thereof; and
(c) the right of an incoming tenant to claim compensation in respect of the whole or part of an improvement which he has purchased may be

exercised although the landlord has not consented in writing to the purchase.

(5) Where a tenancy of a kind described in subsection (2) above was a tenancy from year to year, the compensation payable in respect of an improvement of a kind referred to in that subsection shall be such (if any) as could have been claimed if the 1949 Act had not been passed.

(6) Where the land to which this section applies consists of part only of an agricultural holding this section shall apply as if that part were a separate holding.

(7) Nothing in this section shall confer a right to compensation for the alteration of a building (not being an alteration constituting an enlargement of the building) where the alteration was begun before November 1, 1948.

DEFINITIONS
"agricultural holding": s.1(1).
"building": s.85(1).
"improvement": s.85(1).
"landlord": s.85(1).
"lease": s.85(1).
"market garden": s.85(1).
"tenant": s.85(1).

DERIVATIONS
Agricultural Holdings (Scotland) Act 1949, s.65

GENERAL NOTE
See Gill, paras. 541–548. (For the corresponding English provision see the Agricultural Holdings Act 1986, s.79 and Sched. 10).

Subs. (1)
A market garden is defined in s.85(1) as a holding cultivated wholly or mainly for the purpose of the trade or business of market gardening. That trade or business has been judicially described as one producing the class of goods characteristic of a greengrocer's shop which in ordinary course would reach the shop via the early morning market where such goods are disposed of wholesale (*Watters* v. *Hunter*, 1927 S.C. 310, *per* Lord President Clyde at p. 317). In a very recent case concerning rating, a market garden was described as supplying a market for buying and selling produce for consumption (*Twygen* v. *Assessor for Tayside*, 1991 4 G.W.D. 226. Questions have arisen as to whether a particular holding, *e.g.* one used wholly or mainly for growing flowers, constituted a market garden (see Gill, para. 542, and authorities there cited).

Special compensation provisions favouring the tenants of market gardens originated in the Market Gardeners Compensation (Scotland) Act 1897, coming into force on January 1, 1898.

For an agricultural holding to be used as and constitute a market garden there must be agreement in the lease or some other document, or a direction by the Land Court under s.41.

Subs. (2)
These provisions as appearing in the 1949 Acts and earlier legislation for holdings being used as market gardens when the 1897 Act as above mentioned took effect, are discussed in some detail in Connell (*op. cit.* pp. 179/180) but seem unlikely to be of practical significance now.

Subs. (3)
The effect of the inclusion of the market garden improvements listed in Sched. 6 in the improvements specified in Pt. III of the schedules of old and new improvements is that market garden improvements can be carried out and qualify for outgoing compensation without the consent of or notification to the landlord being required.

Subs. (4)
This covers certain privileges enjoyed by the market garden tenant. Firstly, his right of removal of fixtures and buildings under s.18 extends to every fixture or building provided by him for the purposes of his trade or business at any time since December 31, 1900, including buildings for which he could have claimed compensation. Secondly, he is entitled to remove fruit trees and fruit bushes planted by him but not permanently set out. It has been suggested that he may in any case have this right by implication at common law (see Connell, *op. cit.* p. 179). In any event, he is not entitled to compensation if and in so far as he does not exercise it.

Finally, he can claim compensation for an improvement purchased from the outgoing tenant without the consent of the landlord, which consent under s.35(4) is normally required for a tenant to make such a claim.

Subs. (5)
This, like subs. (2), concerns holdings leased as market gardens on January 1, 1898. As to the position with year-to-year tenancies of such holdings, see Connell, *op. cit.*, p. 180.

Subs. (6)
This provides for the situation in which the parties have agreed that part of an agricultural holding shall be a market garden for the purposes of the Act. The location of the ground allocated to market gardening may, by agreement, be varied during the course of the tenancy, but the tenant's right of freedom of cropping under s.7 does not apply to the market gardening ground (*Taylor* v. *Steel Maitland*, 1913 S.C. 562).

Subs. (7)
Item 4 of Sched. 6 covers the erection, alteration or enlargement of buildings. For the landlord, this can represent a substantial potential liability. A farm tenant, if intending to claim outgoing compensation, would need to have notified his landlord before proceeding. The potential liability of the landlord in a market garden tenancy is limited by this subsection but only as regards an old improvement to a building.
Recent cases illustrating the liabilities incurred by landlords for Sched. 6 market gardening improvements are *Macdonald's Trs.* v. *Taylor*, 1983 S.L.C.R. 9, and *Ritson* v. *McIntyre*, 1982 S.L.C.R. 13.

Direction by Land Court that holding be treated as market garden

41.—(1) Where—
  (a) the tenant of an agricultural holding intimates to the landlord in writing his desire to carry out on the holding or any part thereof an improvement specified in Schedule 6 to this Act;
  (b) the landlord refuses, or within a reasonable time fails, to agree in writing that the holding, or that part thereof, shall be treated as a market garden;
  (c) the tenant applies to the Land Court for a direction under this subsection; and
  (d) the Land Court is satisfied that the holding or that part thereof is suitable for the purposes of market gardening;
the Land Court may direct that section 40 of this Act shall apply to the holding or, as the case may be, part of a holding, either—
  (i) in respect of all the improvements specified in Schedule 6 to this Act, or
  (ii) in respect of some only of those improvements,
and that section shall apply accordingly as respects any improvement carried out after the date on which the direction is given.

(2) A direction under subsection (1) above may be given subject to such conditions, if any, for the protection of the landlord as the Land Court may think fit and, in particular, where the direction relates to part only of the holding, the direction may, on the application of the landlord, be given subject to the condition that the tenant shall consent to the division of the holding into two parts (one such part being the part to which the direction relates) to be held at rents agreed by the landlord and tenant or in default of agreement determined by arbitration, but otherwise on the same terms and conditions (so far as applicable) as those on which the holding is held.

(3) Where a direction is given under subsection (1) above, if the tenancy is terminated—
  (a) by notice of intention to quit given by the tenant, or
  (b) by reason of the tenant's apparent insolvency being constituted under section 7 of the Bankruptcy (Scotland) Act 1985,
the tenant shall not be entitled to compensation in respect of improvements specified in the direction unless he produces an offer which complies with

subsection (4) below and the landlord fails to accept the offer within 3 months after the production thereof.

(4) An offer complies with this subsection if—

(a) it is in writing;

(b) it is made by a substantial and otherwise suitable person;

(c) it is produced by the tenant to the landlord not later than one month after the date of the notice of intention to quit or constitution of apparent insolvency as the case may be, or at such later date as may be agreed;

(d) it is an offer to accept a tenancy of the holding from the termination of the existing tenancy on the terms and conditions of the existing tenancy so far as applicable;

(e) it includes an offer, subject to subsection (5) below, to pay to the outgoing tenant all compensation payable under this Act or under the lease;

(f) it is open for acceptance for a period of 3 months from the date on which it is produced.

(5) If the landlord accepts an offer which complies with subsection (4) above the incoming tenant shall pay to the landlord on demand all sums payable to him by the outgoing tenant on the termination of the tenancy in respect of rent or breach of contract or otherwise in respect of the holding.

(6) Any amount paid by the incoming tenant under subsection (5) above may, subject to any agreement between the outgoing tenant and incoming tenant, be deducted by the incoming tenant from any compensation payable by him to the outgoing tenant.

(7) A tenancy created by the acceptance of an offer which complies with subsection (4) above shall be deemed for the purposes of section 13 of this Act not to be a new tenancy.

DEFINITIONS

"agricultural holding": s.1(1).

"improvement": s.85(1).

"landlord": s.85(1).

"lease": s.85(1).

"market garden": s.85(1).

"notice of intention to quit": s.21(2).

"tenant": s.85(1).

"termination of tenancy": s.85(1).

DERIVATIONS

Agricultural Holdings (Scotland) Act 1949, s.66.

Agriculture Act 1958, Sched. 1, Pt. II, para. 43.

GENERAL NOTE

See Gill, paras. 549, 552. (For the corresponding English provision see the Agricultural Holdings Act 1986, s.80).

Subs. (1)

The onus is on the tenant who wishes to carry on market gardening but has been unable to obtain the agreement of his landlord to satisfy the Land Court that the holding or part of it is suitable for market gardening. A direction by the Court applies only to market garden improvements subsequently carried out.

Subs. (2)

Connell (*op. cit.*, p. 182) suggests that the only obvious way of protecting the landlord's interest would be to require an increase in rent. Where the holding is divided as provided for in this subsection the aggregate rental may well be greater than the rent of the original holding.

Subs. (3)

This gives effect to what is known as the Evesham Custom, whereby, when the use of the holding for market garden purposes depends on a direction of the Land Court, the tenant, if responsible for the tenancy terminating, is not to be entitled to compensation for his market garden improvements unless he can produce an offer from a third party to take on the tenancy and pay to the outgoing tenant all compensation due to him under this Act or the lease.

Subs. (4)

This prescribes certain requirements for such an offer. Connell (*op. cit.* p. 181–2), referring to the words "substantial and otherwise suitable person" (para. (b)) suggests that the offer must come from someone having sufficient capital resources and being otherwise capable, from experience and character, of undertaking the obligations of tenant. He indicates that objections similar to those which can be stated against a legatee or intestate successor under ss.11 and 12 could apply here. Should the landlord not, within the period prescribed, accept an offer complying with these requirements, the outgoing tenant will be entitled to compensation for his Sched. 6 improvements as well as his other outgoing claims.

Subss. (5) and (6)

This has the result that if the landlord accepts an offer complying with the requirements of subs. (4), the incoming tenant is in effect substituted for the outgoing tenant in respect of the latter's liability of any kind to the landlord at the termination of the tenancy. However, the incoming tenant can set off this liability against his liability to the outgoing tenant whose claims he will have undertaken to meet.

Subs. (7)

But for this provision, a new tenancy having been created by the change of tenant, the three-year period for review of the rent under s.13 would have started at the incoming tenant's entry. This subsection has the result that the three-year period is counted as if the original tenant had remained under tacit relocation.

Agreements as to compensation relating to market gardens

42.—(1) Where under an agreement in writing a tenant of an agricultural holding is entitled to compensation which is fair and reasonable having regard to the circumstances existing at the time of making the agreement, for an improvement for which compensation is payable by virtue of section 40 of this Act, such compensation shall, as respects that improvement, be substituted for compensation under this Act.

(2) The landlord and the tenant of an agricultural holding who have agreed that the holding shall be let or treated as a market garden may by agreement in writing substitute, for the provisions as to compensation which would otherwise be applicable to the holding, the provisions as to compensation in section 41(3) to (6) of this Act.

DEFINITIONS
   "agricultural holding": s.1(1).
   "improvement": s.85(1).
   "landlord": s.85(1).
   "market garden": s.85(1).
   "tenant": s.85(1).

DERIVATIONS
Agricultural Holdings (Scotland) Act 1949, s.67.

GENERAL NOTE
   See Gill, para. 553. (For the corresponding English provision see the Agricultural Holdings Act 1986, s.81).

Subs. (1)

This authorises the adoption of substituted compensation in respect of market garden improvements, although substituted compensation is inapplicable to other improvements in Pt. III of the Schedules unless the lease was entered into before January 1, 1921.

Subs. (2)

This results that where a holding is created as a market garden by agreement as opposed to Land Court direction, the parties can agree for substituted compensation on the basis of the Evesham Custom as embodied in s.41.

Miscellaneous

Compensation for disturbance

43.—(1) Where the tenancy of an agricultural holding terminates by reason of—

(a) a notice to quit given by the landlord; or

(b) a counter-notice given by the tenant under section 30 of this Act, and in consequence the tenant quits the holding, subject to subsections (2) to (8) below, compensation for the disturbance shall be payable by the landlord to the tenant.

(2) Compensation shall not be payable under this section where the application of section 22(1) of this Act to the notice to quit is excluded by any of paragraphs (a) or (c) to (f) of subsection (2) of that section.

(3) Subject to subsection (4) below, the amount of the compensation payable under this section shall be the amount of the loss or expense directly attributable to the quitting of the holding which is unavoidably incurred by the tenant upon or in connection with the sale or removal of his household goods, implements of husbandry, fixtures, farm produce or farm stock on or used in connection with the holding, and shall include any expenses reasonably incurred by him in the preparation of his claim for compensation (not being expenses of an arbitration to determine any question arising under this section).

(4) Where compensation is payable under this section—

(a) the compensation shall be an amount equal to one year's rent of the holding at the rate at which rent was payable immediately before the termination of the tenancy without proof by the tenant of any such loss or expense as aforesaid;

(b) the tenant shall not be entitled to claim any greater amount than one year's rent of the holding unless he has given to the landlord not less than one month's notice of the sale of any such goods, implements, fixtures, produce or stock as aforesaid and has afforded him a reasonable opportunity of making a valuation thereof;

(c) the tenant shall not in any case be entitled to compensation in excess of 2 years' rent of the holding.

(5) In subsection (4) above "rent" means the rent after deduction of such an amount as, failing agreement, the arbiter finds to be the amount payable by the landlord in respect of the holding for the year in which the tenancy was terminated by way of any public rates, taxes or assessments or other public burdens, the charging of which on the landlord would entitle him to relief in respect of tax under Part II of the Income and Corporation Taxes Act 1988.

(6) Where the tenant of an agricultural holding has lawfully sub-let the whole or part of the holding, and in consequence of a notice to quit given by his landlord becomes liable to pay compensation under this section to the sub-tenant, the tenant shall not be debarred from recovering compensation under this section by reason only that, owing to not being in occupation of the holding or part of the holding, on the termination of his tenancy he does not quit the holding or that part.

(7) Where the tenancy of an agricultural holding terminates by virtue of a counter-notice given by the tenant under section 30 of this Act and—

(a) the part of the holding affected by the notice to quit given by the landlord, together with any part of the holding affected by any previous notice to quit given by the landlord which is rendered valid by section 29 of this Act, is either less than a quarter of the area of the original holding or of a rental value less than one quarter of the rental value of the original holding, and

(b) the holding as proposed to be diminished is reasonably capable of being farmed as a separate holding,

compensation shall not be payable under this section except in respect of the part of the holding to which the notice to quit relates.

(8) Compensation under this section shall be in addition to any compensation to which the tenant may be entitled apart from this section.

DEFINITIONS
"agricultural holdings": s.1(1).
"landlord": s.85(1).
"notice to quit": s.21(2).
"produce": s.85(1).
"tenant": s.85(1).
"termination of tenancy": s.85(1).

DERIVATIONS
Agricultural Holdings (Scotland) Act 1949, s.35.

GENERAL NOTE
See Gill, paras. 502–508. (For the corresponding English provision see the Agricultural Holdings Act 1986, ss.60, 61, 63).

Subs. (1)
It appears that a defective notice to quit, if acted upon by the tenant, entitles him to compensation for disturbance (*Kestell* v. *Longmaid* [1950] 1 K.B. 233), the contrary view being, however, taken in two Sheriff Court Cases: *Forbes* v. *Pratt*, 1923 S.L.T. (Sh. Ct.) 91 and *Earl of Galloway* v. *Elliot*, 1926 S.L.T. (Sh. Ct.) 123. The tenant retains his claim to compensation for disturbance, although his waygoing is delayed as a result of his serving a counter-notice or demanding arbitration as the case may be (see s.23(3)(4)). Again, the better view appears to be that the unsuccessful defence of the action of removing does not deprive the tenant of his claim (*Preston* v. *Norfolk County Council* [1947] K.B. 775).

In addition to the two instances mentioned in this subsection, compensation for disturbance is payable (a) when the tenant has lawfully sublet and becomes liable to compensate his sub-tenant in consequence of a notice to quit issued by the landlord (see subs. (6)); and (b) in terms of s.49(1)(a) where the tenancy is terminated *quoad* part of the holding under s.29; and (c) in terms of s.49(1)(b) where part of the holding is resumed in exercise of a power of resumption in the lease.

Subs. (2)
In a case coming under para. (a) of s.22(2) the temporary nature of the let makes compensation for its termination unjustifiable. Again, in the cases covered by paras. (c) to (f) of s.22(2), the tenant's default as a result of which the tenancy is being terminated justifies the exclusion of this compensation. On the other hand, the compensation will be payable under para. (b) of that subsection where termination is taking place at the instigation of the landlord to make the holding or part of it available for non-agricultural use.

Other cases in which compensation for disturbance is not payable are termination of the tenancy by the tenant's notice of intention to quit, termination by notice served on an executor under s.16 of the Succession (Scotland) Act 1964 and again termination by conventional irritancy. As to terination by legal irritancy see note to s.20.

Subs. (3)
For reasons referred to below it is not often that a tenant will submit a detailed claim in terms of this provision. As to matters arising, where this is to be done see Connell (*op. cit.* pp. 153–154).

Subs. (4)
Compensation of a year's rent as provided for in para. (a) is usually accepted particularly as the maximum that can be recovered by making a detailed claim is two years' rent. When a detailed claim is made, however, it is a question of fact whether the landlord has had a reasonable opportunity of valuing the items included (*Barbour* v. *McDonall*, 1914 S.C. 844).

Subs. (5)
With owner's rates abolished in 1956 and agricultural land and farm buildings exempt from

rates since then, it seems unlikely that the rent forming the measure of compensation will require to be abated as provided for in this subsection. It appears that the rent payable for the last year of the tenancy should always form the criterion for compensation, disregarding any variation there may have been in earlier years.

Subs. (6)
The effect of this provision is to protect the position of the tenant who has lawfully sublet the holding wholly or partially and having received notice to quit from his landlord has required to give notice to quit to his sub-tenant, making him liable to the latter for compensation for disturbance. The tenant's own claim for compensation is preserved although he will not himself be quitting the holding or the part of it sub-let.

Subs. (7)
This gives significant relief to the landlord where, in response to a notice to quit a limited part of the holding, given under s.29, the tenant serves counter-notice in terms of s.30. The effect of this provision is that compensation for disturbance will be restricted to the rental value of the part of the holding affected by the notice to quit unless that part and any other part of the holding previously repossessed by the landlord under s.29 amounts to not less than a quarter of the holding in area or rental value and the holding as it remains is not reasonably capable of being worked as a separate unit.

Subs. (8)
This confirms the existence of compensation for disturbance as a separate claim which will be unaffected by any arrangements landlord and tenant may have made in respect of any other waygoing claims.

Compensation for continuous adoption of special standard of farming

44.—(1) Where the tenant of an agricultural holding proves that the value of the holding to an incoming tenant has been increased during the tenancy by the continuous adoption of a standard of farming or a system of farming which has been more beneficial to the holding than—

(a) the standard or system required by the lease, or

(b) in so far as no system of farming is so required, the system of farming normally practised on comparable holdings in the district,

the tenant shall be entitled, on quitting the holding, to obtain from the landlord such compensation as represents the value to an incoming tenant of the adoption of that more beneficial standard or system.

(2) Compensation shall not be recoverable under subsection (1) above unless—

(a) the tenant has, not later than one month before the termination of the tenancy, given to the landlord notice in writing of his intention to claim such compensation; and

(b) a record of the condition of the fixed equipment on, and the cultivation of, the holding has been made under section 8 of this Act;

and shall not be so recoverable in respect of any matter arising before the date of the record so made or, where more than one such record has been made during the tenancy, before the date of the first such record.

(3) In assessing the compensation to be paid under subsection (1) above, due allowance shall be made for any compensation agreed or awarded to be paid to the tenant under Part IV of this Act for any improvement which has caused or contributed to the benefit.

(4) Nothing in this section shall entitle a tenant to recover, in respect of any improvement, any compensation which he would not be entitled to recover apart from this section.

DEFINITIONS
"agricultural holding": s.1(1).
"improvement": s.85(1).
"landlord": s.85(1).
"lease": s.85(1).
"tenant": s.85(1).

DERIVATIONS
Agricultural Holdings (Scotland) Act 1949, s.56.

GENERAL NOTE
See Gill, paras. 497–501. (For the corresponding English provision see the Agricultural Holdings Act 1986, s.70).

Subs. (1)
While this subsection speaks of the continuous adoption of a standard or system of farming, it would appear that the tenant's claim will not be excluded because he has needed, in compliance with his lease, to depart from the system in the last year of his tenancy when his freedom of cropping and disposal of produce, as derived from s.7, does not apply. In practice, however, the possibility of a claim for what is termed "high farming" will often be excluded by requirements of the lease going beyond the normal standards of good husbandry. "High farming" as an independent statutory qualification for compensation was introduced by the 1923 Act. For the purpose of rent review s.13(6) directs that it be treated as a tenant's improvement but it does not fall within the category of improvements generally. Thus a tenant who has had successive tenancies of a holding does not have the benefit of s.34(5) as regards a high farming claim. Such a claim has to be as at the conclusion of the tenancy during which it has been earned. As with improvements generally, the criterion of assessment is the value to an incoming tenant assumed to be farming the holding on the same lines as his predecessor.

Subs. (2)
While outgoing claims generally have to be intimated within two months of the tenant's waygoing, this is a claim of which intimation prior to waygoing is required. Again, a record of the state of cultivation prior to the application of the special standard or system is essential for the assessment of the claim.

Subs. (3)
This is required to prevent duplication as between the allowance to be made for "high farming" and any amounts allowed for items of improvement which have contributed to the benefit derived from the tenant's operations.

Subs. (4)
This is intended to obviate the possibility of a "high farming" claim enabling a tenant to recover compensation for some improvement which does not qualify for compensation, *e.g.* because it does not have the required consent of the landlord or because it had not been notified to him in conformity with the relevant statutory provision.

Compensation to landlord for deterioration etc. of holding

45.—(1) The landlord of an agricultural holding shall be entitled to recover from the tenant, on his quitting the holding on termination of the land tenancy compensation—
(a) where the landlord shows that the value of the holding has been reduced by dilapidation, deterioration or damage caused by;
(b) where dilapidation, deterioration or damage has been caused to any part of the holding or to anything in or on the holding by;
non-fulfilment by the tenant of his responsibilities to farm in accordance with the rules of good husbandry.

(2) The amount of compensation payable under subsection (1) above shall be—
(a) where paragraph (a) of that subsection applies, (insofar as the landlord is not compensated for the dilapidation, deterioration or damage under paragraph (b) thereof) an amount equal to the reduction in the value of the holding;
(b) when paragraph (b) of that subsection applies, the cost, as at the date of the tenant's quitting the holding, of making good the dilapidation, deterioration or damage.

(3) Notwithstanding anything in this Act, the landlord may, in lieu of claiming compensation under subsection (1)(b) above, claim compensation in respect of matters specified therein, under and in accordance with a lease in writing, so however that—

(a) compensation shall be so claimed only on the tenant's quitting the holding on the termination of the tenancy;

(b) subject to section 46(4) of this Act compensation shall not be claimed in respect of any one holding both under such a lease and under subsection (1) above;

and compensation under this subsection shall be treated, for the purposes of subsection (2)(a) above and of section 46 (2) of this Act as compensation under subsection (1)(b) above.

DEFINITIONS
"agricultural holding": s.1(1).
"landlord": s.85(1).
"lease" s.85(1).
"rules of good husbandry": s.85(1); Agriculture (Scotland) Act 1948, Sched. 6.
"tenant": s.85(1).
"termination of tenancy": s.85(1).

DERIVATIONS
Agricultural Holdings (Scotland) Act 1949, ss.57, 58.

GENERAL NOTE
See Gill, paras. 555–557. (For the corresponding English provision see the Agricultural Holdings Act 1986, ss.71, 72).

Subs. (1)
The section replaces s.58 of the 1949 Act, covering general depreciation of the holding and s.57 of the 1949 Act, covering dilapidation or deterioration of, or damage to, particular parts of the holding or anything thereon, the two matters being dealt with in paras. (a) and (b) respectively of this subsection.

There are no statutory definitions of the terms "dilapidation" and "deterioration" but in Scammell and Densham, *The Law of Agricultural Holdings* (7th ed.), pp. 34 *et seq.*, where the matter is discussed at some length, it is indicated that "dilapidation" arises from a failure to repair items such as gates, fences or drains while "deterioration" applies to conditions not readily curable such as the loss of soil fertility resulting from lack of fertilisation or other forms of neglect.

Subs. (2)
For general depreciation, the measure of compensation is the decrease in value of the holding for which the tenant has been responsible in so far as not covered by compensation due for specific instances of dilapidation, etc.

Subs. (3)
Subsections (1) and (2) having dealt with the landlord's statutory claims for dilapidation, etc., this subsection preserves his right to claim in terms of a written lease where there is one, the measure of damages being that specified in the lease or applying by legal implication. Like the statutory claim, however, the claim under the lease as authorised by this subsection can be brought only on the tenant quitting the holding. The view has been expressed that the claim for compensation under s.57 of the 1949 Act did not prevent the landlord from proceeding against the tenant at any time during the currency of the tenancy for breaches of the lease (Gill, para. 554) but s.100 of the 1949 Act, which is referred to in support of that view, has not been reproduced in this Act.

The landlord cannot adopt the statutory basis for some items of a claim and the contractual basis for others, but it appears that he may present his claim in alternative terms and subsequently elect on which basis he is to pursue it (*Boyd* v. *Wilton* [1957] 2 Q.B. 277). In this connection a claim under s.46 is regarded as a separate matter. The concluding words of this subsection appear to be intended to make it clear that compensation recovered on a contractual basis for specific items is to be set against any statutory claim for general depreciation of the holding, it being permissible to present the respective claims on different grounds.

Compensation for failure to repair or maintain fixed equipment

46.—(1) This section applies where, by virtue of section 4 of this Act, the liability for the maintenance or repair of an item of fixed equipment is transferred from the tenant to the landlord.

(2) Where this section applies, the landlord may within the period of one month beginning with the date on which the transfer takes effect require that there shall be determined by arbitration, and paid by the tenant, the amount of any compensation which would have been payable under section 45(1)(b) of this Act in respect of any previous failure by the tenant to discharge the said liability, if the tenant had quitted the holding on the termination of his tenancy at the date on which the transfer takes effect.

(3) Where this section applies, any claim by the tenant in respect of any previous failure by the landlord to discharge the said liability shall, if the tenant within the period of one month referred to in subsection (2) above so requires, be determined by arbitration, and any amount directed by the award to be paid by the landlord shall be paid by him to the tenant.

(4) For the purposes of section 45(3)(b) of this Act any compensation under this section shall be disregarded.

DEFINITIONS
"fixed equipment": s.85(1).
"landlord": s.85(1).
"tenant": s.85(1).
"termination": s.85(1).

DERIVATIONS
Agricultural Holdings (Scotland) Act 1949, ss.6(1)(2), 57(3).
Agriculture Holdings (Scotland) Regulations 1950 (S.I. 1950 No. 1553).

GENERAL NOTE
See Gill, para. 96. (For the corresponding English provision see the Agricultural Holdings Act 1986, s.9).

Subs. (1)
This relates to the application of this section to the provisions of s.4 for the revision of written leases which may involve a transfer of liability for the repair and maintenance of items of fixed equipment from tenant to landlord.

Subs. (2)
This proceeds on the basis that where a transfer of liabilities takes place, the tenant, having been previously liable, should make good any default by paying forthwith to the landlord compensation computed as it would be at the tenant's outgoing.

Subs. (3)
Subsections (1) and (2) having dealt with the case of a transfer of liability from tenant to landlord as provided for in s.6(1) of the 1949 Act, this subsection could have been expected to deal with the transfer of liability from landlord to tenant as provided for in s.6(2) of the 1949 Act. It appears, however, that s.6(2) has been treated as spent, having been regarded as misconceived and unnecessary in respect of the fact that s.5 (in this Act and in the 1949 Act) determines the tenant's liability for the maintenance of fixed equipment, making an arbitration on that matter unnecessary and inappropriate. Whether or not that view is justified even in the case of leases to which s.5 applies it is clear that without the transfer provisions of s.6(2) of the 1949 Act, this subsection is meaningless and ineffective.

Subs. (4)
The effect of this provision is that a landlord who has proceeded either on the basis of the lease or under the Act in making a claim under this section is to be entitled, if he chooses, to make his claim for dilapidations, etc. at the tenant's outgoing on the other basis.

Provisions supplementary to ss.45 and 46

47.—(1) Compensation shall not be recoverable under section 45 of this Act, unless the landlord has, not later than 3 months before the termination of the tenancy, given notice in writing to the tenant of his intention to claim compensation thereunder.

(2) Subsection (3) below shall apply to compensation—

(a) under section 45 of this Act, where the lease was entered into after July 31, 1931; or

(b) where the lease was entered into on or after November 1, 1948.

(3) When this subsection applies, no compensation shall be recoverable—

(a) unless during the occupancy of the tenant a record of the condition of the fixed equipment on, and cultivation of, the holding has been made under section 8 of this Act;

(b) in respect of any matter arising before the date of the record referred to in paragraph (a) above; or

(c) where more than one such record has been made during the tenant's occupancy, in respect of any matter arising before the date of the first such record.

(4) If the landlord and the tenant so agree in writing a record of the condition of the holding shall, notwithstanding that it was made during the occupancy of a previous tenant, be deemed, for the purposes of subsection (3) above, to have been made during the occupancy of the tenant and on such date as may be specified in the agreement and shall have effect subject to such modifications (if any) as may be so specified.

(5) Where the tenant has remained in his holding during 2 or more tenancies, his landlord shall not be deprived of his right to compensation under section 45 of this Act in respect of any dilapidation, deterioration or damage by reason only that the tenancy during which the relevant act or omission occurred was a tenancy other than the tenancy at the termination of which the tenant quit the holding.

DEFINITIONS
"landlord": s.85(1).
"lease": s.85(1).
"tenant": s.85(1).
"termination": s.85(1).

DERIVATIONS
Agricultural Holdings (Scotland) Act 1949, s.59.

GENERAL NOTE
See Gill, paras. 558–560.

Subs. (1)
In contrast with claims by the tenant, whether on a statutory or contractual basis, and claims by the landlord on a contractual basis, which in terms of s.62(2) can be intimated at any time not later than two months after the termination of the tenancy, claims by the landlord under the Act have to be intimated at least three months before the termination. This has the result that in practice a landlord may be unable to make a statutory claim for dilapidation, deterioration or damage emerging during the last three months of the tenancy.

Subss. (2) and (3)
These relate to the existence of a record as a condition of the landlord's right to make outgoing claims. A record is required for a claim under the Act if the lease was entered into after July 31, 1931, when the 1931 Act took effect, and for a claim under any lease entered into after November 1, 1948, when the 1948 Act took effect. Since the provisions of s.5(1) for the making of a record of fixed equipment at the commencement of the tenancy tend, in practice, to be disregarded, a landlord, if he is to be in a position to make claims at the tenant's outgoing, will have to ensure that at some time during the course of the tenancy the provisions of s.8(1) are invoked by him or his tenant. Subs. (3) of this section has the result that a record made at a late stage in the tenancy may be of little or no value for this purpose.

Subs. (4)
This appears to recognise that the making of a record can entail considerable expense which can be minimised by the parties agreeing to adapt, as necessary, and accept a record made during the occupancy of a previous tenant.

Subs. (5)

This may be compared with s.34(5) in extending the scope of outgoing claims to events or happenings taking place during a previous tenancy of the outgoing tenant.

Landlord not to have right to penal rent or liquidated damages

48. Notwithstanding any provision to the contrary in a lease of an agricultural holding, the landlord shall not be entitled to recover any sum, by way of higher rent, liquidated damages or otherwise, in consequence of any breach or non-fulfilment of a term or condition of the lease, which is in excess of the damage actually suffered by him in consequence of the breach or non-fulfilment.

DEFINITIONS

"agricultural holding": s.1(1).
"landlord": s.85(1).
"lease": s.85(1).

DERIVATIONS

Agricultural Holdings (Scotland) Act 1949, s.16.

GENERAL NOTE

See Gill, paras. 2 and 145, Connell (*op. cit.* p. 127). (For the corresponding English provision see the Agricultural Holdings Act 1986, s.24).

This section strikes at penalty clauses in leases such as those exacting inflated amounts for breach of conditions affecting cultivation or cropping. The English case of *Wilson* v. *Love* [1896] 1 Q.B. 626 exemplifies the limitation of damages for such a breach to the loss actually incurred.

Compensation provisions to apply to parts of holdings in certain cases

49.—(1) Where—

(a) the tenancy of part of an agricultural holding terminates by reason of a notice to quit which is rendered valid by section 29 of this Act; or

(b) the landlord of an agricultural holding resumes possession of part of the holding in pursuance of a provision in that behalf contained in the lease;

the provisions of this Act with respect to compensation shall apply as if that part of the holding were a separate holding which the tenant had quitted in consequence of a notice to quit.

(2) In a case falling within subsection (1)(b) above, the arbiter, in assessing the amount of compensation payable to the tenant, shall take into account any benefit or relief allowed to the tenant under the lease in respect of the land possession of which is resumed by the landlord.

(3) Where any land comprised in a lease is not an agricultural holding within the meaning of this Act by reason only that the land so comprised includes land to which subsection (4) below applies, the provisions of this Act with respect to compensation for improvements and for disturbance shall, unless it is otherwise agreed in writing, apply to the part of the land exclusive of the land to which subsection (4) below applies as if that part were a separate agricultural holding.

(4) This subsection applies to land which, owing to the nature of the building thereon or the use to which it is put, would not, if it had been separately let, be an agricultural holding.

DEFINITIONS

"agricultural holding": s.1(1).
"improvements": s.85(1).
"landlord": s.85(1).
"lease": s.85(1).
"tenant": s.85(1).

DERIVATIONS
Agricultural Holdings (Scotland) Act 1949, s.60.

GENERAL NOTE
See Gill, paras. 233, 244–247, 422, 507, 508.

Subs. (1)
This provides for the payment of compensation in the same two situations in which s.31
provides for reduction of rent, namely the landlord's repossession of part of the holding as a
result of a notice to quit affecting that part or his exercise of a power of resumption. The
compensation will include the value of any improvements qualifying for compensation on the
area repossessed, as well as compensation for disturbance under s.43, and reorganisation
compensation under s.54, both based on the rental value of the area vacated. In the case of a
resumption, the tenant will also be entitled to compensation in terms of s.58.

Subs. (2)
As in the case of s.31(2), the practical effect of this provision is that where, as often happens,
the lease contains provisions for compensation payable to the tenant on resumption, the tenant
has the option of accepting these provisions or claiming his statutory rights, whichever is the
more advantageous course for him.

Subss. (3) and (4)
These deal with the special case where a tenancy which is predominantly non-agricultural,
and consequently does not comprise an agricultural holding within the meaning of this Act,
includes land used for agricultural purposes. Such land is to be treated for purposes of
compensation for improvements and for disturbance (and reorganisation compensation if
applicable) as a separate agricultural holding. The situation is one not often occurring in
practice, subs. (3) permitting the parties to contract out of the operation of the statutory
provisions.

Determination of claims for compensation where holding is divided

50. Where the interest of the landlord in an agricultural holding has
become vested in several parts in more than one person and the rent payable
by the tenant of the holding has not been apportioned with his consent or
under any statute, the tenant shall be entitled to require that any compensation payable to him under this Act shall be determined as if the holding had
not been divided; and the arbiter shall, where necessary, apportion the
amount awarded between the persons who for the purposes of this Act
together constitute the landlord of the holding, and any additional expenses
of the award caused by the apportionment shall be directed by the arbiter to
be paid by those persons in such proportions as he shall determine.

DEFINITIONS
"agricultural holding": s.1(1).
"landlord": s.85(1).
"tenant": s.85(1).

DERIVATIONS
Agricultural Holdings (Scotland) Act 1949, s.61.

GENERAL NOTE
See Gill, para. 437. (For the corresponding English provision see the Agricultural Holdings
Act 1986, s.75).
In addition to affecting the settlement of compensation for improvements and compensation
for disturbance, this provision applies under s.55(5) to reorganisation compensation and under
the Agriculture Act 1986, Sched. 2, para. 11(5) (as amended in terms of Sched. 11, para. 52(c))
to a claim for compensation for milk quota. On the rent being apportioned as directed the
tenant's claim will be payable by each proprietor in proportion to the rent payable for his
property.

Compensation not to be payable for things done in compliance with this Act

51.—(1) Notwithstanding anything in the foregoing provisions of this Act
or any custom or agreement—

(a) no compensation shall be payable to the tenant of an agricultural holding in respect of anything done in pursuance of a direction under section 9(2) of this Act;

(b) in assessing compensation to an outgoing tenant of an agricultural holding where land has been ploughed up in pursuance of a direction under section 9(2) of this Act, the value per hectare of any tenant's pasture comprised in the holding shall be taken not to exceed the average value per hectare of the whole of the tenant's pasture comprised in the holding on the termination of the tenancy.

(2) In subsection (1)(b) above "tenant's pasture" means pasture laid down at the expense of the tenant or paid for by the tenant on entering the holding.

(3) The tenant of an agricultural holding shall not be entitled to compensation for an improvement specified in Part III of any of Schedules 3 to 5 to this Act, being an improvement carried out for the purposes of—

(a) the proviso to section 35(1) of the Agricultural Holdings (Scotland) Act 1923;

(b) the proviso to section 12(1) of the 1949 Act; or

(c) section 9 of this Act.

DEFINITIONS
"agricultural holding": s.1(1).
"tenant": s.85(1).
"termination of tenancy": s.85(1).

DERIVATIONS
Agricultural Holdings (Scotland) Act 1949, s.63.
Agriculture (Adaptation of Enactments) (Scotland) Regulations 1977 (S.I. 1977 No. 2007).
Agriculture (Scotland) Act 1948, Sched. 1, Pt. II, para. 42.

GENERAL NOTE
See Gill, paras. 164 (subs. (1)), 476 (subs. (2)). (For the corresponding English provision see the Agricultural Holdings Act 1986, s.76).

Subss. (1) and (2)
Where land which the lease provided should remain as permanent pasture has been ploughed up in pursuance of an order under s.9 the order may require that a specified area in addition to the reduced area of permanent pasture should be left at the tenant's waygoing as permanent pasture or temporary pasture sown with a specified mixture of seeds. Such restoration of pasture does not qualify for compensation and the intention of subs. (1)(b) is to prevent a tenant who has a claim for pasture other than that left in accordance with the order nominating his inferior pasture as that laid down in terms of the order and claiming compensation for better pasture.

Subs. (3)
The provisos referred to in paras. (a) and (b) concern the tenant's obligation to restore fertility in cases where he has exercised his statutory rights of freedom of cropping and disposal of produce. Para. (c) is referring to action taken by a tenant in accordance with an order authorising the reduction of the area prescribed by the lease to be retained as permanent pasture. The effect of this subsection is that the tenant is not entitled to compensation for an improvement old or new in the part of the respective Schedules listing improvements for which no consent or notice is required if carried out for the purposes of any of the provisions listed. Section 9 having already been referred to in subs. (1), its inclusion here is perhaps *ob majorem cautelam*. Only the provisos referred to in paras. (a) and (b) appeared in the corresponding provision, being s.63(2) of the 1949 Act.

Compensation for damage by game

52.—(1) Subject to subsection (2) below, where the tenant of an agricultural holding has sustained damage to his crops from game, the right to kill and take which is vested neither in him nor in anyone claiming under him other than the landlord, and which the tenant has not permission in writing to kill, he shall be entitled to compensation from his landlord for the damage if it exceeds in amount the sum of 12 pence per hectare of the area over which it extends.

(2) Compensation shall not be recoverable under subsection (1) above, unless—

(a) notice in writing is given to the landlord as soon as is practicable after the damage was first observed by the tenant, and a reasonable opportunity is given to the landlord to inspect the damage—

(i) in the case of damage to a growing crop, before the crop is begun to be reaped, raised or consumed;

(ii) in the case of damage to a crop reaped or raised, before the crop is begun to be removed from the land; and

(b) notice in writing of the claim, together with the particulars thereof, is given to the landlord within one month after the expiry of the calendar year, or such other period of 12 months as by agreement between the landlord and the tenant may be substituted therefor, in respect of which the claim is made.

(3) The amount of compensation payable under subsection (1) above shall, in default of agreement made after the damage has been suffered, be determined by arbitration.

(4) Where the right to kill and take the game is vested in some person other than the landlord, the landlord shall be entitled to be indemnified by that other person against all claims for compensation under this section; and any question arising under this subsection shall be determined by arbitration.

(5) In this section "game" means deer, pheasants, partridges, grouse and black game.

DEFINITIONS

"agricultural holding": s.1(1).
"landlord": s.1(1).
"tenant": s.1(1).

DERIVATIONS

Agricultural Holdings (Scotland) Act 1949, s.15.
Agriculture (Adaptation of Enactments) (Scotland) Regulations 1977 (S.I. 1977 No. 2007).

GENERAL NOTE

See Gill, paras. 189–197. (For the corresponding English provision see the Agricultural Holdings Act 1986, s.20).

Subs. (1)

The wording "damage from game the right to kill and take which is vested neither in him (the tenant) nor in anyone claiming under him other than the landlord" is intended to defeat a device whereby the landlord, to avoid liability, would, instead of reserving the shooting rights, require the tenant to sub-let the shootings to him.

To exclude his claim the tenant must have express and unqualified written permission to kill the type of game causing the damage. A limited statutory right to kill deer, as conferred by the now-repealed provisions of s.43(1) of the 1948 Act, was held not to exclude the claim for damage done by deer (*Lady Auckland* v. *Dowie*, 1965 S.L.T. 76). A landlord may, however, restrict the tenant's right to kill game to certain species of game, in which case a claim for damage by that species, but not by any other form of game, will be excluded. The tenant was held to have a claim even where the game causing the damage came from an adjacent estate and that during the close season for shooting the type of game in question (*Thomson* v. *Earl of Galloway*, 1919 S.C. 611). While the damage for which a claim can be made has to exceed the minimum stated it appears that where this is so the whole amount and not merely the excess is payable (Connell, *op. cit.* p. 126).

Subs. (2)

A tenant intending to make a claim must give the landlord two notices in writing, the first being a notice of damage and the second a notice of claim. The notice of damage has to be given "as soon as is practicable" after the tenant's first observance of the damage. In the corresponding provision of the 1949 Act (s.15(1), proviso (a)) the words used are "as soon as may be" but the difference would appear to be insignificant. As regards the reasonable opportunity to be given for the landlord to inspect the damage, a distinction is made between the growing crop and a crop which has been reaped or raised but is still on the ground. Connell (*op. cit.* p. 126) recommends that if harvesting is imminent the landlord should be so advised and that the reference to crop in this context should be regarded as meaning the whole crop, including any part of it undamaged. As regards the notice of claim, it is convenient and customary for the lease to relate its terms to the rental year rather than to the calendar year, as the latter may result in the claim being received some considerable time after the tenant's outgoing. Specimen forms of notice of damage and notice of claim will be found in Connell (*op. cit.* pp. 239–240). The claim may be lodged during the currency of the yearly or rental period but it is doubtful if more than one claim can be lodged in respect of any one period (*Earl of Morton's Trs.* v. *Macdougall*, 1944 S.C. 410).

Subss. (3) and (4)

Here we have the statutory arbitration procedure applying not only as between landlord and tenant but also in a matter involving a third party. Provision is made for the situation in which the landlord has let the shooting rights to someone other than the agricultural tenant. In the absence of contracting out, which could appear to be permissible, the sporting tenant will carry the responsibility for damage by game to the agricultural tenant's crops and, although not a party to the agricultural tenancy, will have his liability determined, if necessary, by arbitration under this Act.

Subs. (5)

The basic principle being that the tenant is able to take action to prevent damage to his crops by any species of game which he is entitled to kill (*Ross* v. *Watson*, 1943 S.C. 406 at p. 419), ground game, comprising hares and rabbits, are excluded from the definition of game for the purposes of this section because of the tenant's rights under the Ground Game Act of 1880 and at common law.

Extent to which compensation recoverable under agreements

53.—(1) Unless this Act makes express provision to the contrary, where provision is made in this Act for compensation to be paid to a landlord or tenant—

(a) he shall be so entitled notwithstanding any agreement, and

(b) he shall not be entitled to compensation except under that provision.

(2) Where the landlord and the tenant of an agricultural holding enter into an agreement in writing for such a variation of the terms of the lease as could be made by direction under section 9 of this Act, the agreement may provide for the exclusion of compensation in the same manner as under section 51(1) of this Act.

(3) A claim for compensation by a landlord or tenant of an agricultural holding in a case for which this Act does not provide for compensation shall not be enforceable except under an agreement in writing.

DEFINITIONS

"agricultural holding": s.1(1).
"landlord": s.85(1).
"tenant": s.85(1).

DERIVATIONS

Agricultural Holdings (Scotland) Act 1949, s.64.

GENERAL NOTE

See Gill, paras. 164 (subs. (2)), 438 (subss. (1)(3)). (For the corresponding English provision see the Agricultural Holdings Act 1986, s.78).

Subs. (1)

"Express provision to the contrary" is to be found, *e.g.* in ss.34(4)(7), 37(2), 38(5), 42 and 45(3), each providing for substituted compensation. The general prohibition of contracting out is exemplified in the case of *Coates* v. *Diment* [1951] 1 All E.R. 890, where a limitation in a lease of the right to compensation for disturbance was held void.

Subs. (2)

This adds another exception to the general rule formulated in subs. (1) by enabling compensation for restriction of permanent pasture to be excluded where the parties to a lease have agreed on a reduction of the prescribed area of permanent pasture instead of having the matter referred to arbitration under the provisions of s.9.

Subs. (3)

It is not necessary that the agreement be a probative document—see s.78.

PART VI

ADDITIONAL PAYMENTS

Additional payments to tenants quitting holdings

54.—(1) Where compensation for disturbance in respect of an agricultural holding or part of such a holding becomes payable—

(a) to a tenant, under this Act; or

(b) to a statutory small tenant, under section 13 of the 1931 Act;

subject to this Part of this Act, there shall be payable by the landlord to the tenant, in addition to the compensation, a sum to assist in the reorganisation of the tenant's affairs of the amount referred to in subsection (2) below.

(2) The sum payable under subsection (1) above shall be equal to 4 times the annual rent of the holding or, in the case of part of a holding, times the appropriate portion of that rent, at the rate at which the rent was payable immediately before the termination of the tenancy.

DEFINITIONS

"agricultural holding": s.1(1).
"landlord": s.85(1)
"statutory small tenant": s.59.
"tenant": s.85(1).
"termination of tenancy": s.85(1).

DERIVATIONS

Agriculture (Miscellaneous Provisions) Act 1968, ss.9, 16, Sched. 5, para. 1.

GENERAL NOTE

See Gill, para. 509. (For the corresponding English provision see the Agricultural Holdings Act 1986, ss.60, 61).

Subs. (1)

Compensation for disturbance is regulated by s.43. While compensation under this provision is intended "to assist in the reorganisation of the tenant's affairs," it is payable without proof of loss in all cases where it applies (*Copeland* v. *McQuaker*, 1973 S.L.T. 186 at p. 191).

The statutory small tenant is a person who would have been a landholder with the security of tenure and other rights provided by crofting legislation but for the fact that the whole or greater part of the buildings and permanent improvements on his holding were not provided by him or by any predecessor in the same family. On being dispossessed by his landlord he has the same rights of compensation, including compensation for disturbance, as would be payable under the Agricultural Holdings legislation.

Subs. (2)

The rent payable immediately before termination is the criterion irrespective of any variation or abatement affecting earlier rents.

Provisions supplementary to s.54

55.—(1) Subject to subsection (2) below no sum shall be payable under section 54 of this Act in consequence of the termination of the tenancy of an agricultural holding or part of such a holding by virtue of a notice to quit where—

(a) the notice contains a statement that the carrying out of the purpose for which the landlord proposes to terminate the tenancy is desirable on any grounds referred to in section 24(1)(a) to (c) of this Act and, if an application for consent in respect of the notice is made to the Land Court in pursuance of section 22(1) of this Act, the Court consent to its operation and state in the reasons for their decision that they are satisfied that termination of the tenancy is desirable on that ground;

(b) the notice contains a statement that the landlord will suffer hardship unless the notice has effect and, if an application for consent in respect of the notice is made to the Land Court in pursuance of section 22(1) of this Act, the Court consent to its operation and state in the reasons for their decision that they are satisfied that greater hardship would be caused by withholding consent than by giving it;

(c) the notice is one to which section 22(1) of this Act applies by virtue of section 25(3) of this Act and the Land Court consent to its operation and specify in the reasons for their decision the Case in Schedule 2 to this Act as regards which they are satisfied; or

(d) section 22(1) of this Act does not apply to the notice by virtue of section 29(4) of the Agriculture Act 1967 (which relates to notices to quit given by the Secretary of State or a Rural Development Board with a view to boundary adjustments or an amalgamation).

(2) Subsection (1) above shall not apply in relation to a notice to quit where—

(a) the reasons given by the Land Court for their decision to consent to the operation of the notice include the reason that they are satisfied as to the matter referred to in section 24(1)(e) of this Act; or

(b) the reasons so given include the reason that the Court are satisfied as to the matter referred to in section 24(1)(b) of this Act or, where the tenant has succeeded to the tenancy as the near relative of a deceased tenant, as to the matter referred to in any of Cases 1, 3, 5 and 7 in Schedule 2 to this Act; but the Court state in their decision that they would have been satisfied also as to the matter referred to in section 24(1)(e) of this Act if it had been specified in the application for consent.

(3) In assessing the compensation payable to the tenant of an agricultural holding in consequence of the compulsory acquisition of his interest in the holding or part of it or the compulsory taking of possession of the holding or part of it, no account shall be taken of any benefit which might accrue to the tenant by virtue of section 54 of this Act.

(4) Any sum payable in pursuance of section 54 of this Act shall be so payable notwithstanding any agreement to the contrary.

(5) The following provisions of this Act shall apply to sums claimed or payable in pursuance of section 54 of this Act as they apply to compensation claimed or payable under section 43 of this Act—

sections 43(6);

section 50;

section 74;

(6) No sum shall be payable in pursuance of section 54 of this Act in consequence of the termination of the tenancy of an agricultural holding or part of such a holding by virtue of a notice to quit where—

(a) the relevant notice is given in pursuance of section 25(2)(a), (b) and (d) of this Act;

(b) the landlord is terminating the tenancy for the purpose of using the land for agriculture only; and

(c) the notice contains a statement that the tenancy is being terminated for the said purpose.

(7) If any question arises between the landlord and the tenant as to the purpose for which a tenancy is being terminated, the tenant shall, notwithstanding section 61(1) of this Act, refer the question to the Land Court for determination.

(8) In this section—

(a) references to section 54 of this Act do not include references to it as applied by section 56 of this Act; and

(b) for the purposes of subsection (1)(a) above, the reference in section 24(1)(c) of this Act to the purposes of the enactments relating to allotments shall be ignored.

DEFINITIONS

"agricultural holding": s.1(1).
"agriculture": s.85(1).
"landlord": s.85(1).
"near relative": Sched. 2, Pt. III, para. 1.
"notice to quit": s.21(2).
"tenant": s.85(1).
"termination of tenancy": s.85(1).

DERIVATIONS

Agriculture (Miscellaneous Provisions) Act 1968, s.11.

GENERAL NOTE

See Gill, paras. 509–511. (For the corresponding English provision see the Agricultural Holdings Act 1986, s.61).

Note: the replacement of s.11 of the 1968 Act by this section would appear to have removed the problems referred to in Gill, para. 5.10 caused by s.11 remaining unamended after the repeal of s.18 of the 1968 Act.

Subs. (1)

Section 54 having linked the payment of reorganisation compensation with compensation for disturbance, this subsection deals with cases in which, although compensation for disturbance is payable, liability for reorganisation compensation can be avoided. Basically this applies where the landlord is obtaining possession of the land to use it for an agricultural purpose or where he establishes a case of hardship. Apart from the provisions made here a landlord does not have to disclose the ground on which he is to seek the Land Court's consent to the operation of a Notice to Quit until, having received counter-notice from the tenant, he applies for consent. If, however, a landlord, on obtaining possession is to avoid liability for reorganisation compensation, his notice to quit must disclose grounds which, if accepted by the Court in the event of the tenant contesting possession, will give him exemption. The tenant, when receiving notice to quit and deciding whether or not to contest possession, is to be made aware of whether or not he will be entitled to reorganisation compensation on quitting the holding.

Paras. (a) and (b) each provide for the landlord's statement of grounds for seeking possession being contained in the notice to quit. In a decision which has been the subject of some criticism, however, the Court of Session, overruling the Land Court's decision, held that the statement, which they regarded as constituting intimation of the plea of hardship, could be contained in a letter accompanying the notice to quit (*Graham* v. *Lamont*, 1971 S.L.T. 341; see also Gill, para. 309 and Articles 1972 S.L.T. (News) 129 and 1973 S.L.T. (News) 141).

In terms of para. (a), the grounds qualifying for exemption are to be taken from the alternatives specified in subs. (1)(a)–(c) of s.24, *i.e.* that interests of good husbandry or sound estate management or the desirability of use for agricultural purposes such as research.

Para. (b) deals with hardship as a ground for exemption. The nature of hardship in its statutory sense and the considerations making for a successful plea have been discussed under reference to s.24. A question has arisen as to what other than a specific reference to hardship in the notice constitutes adequate notice that the plea is to be taken. In *Graham* v. *Lamont* the Court of Session, again overruling the Land Court, accepted as sufficient the reference in the letter accompanying the notice to quit to an agreement made by the tenant when he obtained the tenancy to give it up if the landlord or a member of his family wished to farm the holding, coupled with a statement that the landlord's son, having completed a training in agriculture, wanted to take over the farm. On the other hand, in *Copeland* v. *McQuaker*, 1973 S.L.T. 186, a letter stating that the landlords had purchased the holding after the tenant had declined to exercise an option to purchase it and now required it for their own use was held not to constitute intimation of the hardship plea. A fuller discussion of this matter will be formed in the Articles referred to above and in Gill, paras. 384–385.

Para. (c) deals with the case of a notice to quit served on a near relative successor of a deceased tenant as referred to in s.25(2)(c). As to the procedure to be followed in such cases, see s.25(3) and the note thereon. With s.25(3) applying s.22(1), such a successor is entitled to serve a counter-notice. If, however, the notice to quit specifies a case taken from Sched. 2 (which Schedule lists the various special grounds on which consent to the operation of a notice to quit served on a near relative successor may be given), exemption from reorganisation compensation may, subject to subs. (2), be obtained.

Para. (d) deals with the special case for exemption arising under s.29(4) of the Agriculture Act 1967 where the tenancy being terminated is one granted on a terminable basis by the Secretary of State. In such cases no statement is required in the notice to quit and counter-notice is not competent.

Subs. (2)

This makes important restrictions on the scope of exemptions available under subs. (1).

Para. (a) excludes the case where the Land Court's reasons for consenting to the operation of a notice to quit include their being satisfied on the landlord's proposal to use the land for a non-agricultural purpose as referred to in s.24(1)(e).

Para. (b) excludes the case where the reasons for the court's consent include satisfaction on the matter of sound estate management, as referred to in s.24(1)(b), or, again, in a case involving a near relative successor, include his inadequate training or experience in agriculture (Case 1 or 3 of Sched. 2), or his occupancy of other agricultural land (Case 5 or 7 of Sched. 2), but in any of these cases the court, as stated in their decision, would also have been satisfied on the desirability of non-agricultural use as referred to in s.24(1)(e), had it been specified in the landlord's application.

Subs. (3)

Provisions for the payment of reorganisation compensation in cases of compulsory acquisition are contained in s.56.

Subs. (4)

As with the tenant's other outgoing claims, including compensation for disturbance, contracting-out is made incompetent.

Subs. (5)

This applies the rules applicable to payment of compensation for disturbance to reorganisation compensation payable in respect of holdings affected by sub-letting (s.43(6)), holdings where there has been division of ownership (s.50) and holdings where limited owners are in the position of landlords (s.74).

Subs. (6)

Subs. (1)(c) having dealt with the case of the near relative successor, this subsection is concerned with that of the successor who is not a near relative of the deceased tenant. Provided that notice to quit is given in conformity with the timing requirements of s.25(2) (*q.v.* with note thereon), counter-notice cannot be given. However, to secure exemption from liability for reorganisation compensation, the notice to quit must state that the tenancy is being terminated for the purpose of using the land for agriculture only.

Subs. (7)

The content of this subsection appeared in the 1968 Act as a proviso to subs. (7) of s.11, the subsection replaced by subs. (6). This restricted its effect in referring questions as to the purpose for which a tenancy is being terminated to the Land Court instead of to an arbitrator, to cases arising under the subsection of which it formed part. As a separate subsection, however, the provision may have a wider application. While it is not necessary for it to be invoked to give the Land Court jurisdiction in cases arising under subss. (1) and (2) of this section in which Land Court decisions follow upon counter-notices served by tenants, it could be significant in relation to what Gill, para. 510, describes as a lacuna in the 1968 Act not expressly remedied by this Act. This lacuna, which is discussed in the Article in 1973 S.L.T. (News) 41 referred to above, is represented by the absence of provisions enabling a tenant who is not seeking to retain possession to dispute the landlord's intentions as stated in the notice to quit, with a view to maintaining a claim for reorganisation compensation. If one can assume that a tenant can take this course although not serving a counter-notice, this subsection would seem to have the result that the dispute will be resolved by the Land Court and not referred to arbitration.

Subs. (8)

In s.56, s.54 is applied in relation to the compulsory acquisition of the tenant's interest.

The law relative to allotments is contained in the Allotment (Scotland) Acts 1892–1950, but the facilities for the creation of allotments are now seldom used.

Additional payments in consequence of compulsory acquisition etc. of agricultural holdings

56.—(1) This section applies where, in pursuance of any enactment providing for the acquisition or taking of possession of land compulsorily, any person (referred to in this section and in sections 57 and 58 of and Schedule 8 to this Act as "an acquiring authority") acquires the interest of the tenant in, or takes possession of, an agricultural holding or any part of an agricultural holding or the holding of a statutory small tenant.

(2) Subject to subsection (3) below and sections 57 and 58 of this Act, where this section applies section 54 of this Act shall apply as if the acquiring authority were the landlord of the holding and compensation for disturbance in respect of the holding or part in question had become payable to the tenant on the date of the acquisition or taking of possession.

(3) No compensation shall be payable by virtue of this section in respect of an agricultural holding held under a tenancy for a term of 2 years or more unless the amount of such compensation is less than the aggregate of the amounts which would have been payable by virtue of this section if the tenancy had been from year to year: and in such a case the amount of compensation payable by virtue of this section shall (subject to section 57(4) of this Act) be equal to the difference.

DEFINITIONS
"acquisition": s.59.
"agricultural holding": s.1(1).
"landlord": s.85(1).
"tenant": s.85(1).

DERIVATIONS
Agriculture (Miscellaneous Provisions) Act 1968, ss.12, 16.

GENERAL NOTE
See Gill, paras. 562 and 563. (For the corresponding English provision see the Agricultural Holdings Act 1986, s.12).

Subs. (1)
This defines the application of the section as relating to a compulsory acquisition of an agricultural tenancy interest or all interests in land subject to an agricultural tenancy.

Subs. (2)
This gives the tenant thus dispossessed a claim against the acquiring authority for reorganisation compensation as payable under s.54.
In the case of a compulsory acquisition this claim, like the dispossessed tenant's other claims against the acquiring authority, is tax free in the hands of the tenant.

Subs. (3)
This restricts the scope of the tenant's claim by excluding it if the duration of the tenancy is two years or more, unless the tenant would otherwise receive less than a tenant from year to year. It is assumed that with the tenancy of longer duration the compensation payable by the acquiring authority other than reorganisation compensation will adequately compensate the tenant dispossessed. That will not be so in the case of a year-to-year tenancy but if the exclusion of reorganisation compensation in the case of a longer tenancy is to have the result that the tenant receives less compensation than he would have received in aggregate as a yearly tenant, he will be entitled to receive reorganisation compensation to the extent of the difference.
The foregoing is thought to represent the intended meaning of the subsection. Its effect, however, would seem to have been rendered at least doubtful by a drafting error involving the omission in line 4, after the word "payable," of the words "by way of compensation and." Without these words, which appeared in s.12(2) of the 1949 Act, which this subsection replaces, the term "aggregate," as used in this subsection, would seem to be inapplicable.

Provisions supplementary to s.56

57.—(1) For the purposes of section 56 of this Act, a tenant of an agricultural holding shall be deemed not to be a tenant of it in so far as, immediately before the acquiring of the interest or taking of possession referred to in that section, he was neither in possession, nor entitled to take possession, of any land comprised in the holding: and in determining, for those purposes, whether a tenant was so entitled, any lease relating to the land of a kind referred to in section 2(1) of this Act which has not taken effect as a lease of the land from year to year shall be ignored.

(2) Section 56(1) of this Act shall not apply—

(a) where the acquiring authority require the land comprised in the holding or part in question for the purposes of agricultural research or experiment or of demonstrating agricultural methods or for the purposes of the enactments relating to smallholdings;

(b) where the Secretary of State acquires the land under section 57(1)(c) or 64 of the Agricultural (Scotland) Act 1948.

(3) Where an acquiring authority exercise, in relation to any land, power to acquire or take possession of land compulsorily which is conferred on the authority by virtue of section 102 or 110 of the Town and Country Planning (Scotland) Act 1972 or section 7 of the New Towns (Scotland) Act 1968, the authority shall be deemed for the purposes of subsection (2) above not to require the land for any of the purposes mentioned in that subsection.

(4) Schedule 8 to this Act shall have effect in relation to payments under section 56 of this Act.

DEFINITIONS
"acquiring authority": ss.56(1); 59.
"agricultural holding": s.1(1).
"tenant": s.85(1).

DERIVATIONS
Agriculture (Miscellaneous Provisions) (Scotland) Act 1968, s.14.
Town and Country Planning (Scotland) Act 1972, Sched. 21, Pt. II.

GENERAL NOTE
See Gill, paras. 562–563.

Subs. (1)
This excludes the right to compensation under s.56 where the tenant is neither in possession nor entitled to take possession of any land comprised in the holding. "Possession" is apparently intended to mean "actual possession." This was made clear in an interpretation provision (see s.17 of the 1968 Act) but it is not referred to in s.59, the interpretation section for this part of this Act. The particular situation contemplated appears to be one where the tenant has sublet but not where the sub-let is for less than from year to year and has not taken effect as a lease from year to year under s.2(1).

Subs. (2)
This excludes the right to compensation when the land is required for such purposes as agricultural research or the creation of smallholdings (cf. ss.24(1)(c) and 55(1)(a)) and again when the Secretary of State is acquiring land affected by severance in order to secure its full and efficient use (s.57(1)(c) of the 1948 Act) or land to be used for providing agricultural holdings of limited size (s.64 of the 1948 Act).

Subs. (3)
This limits the operation of subs. (2) by excluding from the acquiring authority's exemption from reorganisation compensation certain cases of acquisition for development purposes by local authorities or development corporations as authorised by the Secretary of State.

Subs. (4)
The assessment and payment of claims arising under s.56 is dealt with in Sched. 8 (q.v.), the claims being determined by the Lands Tribunal for Scotland.

Effect of early resumption clauses on compensation

58.—(1) Where—

    (a) the landlord of an agricultural holding resumes land under a provision in the lease entitling him to resume land for building, planting, feuing or other purposes (not being agricultural purposes); or

    (b) the landlord of the holding of a statutory small tenant resumes the holding or part thereof on being authorised to do so by the Land Court under section 32(15) of the 1911 Act; and

    (c) in either case, the tenant has not elected that section 55(2) of the Land Compensation (Scotland) Act 1973 (right to opt for notice of entry compensation) should apply to the notice;

compensation shall be payable by the landlord to the tenant (in addition to any other compensation so payable apart from this subsection) in respect of the land.

(2) The amount of compensation payable under subsection (1) above shall be equal to the value of the additional benefit (if any) which would have accrued to the tenant if the land had, instead of being resumed at the date of resumption, been resumed at the expiry of 12 months from the end of the current year of the tenancy.

(3) Section 55(4) and (5) of this Act shall apply to compensation claimed or payable under subsection (1) above with the substitution for references to section 54 of this Act of references to this section.

(4) In the assessment of the compensation payable by an acquiring authority to a statutory small tenant in the circumstances referred to in section 56(1) of this Act, any authorisation of resumption of the holding or part thereof by the Land Court under section 32(15) of the 1911 Act for any purpose (not being an agricultural purpose) specified therein shall—

    (a) in the case of an acquisition, be treated as if it became operative only on the expiry of 12 months from the end of the year of the tenancy current when notice to treat in respect of the acquisition was served or treated as served on the tenant; and

    (b) in the case of a taking of possession, be disregarded;

unless compensation assessed in accordance with paragraph (a) or (b) above would be less than would be payable but for this subsection.

(5) For the purposes of subsection (1) above, the current year of a tenancy for a term of 2 years or more is the year beginning with such day in the period of 12 months ending with a date 2 months before the resumption mentioned in that subsection as corresponds to the day on which the term would expire by the effluxion of time.

DEFINITIONS

"acquiring authority": s.59.

"acquisition": s.59.

"agricultural": s.85(1).

"landlord": s.85(1).

"lease": s.85(1).

"statutory small tenant": s.59.

"tenant": s.85(1).

DERIVATIONS

Agriculture (Miscellaneous Provisions) Act 1968, ss.15, 14, Sched. 5, para. 5.

GENERAL NOTE

See Gill, paras. 562–569, particularly paras. 563 and 566. (For the corresponding English provision see the Agricultural Holdings Act 1986, s.62).

Subs. (1)

This shows that the section applies to resumption in respect of agricultural holdings under the provisions of leases as referred to in s.21(7)(a) and resumptions affecting statutory small tenants made with the authority of the Land Court under the relevant statutory provisions. In either case, however, the tenant's right to compensation under this section does not apply if the tenant is being dispossessed as a result of a notice to quit or notice of resumption under s.55(8) of the Land Compensation (Scotland) Act 1973, given by the landlord by reason of a compulsory acquisition scheme and the tenant has opted under s.55(2)(b) of that Act (as amended in terms of Sched. 11, para. 2(c)) for the wider measure of compensation available to him under the compulsory purchase code.

Subs. (2)

Compensation under this section is in effect being given for dispossession without the normal period of notice and so is based on the additional benefit (if any) which the tenant would have obtained from the land affected had he been vacating it on the normal period of notice. The subsection postulates the land being due to be vacated on the expiry of twelve months from the end of the year of the tenancy current at a date two months before the date of resumption. The two-month period appears to be prescribed on the basis of the rules established in England as regards the minimum notice for resumption—see notes to s.21(7). It is necessary to read, along with this subsection, subs. (5), which defines the current year in the case of a tenancy of two years or more. The practical effect of these provisions is exemplified in Connell (*op. cit.* p. 29) the period covered by the claim varying according to the point within the tenancy year at which resumption takes effect. Failing agreement, the tenant's claim will go to statutory arbitration. In the case of arable land the arbiter will estimate the value of the crop or other produce of the land and make deduction for such disbursements as rent and expense of cultivation to arrive at the amount due. Where the land is in grass its potential letting value as grazings, less rent and expenses, will usually form the basis of assessment.

Subs. (3)

This renders contracting out incompetent and applies the provisions of the Act as regards divided holdings, holdings affected by sub-letting and holdings with limited owners in the position of landlords.

Subs. (4)

This puts resumption affecting statutory small tenancies in a similar position to resumption affecting agricultural holdings, which under s.44 of the Land Compensation (Scotland) Act 1973 (as amended in terms of Sched. 11, para. 34) are disregarded in assessing the compensation payable by an acquiring authority (see Gill, para. 564) except in the special circumstances specified.

Subs. (5)

See notes to subs. (2).

Interpretation etc. of Part VI

59. In sections 54 to 58 of and Schedule 8 to this Act—

"acquiring authority" has the meaning assigned to it by section 56(1) of this Act;

"statutory small tenant" and "holding" in relation to a statutory small tenant have the meanings given in section 32(1) of the 1911 Act; and

references to the acquisition of any property are references to the vesting of the property in the person acquiring it.

DERIVATIONS

Agriculture (Miscellaneous Provisions) Act 1968, ss.16, 17.

GENERAL NOTE

With regard to statutory small tenants, see note to s.54(1).

"Acquisition" applies to the transfer of ownership to the acquiring authority as contrasted with the "taking of possession," signifying a temporary requisition.

PART VII

ARBITRATION AND OTHER PROCEEDINGS

Questions between landlord and tenant

60.—(1) Subject to subsection (2) below and except where this Act makes express provision to the contrary, any question or difference between the landlord and the tenant of an agricultural holding arising out of the tenancy or in connection with the holding (not being a question or difference as to liability for rent) shall, whether such question or difference arises during the currency or on the termination of the tenancy, be determined by arbitration.

(2) Any question or difference between the landlord and the tenant of an agricultural holding which by or under this Act or under the lease is required to be determined by arbitration may, if the landlord and the tenant so agree, in lieu of being determined by arbitration be determined by the Land Court, and the Land Court shall, on the joint application of the landlord and the tenant, determine such question or difference accordingly.

DEFINITIONS
"agricultural holding": s.1(1).
"landlord": s.85(1).
"tenant": s.85(1).
"termination of tenancy": s.85(1).

DERIVATIONS
Agricultural Holdings (Scotland) Act 1949, ss.74, 78.

GENERAL NOTE
See Gill, paras. 606–610, 613, 662.

Subs. (1)
This provision, as previously embodied in s.74 of the 1949 Act, has a wide scope, being excluded only where the Act otherwise "expressly" provides (for instances of its exclusion such as existing under ss.20, 22 and 39 and 41, see Gill, para. 613). While the provision covers all questions arising during or at the termination of a tenancy it does not apply to questions concerning the creation or existence of a landlord-tenant relationship in an agricultural tenancy (*Houison Cranfords Trs.* v. *Davies*, 1951 S.C. 1; *Brodie* v. *Kerr: McCallum* v. *McNair*, 1952 S.C. 216, *Cormack* v. *McIldowie's Executor*, 1974 S.L.T. 178 (O.H.), *Craig and Another*, 1981 S.L.T. (Land Ct.) 12). For its application there must be a subsisting relationship of landlord and tenant between the parties. Thus it does not affect questions between incoming and outgoing tenants.

Where the statutory arbitration applies, the jurisdiction of the court cannot be expressly prorogated nor can it be impliedly prorogated by the failure of a defender in a court action to plead the provision (*Craig and Another*, above; see also *Taylor* v. *Brick*, 1982 S.L.T. 25). Thus any action of removing, whether based on irritancy, resumption or notice to quit if defended on the merits, must be sisted for the statutory arbitration. In other processes a defender seeking to invoke this subsection must aver specifically and relevantly that a question or difference falling within the subsection exists (*Brodie* v. *Kerr, supra,* at p. 227).

It appears, however, that a claim of damages arising *ex delicto* but involving the parties to a tenancy is not a matter for the statutory arbitration (*McDiarmid* v. *Secretary of State*, 1971 S.L.T. (Land Ct.) 4).

The wording "question or difference" involves that except in relation to waygoing claims covered by s.61(7) there is no distinction to be made between matters of arbitration and matters of valuation. The exclusion, however, of any "question or difference as to liability of rent" places a certain limitation on the scope of the statutory arbitration, but this is restricted to cases where the liability to pay the rent sued for is disputed upon grounds which, if sustained, would extinguish that liability. Hence it does not apply where the tenant claims to be entitled to withhold payment in respect of some default in performance of the landlord's obligations under the lease (*Brodie* v. *Kerr* (*supra*, at p. 226)). Again, a rent review under s.13 does not involve a question of difference as to liability for rent (*Boyd* v. *Macdonald*, 1958 S.L.C.R. 10).

Subs. (2)
The subsection does not extend the scope of the statutory arbitration (*Craig and Another*), but the practical advantages of the facility as compared with the statutory arbitration procedure are brought out in Gill, para. 662. To what is said there may be added the comment that the Fee Fund or court fees paid in the Land Court will normally be much less than the cost of an arbitration: again, the fact that the facility exists, even although it is not as widely used as it might be, has resulted in there being available reports of important cases, which would not have been published in any way had they been dealt with by arbitration.

Arbitrations

61.—(1) Any matter which by or under this Act, or by regulations made thereunder, or under the lease of an agricultural holding is required to be determined by arbitration shall, whether the matter arose before or after the passing of this Act, be determined, notwithstanding any agreement under the lease or otherwise providing for a different method of arbitration, by a single arbiter in accordance with the provisions of Schedule 7 to this Act, and the Arbitration (Scotland) Act 1894 shall not apply to any such arbitration.

(2) An appeal by application to the Land Court by any party to an aribitration under section 13(1) of this Act (variation of rent) against the award of an arbiter appointed by the Secretary of State or the Land Court on any question of law or fact (including the amount of the award) shall be competent.

(3) An appeal under subsection (2) above must be brought within 2 months of the date of issue of the award.

(4) The Secretary of State may by regulations made by statutory instrument subject to annulment in pursuance of a resolution of either House of Parliament make such provision as he thinks desirable for expediting, or reducing the expenses of, proceedings on arbitrations under this Act.

(5) The Secretary of State shall not make regulations under subsection (4) above which are inconsistent with the provisions of Schedule 7 to this Act.

(6) Section 62 of this Act shall apply to the determination by arbitration of any claims which arise—

   (a) under this Act or any custom or agreement, and

   (b) on or out of the termination of the tenancy of an agricultural holding or part thereof.

(7) This section and section 60 of this Act shall not apply to valuations of sheep stocks, dung, fallow, straw, crops, fences and other specific things the property of an outgoing tenant, agreed under a lease to be taken over from him at the termination of a tenancy by the landlord or the incoming tenant, or to any questions which it may be necessary to determine in order to ascertain the sum to be paid in pursuance of such an agreement, whether such valuations and questions are referred to arbitration under the lease or not.

(8) Any valuation or question mentioned in subsection (7) above falling to be decided by reference to a date after May 16, 1975, which would, if it had fallen to be decided by reference to a date immediately before that day, have been decided by reference to fiars prices, shall be decided in such manner as the parties may by agreement determine or, failing such agreement, shall, notwithstanding the provisions of that subsection, be decided by arbitration under this Act.

DEFINITIONS

   "agricultural holding": s.1(1).
   "landlord": s.85(1).
   "lease": s.85(1).
   "tenant": s.85(1).
   "termination of tenancy": s.85(1).

DERIVATIONS

   Agricultural Holdings (Scotland) Act 1949, ss.68, 75.
   Local Government (Scotland) Act 1973, s.228(5).
   Agricultural Holdings (Scotland) Act 1983, s.5(1).

GENERAL NOTE

   See Gill, paras. 219, 448, 611, 612, 614. (For the corresponding English provision see the Agricultural Holdings Act 1986, s.84 and Sched. 11).

Subs. (1)

   This establishes the form of the statutory arbitration involving a reference to a single arbiter applying to all questions or disputes between landlord and tenant apart from the matters referred to in subs. (7). When subs. (1) operates, a reference to two arbiters and an oversman, as sometimes prescribed in leases or agreements, is incompetent. The same rule has been applied to arbitrations on milk quota compensation (Agriculture Act 1986, Sched. 2, paras. 10(1) and 11(4) as amended in terms of Sched. 11, paras. 51 and 52).

Subss. (2) and (3)

This right of appeal, restricted to arbitrations for variation of rent, and available within two months of the issue of the arbiter's award, was introduced by the 1983 Act. Certain procedural matters arising in connection with these appeals are discussed in Gill, para. 219. It should be noted that if the court sustains the appeal it must make its own determination of the question at issue, a remit to the arbiter, who is by then *functus*, not being competent.

Subss. (4) and (5)

The Secretary of State's power, which has not yet been exercised, has been extended to arbitrations under the Opencast Coal Act 1958 (Sched. 7, paras. 4(4) and 25, as amended in terms of Sched. 11, para. 21), the Agriculture Act 1967 (Sched. 3, para. 7(5) as amended in terms of Sched. 11, para. 31 on breach of conditions applying to amalgamated agricultural units), and the Agriculture Act 1986 (Sched. 2, paras. 10(1) and 11(4) as amended in terms of Sched. 11, paras. 51, 52 dealing with milk quota compensation). Any regulations made under these powers must not be inconsistent with the code of rules for arbitration procedure contained in Sched. 7 to this Act.

Subs. (6)

The substantive content of this provision is repeated in s.62(1) (*q.v.*).

Subs. (7)

The exclusion of the statutory arbitration procedure applies only where the items in question belong to an outgoing tenant. It does not apply to transactions between an incoming tenant and a landlord who has been in possession (*Methven* v. *Burn*, 1923 S.L.T. (Sh. Ct.) 25) nor to the valuation of milk quota compensation (Agriculture Act 1986, Sched. 2, para. 11(4) as amended *ut sup.*). The excluded transactions may be referred to a single arbiter along with the statutory claims, but in the past, at least, it has been customary for the quantification and valuation of such items, as dung or crops for which an outgoing tenant is entitled to payment, to be covered by a reference to two arbiters and an oversman. These are common law arbitrations but are subject, where applicable, to provisions of the Arbitration (Scotland) Act 1894 and the Administration of Justice (Scotland) Act 1972 (see Gill, para. 615).

Subs. (8)

In the past Fiars Prices of grain, as fixed annually at the Fiars Court for determination of minister's stipends where there had not been created standard charges under the legislation of 1925, were sometimes prescribed as a measure of value in the claims of outgoing tenants for crops. The Local Government (Scotland) Act 1973, in abolishing Fiars Prices, provided by s.228(4) that any valuation or question which would have been decided on the basis of Fiars Prices should in future be decided, failing agreement on some other method, by a statutory arbitration.

Claims on termination of tenancy

62.—(1) Without prejudice to any other provision of this Act, any claim by a tenant of an agricultural holding against his landlord or by a landlord of an agricultural holding against his tenant, being a claim which arises, under this Act or under any custom or agreement, on or out of the termination of the tenancy (or of part thereof shall, subject to subsections (2) to (5) below, be determined by arbitration.

(2) Without prejudice to any other provision of this Act, no claim to which this section applies shall be enforceable unless before the expiry of 2 months after the termination of the tenancy the claimant has given notice in writing to his landlord or his tenant, as the case may be, of his intention to make the claim.

(3) A notice under subsection (2) above shall specify the nature of the claim, and it shall be a sufficient specification thereof if the notice refers to the statutory provision, custom, or term of an agreement under which the claim is made.

(4) The landlord and the tenant may within 4 months after the termination of the tenancy by agreement in writing settle any such claim and the Secretary of State may upon the application of the landlord or the tenant made within that period extend the said period by 2 months and, on a second such application made during these 2 months, by a further 2 months.

(5) Where before the expiry of the period referred to in subsection (4) above and any extension thereof under that subsection any such claim has not been settled, the claim shall cease to be enforceable unless before the expiry of one month after the end of the said period and any such extension, or such longer time as the Secretary of State may in special circumstances allow, an arbiter has been appointed by agreement between the landlord and the tenant under this Act or an application for the appointment of an arbiter under those provisions has been made by the landlord or the tenant.

(6) Where a tenant lawfully remains in occupation of part of an agricultural holding after the termination of a tenancy, references in subsections (2) and (4) above to the termination of the tenancy thereof shall be construed as references to the termination of the occupation.

DEFINITIONS
"agricultural holding": s.1(1).
"landlord": s.85(1).
"tenant": s.85(1).
"termination of tenancy": s.85(1).

DERIVATIONS
Agricultural Holdings (Scotland) Act 1949, s.68.

GENERAL NOTE
See Gill, paras. 429–436. (For the corresponding English provision see the Agricultural Holdings Act 1986, s.83).

Subs. (1)
Despite the comprehensive terms of s.60 it has been considered necessary to include in earlier legislation specific provision for arbitration as applying to certain matters. Here we have it applied to outgoing claims generally. As to the application of custom, see s.85(4), and as to "termination" of the tenancy s.85(1).

Subs. (2)
Two months from the termination of the tenancy (modified by subs. (6) if applicable) is the basic period for intimation of outgoing claims, but exceptions involving requirements of earlier notice exist under s.44(2) ("high farming") and s.47(1) (landlord's claims for dilapidation or deterioration). On the wording of this provision there would appear to be no reason why notice should not be given before the termination of the tenancy. Again it would appear that where in one of the exceptional cases notice as required has been given before the termination of the tenancy, further notice within the supervening period should not be required.

Subs. (3)
In contrast with the requirements applying after an arbiter has been appointed (see Sched. 7, para. 5), notice given at this stage does not require to be in detailed terms, nor need it quantify the claim.

Subs. (4)
The negotiating period, like the period for intimation of claims, runs from the termination of the tenancy. Hence if intimation of the claim has been delayed as long as permissible, the negotiating period may be only two months or slightly more. Any application for extension or further extension of that period must be made before expiry of the period or the initial extension.

Subs. (5)
Where claims are not settled within the negotiating period extended, as the case may be, a further month is allowed for the appointment of an arbiter by agreement (an agreement to appoint an arbiter not being sufficient; see *Chalmers Property Investment Co.* v. *MacCall*, 1951

S.C. 24) or for an application to the Secretary of State to be made for an appointment. That is the alternative available in terms of para. 1 of Sched. 7. The Secretary of State is, however, given a discretion enabling him, in special circumstances, to extend this period of one month. The only reported case bearing on the exercise of this discretion, as contained in previous legislation, appears to be *Crawford's Trs.* v. *Smith*, 1952 S.L.T. (Notes) 5.

Subs. (6)

The statutory interpretation of "termination" of the tenancy (s.85(1)) has been taken to mean the date when the contractual relationship ends rather than the date of complete vacation of the holding or cessation of the tenant's possession. As contained in s.68(5) of the 1949 Act, the provisions of this subsection have been held as not applying where the lease provides for vacation of part of the holding being deferred to enable a crop to be ingathered by the outgoing tenant, but only where a new agreement affecting part of the holding is concluded after the termination of the lease (*Coutts* v. *Barclay Harvey*, 1956 S.L.T. (Sh. Ct.) 54 following decisions of the English courts in *Swinburne* v. *Andrews* [1923] 2 K.B. 483 at p. 487 and *Arden* v. *Rutter* [1923] 2 K.B. 865). This subsection could not be invoked by a tenant unsuccessfully challenging or refusing to obtemper a notice to quit, his occupation beyond the ish not being "lawful" (see *Hendry* v. *Walker*, 1927 S.L.T. 333).

Panel of arbiters, and remuneration of arbiter

63.—(1) Such number of persons as may be appointed by the Lord President of the Court of Session, after consultation with the Secretary of State, shall form a panel of persons from whom any arbiter appointed, otherwise than by agreement, for the purposes of this Act shall be selected.

(2) The panel of arbiters constituted under subsection (1) above shall be subject to revision by the Lord President of the Court of Session, after consultation with the Secretary of State, at such intervals not exceeding 5 years, as the Lord President and the Secretary of State may from time to time agree.

(3)—

(a) the remuneration of an arbiter appointed by the Secretary of State under Schedule 7 to this Act shall be such amount as is fixed by the Secretary of State;

(b) the remuneration of an arbiter appointed by the parties to an arbitration under this Act shall, in default of agreement between those parties and the arbiter, be such amount as, on the application of the arbiter or of either of the parties, is fixed by the auditor of the sheriff court, subject to appeal to the sheriff;

(c) the remuneration of an arbiter, when agreed or fixed under this subsection, shall be recoverable by the arbiter as a debt due from either of the parties;

(d) any amount paid in respect of the remuneration of the arbiter by either of the parties in excess of the amount (if any) directed by the award to be paid by that party in respect of the expenses of the award shall be recoverable from the other party.

DERIVATIONS

Agricultural Holdings (Scotland) Act 1949, s.76.
Sheriffs Courts (Scotland) Act 1971, s.4.

GENERAL NOTE

With reference to subs. (3) it is pointed out by Connell (*op. cit.* p. 188) that it is for the arbiter to apply to the Secretary of State to fix his fee which is over and above his out-of-pocket expenses and that his application should give details of work done and time occupied, the process in the arbitration being submitted for reference in important or complex cases.

Appointment of arbiter in cases where Secretary of State is a party

64. Where the Secretary of State is a party to any question or difference which under this Act is to be determined by arbitration or by an arbiter appointed in accordance with this Act, the arbiter shall, in lieu of being appointed by the Secretary of State, be appointed by the Land Court, and the remuneration of the arbiter so appointed shall be such amount as may be fixed by the Land Court.

DERIVATIONS
   Agricultural Holdings (Scotland) Act 1949, ss.77, 87(2).
   Agriculture (Miscellaneous Provisions) Act 1968, s.17(3).

GENERAL NOTE
   With the Secretary of State, through the Department of Agriculture, being a party to many tenancy contracts of agricultural land, a provision avoiding a situation of *auctor in rem suam* is appropriate and indeed necessary. This section is confined in its application to the appointment and remuneration of an arbiter but the position of the Secretary of State as landlord or tenant is dealt with on a more general basis by s.80.

Recovery of compensation and other sums due

65. Any award or agreement under this Act as to compensation, expenses or otherwise may, if any sum payable thereunder is not paid within one month after the date on which it becomes payable, be recorded for execution in the Books of Council and Session or in the sheriff court books, and shall be enforceable in like manner as a recorded decree arbitral.

DERIVATIONS
   Agricultural Holdings (Scotland) Act 1949, s.69.

GENERAL NOTE
   See Gill, para. 438.
   It is suggested by Connell (*op. cit.* p. 185) that the submission or award would not require to contain a warrant of registration for execution. It would seem, however, to be advisable that any agreement intended to be enforceable under this provision should contain a consent to registration for execution. The provisions of this section apply to compensation for milk quotas in terms of the Agriculture Act 1986, Sched. 2, para. 2 as amended in terms of para. 53 of Sched. 11 to this Act.

Power to enable demand to remedy a breach to be modified on arbitration

66.—(1) Where a question or difference required by section 60 of this Act to be determined by arbitration relates to a demand in writing served on a tenant by a landlord requiring the tenant to remedy a breach of any term or condition of his tenancy by the doing of any work of provision, repair, maintenance or replacement of fixed equipment, the arbiter may—
   (a) in relation to all or any of the items specified in the demand, whether or not any period is specified as the period within which the breach should be remedied, specify such period for that purpose as appears in all the circumstances to the arbiter to be reasonable;
   (b) delete from the demand any item or part of an item which, having due regard to the interests of good husbandry as respects the holding and of sound-management of the estate of which the holding forms part or which the holding constitutes, the arbiter is satisfied is unnecessary or unjustified;
   (c) substitute, in the case of any item or part of an item specified in the demand, a different method or material for the method or material which the demand would otherwise require to be followed or used where, having regard to the purpose which that item or part is intended to achieve, the arbiter is satisfied that—
      (i) the latter method or material would involve undue difficulty or expense,
      (ii) the first-mentioned method or material would be substantially as effective for the purpose, and
      (iii) in all the circumstances the substitution is justified.

(2) Where under subsection (1)(a) above an arbiter specifies a period within which a breach should be remedied or the period for remedying a breach is extended by virtue of subsection (4) below, the Land Court may, on the application of the arbiter or the landlord, specify a date for the termination of the tenancy by notice to quit in the event of the tenant's failure to remedy the breach within that period, being a date not earlier than whichever of the two following dates is the later, that is to say—

(a) the date on which the tenancy could have been terminated by notice to quit served on the expiry of the period originally specified in the demand, or if no such period is so specified, on the date of the giving of the demand, or

(b) 6 months after the expiry of the period specified by the arbiter or, as the case may be, of the extended period.

(3) A notice to quit on a date specified in accordance with subsection (2) above shall be served on the tenant within one month after the expiry of the period specified by the arbiter or the extended time, and shall be valid notwithstanding that it is served less than 12 months before the date on which the tenancy is to be terminated or that that date is not the end of a year of the tenancy.

(4) Where—

(a) notice to quit to which 22(2)(d) of this Act applies is stated to be given by reason of the tenant's failure to remedy within the period specified in the demand a breach of any term or condition of his tenancy by the doing of any work of provision, repair, maintenance or replacement of fixed equipment, or within that period as extended by the landlord or the arbiter; and

(b) it appears to the arbiter on an arbitration required by notice under section 23(2) of this Act that, notwithstanding that the period originally specified or extended was reasonable, it would, in consequence of any happening before the expiry of that period, have been unreasonable to require the tenant to remedy the breach within that period;

the arbiter may treat the period as having been extended or further extended and make his award as if the period had not expired; and where the breach has not been remedied at the date of the award, the arbiter may extend the period as he considers reasonable, having regard to the length of period which has elapsed since the service of the demand.

DEFINITIONS
  "fixed equipment": s.85(1).
  "good husbandry": s.85(1).
  "landlord": s.85(1).
  "notice to quit": s.21(2).
  "sound estate management": s.85(1).
  "tenant": s.85(1).
  "termination of tenancy": s.85(1).

DERIVATIONS
  Agriculture (Miscellaneous Provisions) Act 1976, s.13.

GENERAL NOTE
  See Gill, paras. 342–353.

Subs. (1)
  This subsection, like the remainder of the section, should be read along with the provisions of s.32. It discloses that the breach of the kind inferred to in s.32(1)(b) is one requiring to be remedied by work of provision, repair maintenance or replacement of fixed equipment and results that an arbiter called upon to consider a demand to remedy such a breach has a wide discretion in modifying or altering its content and specifying or extending the time allowed for compliance. From the tenant's point of view the importance of this provision is that whereas

before its introduction in the Act of 1976 he took the risk of losing his tenancy if he did not comply with such a demand to remedy, no modification of the demand nor extension of time allowed being then within the arbiter's powers, he can now invoke the arbiter's discretion on receiving the demand and base his response to it on the resultant ruling.

Subs. (2)

The specification or extension by the arbiter of a period for compliance with the demand to remedy may have the result that even if the tenant defaults in complying with the demand to remedy as modified or amended, the landlord will not be able to serve a notice to quit for the term for which it could otherwise have been served. To prevent a defaulting tenant in this way obtaining an extra year's possession of the holding, provision is made for the Land Court, on the application of the arbiter or the landlord, to specify a date for termination of the tenancy by notice to quit, which date must, however, be not earlier than the later of (a) the date on which the tenancy could have been terminated by notice to quit served on the expiry of the period specified in the demand or the date of the demand when no period is specified; or (b) six months after the expiry of the period specified or extended by the arbiter. The application in practice of this and the following subsections is exemplified in Gill, paras. 351–352.

Subs. (3)

This provides for the situation in which a second notice to quit has to be served. It requires service within a month of the expiry of the period specified or extended by the arbiter but enables a notice to be effective although served less than twelve months before its effective date and/or for a date other than the termination of the tenancy. Section 32(6), however, enables the tenant by serving counter-notice to make the operation of such second notice to quit subject to Land Court consent.

Subs. (4)

This deals with the situation in which the tenant's failure to obtemper timeously a demand to remedy can be attributed to something happening before the period for remedial action has expired which would make it unreasonable to require the breach to be remedied within that period. Although the nature of the occurrence is not specified, the subsection would appear to be referring to some personal disaster affecting the tenant or again to some external factor such as failure of contractors, industrial disputes or exceptional weather conditions. When notice to quit founding on the failure to remedy is served and the tenant calls for arbitration, the arbiter, if the demand has been fulfilled late, may make an award in the tenant's favour by treating the time limit for compliance as having been extended retrospectively. Again, if the breach remains unremedied he can extend the time for compliance to the extent he considers reasonable, having regard to the time which has already passed since the service of the demand.

In either case the notice to quit, as a notice under s.22(2)(d) enforceable without Land Court consent, will be invalidated, but in the latter case the landlord will be able to serve a second notice to quit based on the demand to remedy should the tenant fail to obtemper the demand within the extended period allowed by the arbiter.

Prohibition of appeal to sheriff principal

67. Where jurisdiction is conferred by this Act on the sheriff, there shall be no appeal to the sheriff principal.

DERIVATIONS

Agricultural Holdings (Scotland) Act 1949, s.91.
Sheriffs Courts (Scotland) Act 1971, s.4.

GENERAL NOTE

See Gill, para. 674.

The terms "Sheriff" and "Sheriff Substitute" now fall to be interpreted in accordance with s.49 of the Sheriff Courts (Scotland) Act 1971 and the Interpretation Act 1978, Sched. 1. Either the Sheriff or the Sheriff Substitute is entitled to execute jurisdiction. The section applies only to jurisdiction conferred by this Act and not to any proceedings falling within the Sheriff's normal jurisdiction under the Sheriff Courts (Scotland) Acts 1907 and 1971 (*Cameron* v. *Ferrier* (1912) 28 Sh.Ct.Rep. 220).

Sheep stock valuation

68.—(1) This section and sections 69 to 72 of this Act shall apply where under a lease of an agricultural holding, the tenant is required at the termination of the tenancy to leave the stock of sheep on the holding to be taken over by the landlord or by the incoming tenant at a price or valuation to be fixed by arbitration, referred to in this section and sections 69 to 72 of this Act as a "sheep stock valuation."

(2) In a sheep stock valuation where the lease was entered into before or on November 6, 1946, the arbiter shall in his award show the basis of valuation of each class of stock and state separately any amounts included in respect of acclimatisation or hefting or of any other consideration or factor for which he has made special allowance.

(3) In a sheep stock valuation where the lease was entered into after November 6, 1946, the arbiter shall fix the value of the sheep stock in accordance—

    (a) in the case of a valuation made in respect of a tenancy terminating at Whitsunday in any year, with Part I of Schedule 9 to this Act if the lease was entered into before December 1, 1986, otherwise with Part I of Schedule 10 to this Act; or

    (b) in the case of a valuation made in respect of a tenancy terminating at Martinmas in any year, with the provisions of Part II of Schedule 9 to this Act, if the lease was entered into before December 1, 1986, otherwise with Part II of Schedule 10 to this Act,

and subsection (2) above shall apply in such a case as if for the words from "show the basis" to the end of the subsection there were substituted the words "state separately the particulars set forth in Part III of Schedule 9 (or, as the case may be, Schedule 10) to this Act."

(4) Where an arbiter fails to comply with any requirement of subsection (2) or (3) above, his award may be set aside by the sheriff.

(5) The Secretary of State may, by order made by statutory instrument subject to annulment in pursuance of a resolution of either House of Parliament, vary the provisions of Schedule 10 to this Act, in relation to sheep stock valuations under leases entered into on or after the date of commencement of the order.

DEFINITIONS
    "agricultural holding": s.72.
    "arbiter": s.72.
    "landlord": s.85(1).
    "lease": s.85(1).
    "tenant": s.85(1).
    "termination of tenancy": s.85(1).

DERIVATIONS
    Sheep Stocks Valuation (Scotland) Act 1937, s.1.
    Hill Farming Act 1946, s.28.
    Hill Farming Act 1946 (Variation of Second Schedule) (Scotland) Order 1986 (S.I. 1986 No. 1823).
    Law Reform (Miscellaneous Provisions) (Scotland) Act 1985, s.32.

GENERAL NOTE
    See Gill, paras. 454–470 and paras. 659–660.

Subs. (1)
    The group of sections of which this is the first has the effect of embodying in this Act the statutory provisions previously existing outwith the agricultural holdings legislation, for the valuation of what are generally referred to as bound sheep stocks. This subsection prescribes the basic conditions for the application of these provisions. When the lease requires the outgoing tenant to leave a sheep stock to be taken over by the landlord or incoming tenant the sheep are said to be bound to the ground. The lease may specify the price at which the sheep are to be taken over but such an arrangement, which can operate inequitably with changes in value taking place during a tenancy of even moderate duration, is now uncommon in practice. The usual course is for the lease to provide for the price of the stock to be fixed by arbitration at the

tenant's waygoing and it is to such an arrangement that the legislation first introduced in 1937 has applied. The statutory provisions do not apply unless the outgoing tenant is obliged by the lease to leave the sheep stock. Otherwise any arrangement with the landlord or incoming tenant for the stock to be taken over at valuation will be implemented by a common law arbitration unaffected by these provisions (*Bell* v. *Simpson*, 1965 S.L.T. (Sh. Ct.) 9; see also *Toms* and *Parnell*, 1948 S.L.C.R. 8). Again, arrangements between a landlord who has been in occupation and an incoming tenant for the taking over by the latter of the sheep stock are unaffected, although the parties may agree to have the statutory basis operate at the tenant's entry as it will at his waygoing (*Secretary of State and White*, 1967 S.L.C.R. App. 133).

Subs. (2)

With the exception of the basic provisions of the 1937 Act the legislation on sheep stock valuation has not operated retrospectively. November 6, 1946 is the date on which the Hill Farming Act of 1946 came into force. Section 28 of that Act amended the directions for valuation of sheep stock as contained in s.1(1) of the 1937 Act. These provisions, however, remain unaltered as applying to the terms of leases entered into not later than that date. They require firstly that the arbiter's award disclose the basis of valuation of each class of stock. (The various grades and classes of stock are now conveniently set out in Sched. 2 to the 1946 Act). Secondly, they require that there be stated separately any allowance made for acclimatisation or hefting or other special factors. By acclimatisation is meant the immunity which sheep reared and kept on certain ground acquire to diseases or infections prevalent there. Hefting signifies the tendency of sheep to remain on ground on which they have been reared and kept, thus reducing the costs of fencing and herding. While it was considered that these requirements for specification should counteract a tendency for arbiters to make over-generous awards, particularly for items such as hefting and acclimatisation, these provisions did nothing to limit the arbiter's unrestricted discretion in fixing the value of stock.

Subs. (3)

In the case of a lease to which it applies, the 1946 Act severely restricted the arbiter's discretion in the matters referred to above, conformity with the statutory schedule involving that he base his valuation of female stock and lambs on records of sales off the hill by auction during certain past years. This, however, was found to be an unsatisfactory basis of valuation, inconsistent as it is with the modern practice whereby only the cast ewes are normally disposed of by auction. This practice renders it difficult, if not impossible, to carry out a valuation on the prescribed basis and results that such a valuation may produce unjustified and unfair results. The difficulties experienced by the Land Court in making such valuations are exemplified in *Potts J.F.* v. *Johnston*, 1952 S.L.C.R. 22 and *Garrow and Another*, 1958 S.L.C.R. 13. An example of a result grossly unfair to the tenant is to be found in the case of *Tufnell and Nether Whitehaugh Co.* 1977 S.L.T. (Land Ct.) 14 (see also the article "Valuation of Bound Sheep Stocks," 1978 S.L.T. (News) 37). To resolve, so far as possible, the problems thus arising, the Secretary of State, in exercise of his powers under the equivalent of subs. (5) (*i.e.* s.28(1A) and (1B) of the 1946 Act) by S.I. 1986 No. 1823 provided, in relation to leases entered into on or after December 1, 1986, for a new method of determining basic ewe value, and extended certain limits within which under the 1946 provisions prices for animals in a particular stock could be adjusted. Where this amendment applies the basic ewe value is derived from sales evidence relating to "regular cast ewes" sold off the hill. For regular cast ewes as the term is applied in the locality where the stock is maintained, a true market exists. As introduced in the 1946 Act, the statutory schedule for valuations had to distinguish between and make separate provisions for Whitsunday outgoings in which a lamb crop is involved and Martinmas outgoings where that is not so. As a result of the 1983 S.I. we now have two Schedules, Scheds. 9 and 10, applying respectively to leases entered into before December 1, 1986 and other leases, each Schedule containing provision for a Whitsunday outgoing in Pt. I and a Martinmas outgoing in Pt. II. For fuller details of the valuation process as now operating, reference must be made to these Schedules.

Subs. (4)

As an example of the operation of this provision as contained in s.1(2) of the 1937 Act, see *Dunlop* v. *Mundell*, 1943 S.L.T. 286.

Subs. (5)

As mentioned in relation to subs. (3), the corresponding powers as contained in the previous legislation have been exercised to alter the rules for valuation as contained in the relative schedules.

Submission of questions of law for decision of sheriff

69.—(1) In a sheep stock valuation where the lease was entered into after June 10, 1937 the arbiter may, at any stage of the proceedings, and shall, if so directed by the sheriff (which direction may be given on the application of either party) submit, in the form of a stated case for the decision of the sheriff, any question of law arising in the course of the arbitration.

(2) The decision of the sheriff on questions submitted under subsection (1) above shall be final unless, within such time and in accordance with such conditions as may be prescribed by Act of Sederunt, either party appeals to the Court of Session, from whose decision no appeal shall lie.

(3) Where a question is submitted under subsection (1) above for the decision of the sheriff, and the arbiter is satisfied that, whatever the decision on the question may be, the sum ultimately to be found due will be not less than a particular amount, it shall be lawful for the arbiter, pending the decision of such question, to make an order directing payment to the outgoing tenant of such sum, not exceeding that amount, as the arbiter may think fit, to account of the sum that may ultimately be awarded.

DEFINITIONS
"arbiter": s.72.
"lease": s.85(1).
"sheep stock valuation": ss.68(1) and 72.

DERIVATIONS
Sheep Stocks Valuation (Scotland) Act 1937.

GENERAL NOTE
See Gill, para. 659.

Subs. (1)
June 10, 1937 is the date of passing of the 1937 Act which introduced this form of appeal but did not make it available under existing leases.

Subs. (2)
As in the case of statutory arbitrations concerning matters other than sheep stock valuation, there is, under the Stated Case procedure, no right of appeal to the House of Lords (*cf.* Sched. 7, para. 21).

Subs. (3)
As the preparation and hearing of a Stated Case may take some considerable time, this provision for an interim payment may be useful in preventing hardship to the tenant resulting from the delay.

Determination by Land Court of questions as to value of sheep stock

70.—(1) Any question which would fall to be decided by a sheep stock valuation—
   (a) where the lease was entered into before or on November 6, 1946 may, on the joint application of the parties; and
   (b) where the lease was entered into after that date shall, on the application of either party,
in lieu of being determined in the manner provided in the lease, be determined by the Land Court.

(2) The Land Court shall determine any question or difference which they are required to determine, in a case where subsection (1)(b) above applies, in accordance with the appropriate provisions—
   (a) where the lease was entered into before December 1, 1986, of Schedule 9 to this Act;
   (b) where the lease was entered into on or after that date, of Schedule 10 to this Act.

DEFINITIONS
"lease": s.85(1).
"sheep stock valuation": ss.68(1) and 72.

DERIVATIONS
Sheep Stock Valuation (Scotland) Act 1937, s.3.
Hill Farming Act 1946, s.29.
Hill Farming Act 1946 (Variation of Second Schedule) (Scotland) Order 1986 (S.I. 1986 No. 1823)

GENERAL NOTE
See Gill, paras. 663 and 467.

Subs. (1)
Prior to the passing of the 1946 Act the position as regards referring sheep stock valuations to the Land Court instead of to arbitration was the same as that existing in respect of matters coming under the general statutory arbitration, *i.e.*, it required a joint application of the parties (*cf.* s.60(2)). In the case of leases entered into after its passing, however, the 1946 Act made the application of either party sufficient for this purpose.

Subs. (2)
This contains provisions confirming that in exercising their jurisdiction in the case of a lease entered into after the passing of the 1946 Act, the Land Court are to proceed under the provisions of the appropriate Schedule according to whether the lease was entered into before or after December 1, 1986, when the rules for valuation were amended by statutory instrument.

Statement of sales of stock

71.—(1) Where any question as to the value of any sheep stock has been submitted for determination to the Land Court or to an arbiter, the outgoing tenant shall, not less than 28 days before the determination of the question, submit to the Court or to the arbiter, as the case may be—
    (a) a statement of the sales of sheep from such stock—
        (i) in the case of a valuation made in respect of a tenancy terminating at Whitsunday during the preceding three years; or
        (ii) in the case of a valuation made in respect of a tenancy terminating at Martinmas during the current year and in each of the two preceding years; and
    (b) such sale-notes and other evidence as may be required by the Court or the arbiter to vouch the accuracy of such statement.
(2) Any document submitted by the outgoing tenant in pursuance of this section shall be open to inspection by the other party to the valuation proceedings.

DEFINITIONS
"arbiter": s.72.
"tenant": s.85(1).

DERIVATIONS
Hill Farming Act 1946, s.30.

GENERAL NOTE
See Gill, para. 468.

Subs. (1)
This concerns the documents submission of which by the tenant is regarded as necessary to enable the arbiter or Land Court to value the sheep stock on the basis introduced by the 1946 Act.

Subs. (2)
The documents submitted in compliance with subs. (1) being in effect productions in the valuation procedure, it is appropriate that they be open to inspection by the other party.

Interpretation of sections 68 to 71

72. In sections 68 to 71 of this Act—
    (a) "agricultural holding" means a piece of land held by a tenant which is wholly or in part pastoral, and which is not let to the tenant during and in connection with his continuance in any office, appointment, or employment held under the landlord;
    (b) "arbiter" includes an oversman and any person required to determine the value or price of sheep stock in pursuance of any provision in the lease of an agricultural holding, and "arbitration" shall be construed accordingly; and
    (c) "sheep stock valuation" shall be construed in accordance with section 68(1) of this Act.

DERIVATIONS
Sheep Stocks Valuation (Scotland) Act 1937, s.4.

GENERAL NOTE
See Gill, para. 11.
Agricultural holding. The definition in s.1(1) requires modification as there cannot be a bound sheep stock on a holding which is wholly arable.
Arbiter. In terms of s.61(7) the provisions of s.61 making reference to a single arbiter mandatory in the case of a statutory arbitration under s.60 do not apply to sheep stock valuations, which in practice are frequently carried out by two arbiters with an oversman.
Sheep stock valuation. See s.68(1) and note thereon.

PART VIII

MISCELLANEOUS

Power of Secretary of State to vary Schedules 5 and 6

73.—(1) The Secretary of State may, after consultation with persons appearing to him to represent the interests of landlords and tenants of agricultural holdings, by order vary the provisions of Schedules 5 and 6 to this Act.

(2) An order under this section may make such provision as to the operation of this Act in relation to tenancies current when the order takes effect as appears to the Secretary of State to be just having regard to the variation of the said Schedules effected by the order.

(3) Nothing in any order made under this section shall affect the right of a tenant to claim, in respect of an improvement made or begun before the date on which such order comes into force, any compensation to which, but for the making of the order, he would have been entitled.

(4) Orders under this section shall be made by statutory instrument which shall be of no effect unless approved by resolution of each House of Parliament.

DEFINITIONS
"agricultural holding": s.1(1).
"improvement": s.85(1).
"landlord": s.85(1).
"tenant": s.85(1).

DERIVATIONS
Agricultural Holdings (Scotland) Act 1949, s.79.

GENERAL NOTE
See also the corresponding English provision: Agricultural Holdings Act 1986, s.91.
The Schedules referred to list respectively new improvements as defined in s.33(1) and market garden improvements as referred to in s.40(3). Under s.69 of the 1949 Act, which this section replaces, variations of the Schedule of new improvements which are incorporated in

Sched. 5 were made by the Agricultural Holdings (Scotland) Act 1949 (Variation of First Schedule) Order 1978 (S.I. 1978 No. 798).

Power of limited owners to give consents, etc.

74. The landlord of an agricultural holding, whatever may be his estate or interest in the holding, may for the purposes of this Act give any consent, make any agreement, or do or have done to him any act which he might give or make or do or have done to him if he were the owner of the dominium utile of the holding.

DEFINITIONS
"agricultural holding": s.1(1).
"landlord": s.85(1).

DERIVATIONS
Agricultural Holdings (Scotland) Act 1949, s.80.

GENERAL NOTE
See Gill, paras. 32 and 36. (For the corresponding English provision see the Agricultural Holdings Act 1986, s.88).

This provision is consistent with the definition of "landlord" in s.85(1) which includes a number of parties other than absolute owners. Among these are liferenters, who, while they may act as owners in many respects, would appear to be precluded from granting a lease of agricultural holding since by reason of the tenant's security of tenure it could extend beyond the life of the grantor.

As to "owner of the *dominium utile*" replacing "absolute owner", see notes on s.75. This section does not appear to contemplate the case where the landlord's title takes the form of a registered lease, although that possibility is provided for in s.75.

Power of tenant and landlord to obtain charge on holding

75.—(1) Where any sum has become payable to the tenant of an agricultural holding in respect of compensation by the landlord and the landlord has failed to discharge his liability therefor within one month after the date on which the sum became payable, the Secretary of State may, on the application of the tenant and after giving not less than 14 days' notice of his intention so to do to the landlord, create, where the landlord is the owner of the dominium utile of the holding, a charge on the holding, or where the landlord is the lessee of the holding under a lease recorded under the Registration of Leases (Scotland) Act 1857 a charge on the lease for the payment of the sum due.

(2) For the purpose of creating a charge of a kind referred to in subsection (1) above, the Secretary of State may make in favour of the tenant a charging order charging and burdening the holding or the lease, as the case may be, with an annuity to repay the sum due together with the expenses of obtaining the charging order and recording it in the General Register of Sasines or registering it in the Land Register of Scotland.

(3) Where the landlord of an agricultural holding, not being the owner of the dominium utile of the holding, has paid to the tenant of the holding the amount due to him under this Act, or under custom or agreement, or otherwise, in respect of compensation for an improvement or in respect of compensation for disturbance, or has himself defrayed the cost of an improvement proposed to be executed by the tenant, the Secretary of State may, on the application of the landlord and after giving not less than 14 days notice to the absolute owner of the holding, make in favour of the landlord a charging order charging and burdening the holding with an annuity to repay the amount of the compensation or of the cost of the improvement, as the case may be, together with the expenses of obtaining the charging order and recording it in the General Register of Sasines or registering it in the Land Register of Scotland.

(4) Section 65(2), (4) and (6) to (10) of the Water (Scotland) Act 1980 shall, with the following and any other necessary modifications, apply to any such charging order as is mentioned in subsection (2) or (3) above, that is to say—

(a) for any reference to an islands or district council there shall be substituted a reference to the Secretary of State;

(b) for any reference to the period of 30 years there shall be substituted—

(i) where subsection (1) above applies, a reference to such period (not exceeding 30 years) as the Secretary of State may determine;

(ii) in the case of a charging order made in respect of compensation for, or of the cost of, an improvement, a reference to the period within which the improvement will, in the opinion of the Secretary of State, have become exhausted;

(c) for references to Part V of the said Act of 1980 there shall be substituted references to this Act.

(5) Where subsection (3) above applies, an annuity constituted a charge by a charging order recorded in the General Register of Sasines or registered in the Land Register of Scotland shall be a charge on the holding specified in the order and shall rank after all prior charges heritably secured thereon.

(6) The creation of a charge on a holding under this section shall not be deemed to be a contravention of any prohibition against charging or burdening contained in the deed or instrument under which the holding is held.

DEFINITIONS

"compensation for disturbance": s.43(1).
"improvement": s.85(1).
"landlord": s.85(1).
"lease": s.85(1).
"tenant": s.85(1).

DERIVATIONS

Agricultural Holdings (Scotland) Act 1949, ss.70, 82.
Water (Scotland) Act 1980, Sched. 10.

GENERAL NOTE

See Gill, paras. 437, 438. (For the corresponding English provision see the Agricultural Holdings Act 1986, ss.86, 87).

Subss. (1) and (2)

These provisions give the outgoing tenant to whom the landlord is due money by way of compensation in any form, a remedy additional to that available to him under s.65. They are extended to apply to compensation due for milk quota under para. 12 of Sched. 2 to the 1986 Act, as amended in terms of para. 53 of Sched. 11. While in practice this remedy is seldom used by an outgoing tenant, its existence has the result that where a purchaser is taking over a holding at the tenant's outgoing, although the outgoing claims will be the responsibility of the selling proprietor, the purchaser should be satisfied that these have been settled and so could not be made the subject of a charge in favour of the outgoing tenant.

Subs. (3)

This will apply, for example, where a liferenter exercising the power which he will normally have under s.74, settles an outgoing tenant's claims. The wording of this provision differs from s.82(1) of the 1949 Act, which it replaces, in referring to the limited owner as not being owner of the *dominium utile* of the holding, whereas the 1949 Act used the words "not being absolute owner of the holding." "Absolute owner" is defined by s.93(1) of the 1949 Act as meaning "the owner or person capable of disposing by disposition or otherwise of the fee simple or the *dominium utile* of the whole interest of or in land, although the land or his interest therein is burdened charged or encumbered." It has not, however, been considered necessary to amplify on these lines the wording adopted in this subsection. That wording has been adopted in place of the reference to the absolute owner in the amendment of s.18 of the 1986 Act (concerning restrictions on agricultural use in environmentally sensitive areas) in terms of para. 45 of Sched. 11. The wording could conceivably cause difficulty in the rare case where the land in question is held otherwise than on feudal or leasehold tenure, *e.g.* on udal tenure or as allodial property.

This possibility was apparently envisaged in a now-repealed provision, s.38(1) of the 1948 Act, defining "owner" as "the person who is for the time being proprietor of the *dominium utile* or, in the case of land other than feudal land, is the owner thereof".

Subs. (4)

While the Secretary of State is empowered in terms of para. (b)(i) and (ii) to reduce the basic annuity period of 30 years, the method of repayment over a substantial period makes the arrangement unattractive, particularly to an outgoing tenant, and as a result such charges on agricultural land are seldom encountered in practice.

Subs. (5)

This has the result that the charge in favour of the limited owner will rank after such charges as feuduty or ground annual (if not redeemed) and heritable securities previously recorded.

Subs. (6)

Such prohibitions are not often included in modern deeds but will be found in Deeds of Entail as formerly in use. It has apparently been considered unnecessary to include in this Act the special provisions of s.81 of the 1949 Act, enabling an heir of entail to apply the proceeds of sales of entailed estate in reimbursement of expenditure incurred in settling outgoing tenants' claims.

Power of land improvement companies to advance money

76. Any company incorporated by Parliament or incorporated under the Companies Act 1985 or under the former Companies Acts within the meaning of that Act and having power to advance money for the improvement of land, or for the cultivation and farming of land, may make an advance of money upon a charging order duly made and recorded or registered under this Act, on such terms and conditions as may be agreed upon between the company and the person entitled to the order.

DEFINITIONS

"farming of land": s.85(3).

DERIVATIONS

Agricultural Holdings (Scotland) Act 1949, s.13.

GENERAL NOTE

For the corresponding English provision see the Agricultural Holdings Act 1986, s.87(7).

Charges of this kind are not common in practice, advances made by bodies such as the Scottish Agricultural Securities Corporation or by lenders such as banks being normally secured by Standard Security in terms of the Conveyancing and Feudal Reform (Scotland) Act 1970 granted by the proprietor of the security subjects.

Appointment of guardian to landlord or tenant

77. Where the landlord or the tenant of an agricultural holding is a pupil or a minor or is of unsound mind, not having a tutor, curator or other guardian, the sheriff, on the application of any person interested, may appoint to him, for the purposes of this Act, a tutor or a curator, and may recall the appointment and appoint another tutor or curator if and as occasion requires.

DEFINITIONS

"agricultural holding": s.1(1).
"landlord": s.85(1).
"tenant": s.85(1).

DERIVATIONS

Agricultural Holdings (Scotland) Act 1949, s.84.

GENERAL NOTE

The tutor, curator or other person appointed in terms of these provisions falls within the statutory definitions of "landlord" or "tenant" as the case may be and, in the case of a landlord, will have the powers provided for in s.74.

Validity of consents, etc.

78. It shall be no objection to any consent in writing or agreement in writing under this Act signed by the parties thereto or by any persons authorised by them that the consent or agreement has not been executed in accordance with the enactments regulating the execution of deeds in Scotland.

DERIVATIONS
Agricultural Holdings (Scotland) Act 1949, s.85.

GENERAL NOTE
See Gill, para. 679.
This section has the result that any provision of the Act requiring agreement or consent in writing can be implemented by a document not fulfilling the requirements of probativity by being attested or adopted as holograph. Connell (*op. cit.* p. 192) suggests that this in effect places such documentation in the category of privileged writs such as these *in re mercatoria* on account of the rapidity with which they may have to be prepared.

PART IX

SUPPLEMENTARY

Crown and Secretary of State

Application to Crown land

79.—(1) This Act shall apply to land belonging to Her Majesty in right of the Crown, with such modifications as may be prescribed; and for the purposes of this Act the Crown Estate Commissioners or other proper officer or body having charge of the land for the time being, or if there is no such officer or body, such person as Her Majesty may appoint in writing under the Royal Sign Manual, shall represent Her Majesty and shall be deemed to be the landlord.

(2) This Act shall apply to land notwithstanding that the interest of the landlord or the tenant thereof belongs to a government department or is held on behalf of Her Majesty for the purposes of any government department with such modifications as may be prescribed.

DEFINITIONS
"landlord": s.85(1).
"prescribed": s.85(1).
"tenant": s.85(1).

DERIVATIONS
Agricultural Holdings (Scotland) Act 1949, s.86.
Agriculture (Miscellaneous Provisions) Act 1968, s.17(3).

GENERAL NOTE
See Gill, para. 29. (For the corresponding English provision see the Agricultural Holdings Act 1986, s.95).
These provisions are extended by s.16(7) of the Agriculture Act 1986 (as amended in terms of Sched. 11, para. 44(b)) to apply to rent arbitrations where milk quota is involved.
The power of the Secretary of State to prescribe modifications has not yet been exercised.

Determination of matters where Secretary of State is landlord or tenant

80.—(1) This section applies where the Secretary of State is the landlord or the tenant of an agricultural holding.

(2) Where this section applies, any provision of this Act—
(a) under which any matter relating to the holding is referred to the decision of the Secretary of State; or
(b) relating to an arbitration concerning the holding,
shall have effect with the substitution for every reference to "the Secretary of State" of a reference to "the Land Court," and any provision referred to in paragraph (a) above which provides for an appeal to an arbiter from the decision of the Secretary of State shall not apply.

DEFINITIONS
"agricultural holding": s.1(1).
"landlord": s.85(1).
"tenant": s.85(1).

DERIVATIONS
Agricultural Holdings (Scotland) Act 1949, s.87(1).

GENERAL NOTE
See Gill, para. 666(h).

Subs. (1)
Like s.64 this section is directed to dealing but on a broader basis, with the problem of *auctor in rem suam* as it could arise where the Secretary of State as representing the Department of Agriculture is involved in the letting of holdings to farm tenants. The holding of tenancies departmentally is less common although not unknown. The Land Court's jurisdiction as derived from this section is extended to milk quota arbitrations in terms of paras. 10 and 11 of Sched. 2 to the Agriculture Act 1986 as amended to conform to paras. 51 and 52 of Sched. 11.

Subs. (2)
Examples of cases to which these provisions will apply are to be found in ss.62(4)(5) and 75(1)(2)(3)(4). For a full list of functions of the Secretary of State which may be affected by these provisions, see Gill, para. 675.

Expenses and receipts

81.—(1) All expenses incurred by the Secretary of State under this Act shall be paid out of moneys provided by Parliament.
(2) All sums received by the Secretary of State under this Act shall be paid into the Consolidated Fund.

DERIVATIONS
Agricultural Holdings (Scotland) Act 1949, s.88.

Powers of entry and inspection

82.—(1) Any person authorised by the Secretary of State in that behalf shall have power at all reasonable times to enter on and inspect any land for the purpose of determining whether, and if so in what manner, any of the powers conferred on the Secretary of State by this Act are to be exercised in relation to the land, or whether, and if so in what manner, any direction given under any such power has been complied with.
(2) Any person authorised by the Secretary of State who proposes to exercise any power of entry or inspection conferred by this Act shall, if so required, produce some duly authenticated document showing his authority to exercise the power.
(3) Admission to any land used for residential purposes shall not be demanded as of right in the exercise of any such power unless 24 hours notice of the intended entry has been given to the occupier of the land.
(4) Save as provided by subsection (3) above, admission to any land shall not be demanded as of right in the exercise of any such power unless notice has been given to the occupier of the land that it is proposed to enter during a period, specified in the notice, not exceeding 14 days and beginning at least

24 hours after the giving of the notice and the entry is made on the land during the period specified in the notice.

(5) Any person who obstructs a person authorised by the Secretary of State exercising any such power shall be guilty of an offence and shall be liable on summary conviction to a fine not exceeding level 2 on the standard scale.

DERIVATIONS

Agricultural Holdings (Scotland) Act 1949, s.89.
Criminal Law Act 1977, s.31.
Criminal Procedure (Scotland) Act 1975, s.289.

GENERAL NOTE

The provisions of this section may be compared with these of s.10 giving the landlord power of entry to the holding. These provisions for official inspection are more specific as regards the required notice of entry and the period during which access facilities are to operate. Their terms are virtually identical with those of s.82 of the 1948 Act. The powers concerning the exercise of which access may be required under this Act would appear to include the approval of an alternative provision made by landlord or tenant in lieu of his insurance obligation under paras. 5 and 6 of Sched. 1 or the making of charging orders in favour of outgoing tenants or limited owners in terms of s.75.

Land Court

Proceedings of the Land Court

83. The provisions of the Small Landholders (Scotland) Acts 1886 to 1931 relating to the Land Court shall apply, with any necessary modifications, for the purposes of the determination by the Land Court of any matter referred to them under this Act, as they apply for the purposes of the determination of matters referred to them under those Acts.

DERIVATIONS

Agricultural Holdings (Scotland) Act 1949, s.73.
Agriculture (Miscellaneous Provisions) Act 1976, s.14(6).
Crofting Reform (Scotland) Act 1976, Sched. 2, para. 25.

GENERAL NOTE

See Gill, paras. 668–671.

The general effect of this section is to import into cases in the Land Court concerning agricultural holdings the Rules of the Court made under the Small Landholders Acts, small-holdings and crofts having been the court's original fields of jurisdiction. In addition to making detailed provision as to pleadings and procedure, the Rules, which are reproduced in the Parliament House Book and in Gill, pp. 717 *et seq.*, provide for an appeal by way of special care, on questions of law, from the Land Court to the Court of Session.

Service of notices

Service of notices, etc.

84.—(1) Any notice or other document required or authorised by or under this Act to be given to or served on any person shall be duly given or served if it is delivered to him, or left at his proper address, or sent to him by registered post or recorded delivery.

(2) Any such document required or authorised to be given to or served on an incorporated company or body shall be duly given or served if it is delivered to or sent by registered post or recorded delivery to the registered office of the company or body.

(3) For the purposes of this section and of section 7 of the Interpretation Act 1978, the proper address of any person to or on whom any such document as aforesaid is to be given or served shall, in the case of the secretary or clerk of any incorporated company or body, be that of the registered or principal office of the company or body, and in any other case be the last known address of the person in question.

(4) Unless or until the tenant of an agricultural holding shall have received notice that the person previously entitled to receive the rents and profits of the holding (hereinafter referred to as "the original landlord") has ceased to be so entitled, and also notice of the name and address of the person who has become so entitled, any notice or other document served on or delivered to the original landlord by the tenant shall be deemed to have been served on or delivered to the landlord of the holding.

DEFINITIONS
"agricultural holding": s.1(1).
"landlord": s.85(1).
"tenant": s.85(1).

DERIVATIONS
Agricultural Holdings (Scotland) Act 1949, s.90.
Companies Act 1985, s.725(1).

GENERAL NOTE
See Gill, para. 574 (relating to subs. (41)) and para. 678. (For the corresponding English provision see the Agricultural Holdings Act 1986, s.93).

Subss. (1)–(3)
These contain standard provisions for service of notices as required or authorised by statute. While these apply to notices generally, they would appear to be overridden in the case of notices to quit served by landlords which in terms of s.21(5) require registered post or recorded delivery (see Gill, para. 288).

Subs. (4)
This applies only where the party giving the notice holds the position of tenant. Accordingly, a legatee of a deceased tenant giving notice under s.11(2) or a successor on intestacy given notice under s.12(1), not yet having become tenant, will have to satisfy himself as to the identity and whereabouts of the present owner of the holding if there has been any change of ownership since the commencement of the tenancy.

Interpretation

Interpretation

85.—(1) In this Act, unless the context otherwise requires—
"the 1911 Act" means the Small Landholders (Scotland) Act 1911;
"the 1949 Act" means the Agricultural Holdings (Scotland) Act 1949;
"agricultural holding" (except in sections 68 to 72 of this Act) and "agricultural land" have the meanings assigned to them by section 1 of this Act;
"agricultural unit" means land which is an agricultural unit for the purposes of the Agriculture (Scotland) Act 1948;
"agriculture" includes horticulture, fruit growing; seed growing; dairy farming; livestock breeding and keeping; the use of land as grazing land, meadow land, osier land, market gardens and nursery grounds; and the use of land for woodlands where that use is ancillary to the farming of land for other agricultural purposes: and "agricultural" shall be construed accordingly;
"building" includes any part of a building;
"fixed equipment" includes any building or structure affixed to land and any works on, in, over or under land, and also includes anything grown on land for a purpose other than use after severance from the land, consumption of the thing grown or of produce thereof, or amenity, and, without prejudice to the foregoing generality, includes the following things, that is to say—
(a) all permanent buildings, including farm houses and farm cottages, necessary for the proper conduct of the agricultural holding;

(b) all permanent fences, including hedges, stone dykes, gate posts and gates;

(c) all ditches, open drains and tile drains, conduits and culverts, ponds, sluices, flood banks and main water courses;

(d) stells, fanks, folds, dippers, pens and bughts necessary for the proper conduct of the holding;

(e) farm access or service roads, bridges and fords;

(f) water and sewerage systems;

(g) electrical installations including generating plant, fixed motors, wiring systems, switches and plug sockets;

(h) shelter belts,

and references to fixed equipment on land shall be construed accordingly;

"improvement" shall be construed in accordance with section 33 of this Act, and "new improvement," "old improvement," "1923 Act improvement" and "1931 Act improvement" have the meanings there assigned to them;

"Land Court" means the Scottish Land Court;

"Lands Tribunal" means the Lands Tribunal for Scotland;

"landlord" means any person for the time being entitled to receive the rents and profits or to take possession of an agricultural holding, and includes the executor, assignee, legatee, disponee, guardian, curator bonis, tutor, or permanent or interim trustee (within the meaning of the Bankruptcy (Scotland) Act 1985), of a landlord;

"lease" means a letting of land for a term of years, or for lives, or for lives and years, or from year to year;

"livestock" includes any creature kept for the production of food, wool, skins or fur, or for the purpose of its use in the farming of land;

"market garden" means a holding, cultivated, wholly or mainly, for the purpose of the trade or business of market gardening;

"prescribed" means prescribed by the Secretary of State by regulations made by statutory instrument which shall be subject to annulment in pursuance of a resolution of either House of Parliament;

"produce" includes anything (whether live or dead) produced in the course of agriculture;

"tenant" means the holder of land under a lease of an agricultural holding and includes the executor, assignee, legatee, disponee, guardian, tutor, curator bonis, or permanent or interim trustee (within the meaning of the Bankruptcy (Scotland) Act 1985), of a tenant;

"termination," in relation to a tenancy, means the termination of the lease by reason of effluxion of time or from any other cause;

(2) Schedules 5 and 6 to the Agriculture (Scotland) Act 1948, (which have effect respectively for the purpose of determining for the purposes of that Act whether the owner of agricultural land is fulfilling his responsibilities to manage it in accordance with the rules of good estate management and whether the occupier of such land is fulfilling his responsibilities to farm it in accordance with the rules of good husbandry) shall have effect for the purposes of this Act as they have effect for the purposes of that Act.

(3) References in this Act to the farming of land include references to the carrying on in relation to the land of any agricultural activity.

(4) References to the terms, conditions, or requirements of a lease of or of an agreement relating to, an agricultural holding shall be construed as including references to any obligations, conditions or liabilities implied by the custom of the country in respect of the holding.

(5) Anything which by or under this Act is required or authorised to be done by, to or in respect of the landlord or the tenant of an agricultural holding may be done by, to or in respect of any agent of the landlord or of the tenant.

DERIVATIONS
Agricultural Holdings (Scotland) Act 1949, s.93.

GENERAL NOTE

See Gill, para. 574 (relating to subs. (4)) and para. 678. (For the corresponding English provision see the Agricultural Holdings Act 1986, s.96).

Subs. (1)

This forms the main or general interpretation provision in the Act. The following comments relate to the particular items specified.

Agricultural unit. This is defined in s.86(2) of the 1948 Act (*q.v.*) as land which is occupied as a unit for agricultural purposes. In *Jenners Princes Street Edinburgh* v. *Howe*, 1990 S.L.T. (Land Ct.) 26 it was held that the unit included any land actually occupied for agricultural purposes as a single unit whether formally or informally.

Agriculture. See Gill, paras. 23–25. This definition should be read with the definition of "agricultural land" for the purpose of ss.1 and 2. In the English case of *Rutherford* v. *Maurer* [1962] 1 Q.B. 16 the Court of Appeal held that the use of land let for grazing of horses belonging to a riding school constituted use for agriculture and being related to a business made the land agricultural although the business itself was not of an agricultural nature. That decision, which has been criticised in England (see *Howkins* v. *Jardine* [1951] 1 K.B. 614, *per* Jenkins L.J. at p. 629), has been followed in Scotland in *Crawford* v. *Dun*, 1981 S.L.T. (Sh. Ct.) 66. The definition of "livestock," as appearing later in this subsection, has the result that "livestock breeding and keeping" as a form of agriculture is not confined to ordinary farm animals such as horses, cattle, sheep and poultry. Modern livestock rearing includes activities such as deer farming and the definition refers not only to the production of food but also to that of wool, skins or fur. Where, however, the primary purpose of breeding or keeping certain types of livestock is unconnected with the commercial operation of farming, *e.g.* breeding for sport or for scientific research, it will not come within the statutory definitions of "livestock breeding and keeping" and "agriculture."

Fixed equipment. It should be noted that the items specified include "shelter belts," the creation of which results from "the use of land for woodlands as ancillary to the farming of land or other agriculture purpose" as referred to in the definition of "agriculture."

Lands Tribunal. The Lands Tribunal for Scotland established under the Lands Tribunal Act 1949 has sole jurisdiction in questions of compensation under the Land Compensation (Scotland) Act 1973 as affecting agricultural holdings and likewise under the provisions of this Act so far as relating to their compulsory purchase, *viz.* ss.56 and 57 and Sched. 8.

Landlord. See Gill, paras. 30–36. The term is widely defined so as to cover not only absolute beneficial owners but also limited owners such as liferenters or parties in right in administrative or fiduciary capacities. In all cases it is essential that the party who is to be regarded as holding the position of landlord should be entitled either to take possession of the property or to draw the rents due in respect of it. Steps to recover possession from a tenant may be initiated by a holder of the landlord's interest on an incomplete or unfeudalised title but the title must be completed before decree can be obtained (*Walker* v. *Hendry*, 1925 S.C. 855). A purchaser under Missives is not regarded as a landlord and cannot even initiate proceedings for recovery of possession (*Grandison* v. *Mackay*, 1919 1 S.L.T.). The appointment of a guardian such as tutor may be made under s.77 or under other statutory or common law authority. Liferenters will generally be regarded as landlords *pro tem.*, although it would be inconsistent with the limitation of their interest for them to grant an agricultural lease which by reason of security of tenure could endure beyond the expiry of a liferent.

Where the ownership of the holding is divided, the several proprietors together constitute the landlord and all must concur in any action relating to the tenancy such as proceedings for recovery of rent or steps taken to terminate the lease. A similar position exists in the case of *pro indiviso* ownership.

Lease. See Gill, paras. 57–61. Like other definitions in this subsection, the definition of "lease" which originated in an Act of 1883 applies "unless the context otherwise requires." It does so in the case of a lease of the kind referred to in s.2(1). Even where it applies, however, the definition excludes certain leases which would be valid at common law. A lease for a rotation of cropping but subject to termination in the event of a sale was held invalid (*Stirrat* v. *Whyte*, 1968 S.L.T. 157), while on the other hand a let for four years for cropping in each year (*McKenzie* v. *Buchan* (1889) 5 Sh.Ct.Rep. 40) and a lease for "four years and crops" as from its date (*Stonehaven* v. *Adam*, 1970 S.L.T. (Sh. Ct.) 43) were both held to be within the statutory category. Again, however, the wording "for lives or for lives and years" would seem to exclude a lease for the single life of the tenant. A year-to-year lease as referred to in the definition exists by inference where the tenant enters into possession without any ish being specified (*Gray* v. *Edinburgh University*, 1962 S.C. 157).

Livestock. The definition clearly includes farm animals such as working horses and sheep-dogs. As to its other content see under "agriculture," *supra.*

Market garden. For amplification of this definition see note to s.40(1).

Produce. The wide terms of the definition are consistent with the tenant's freedom of cropping and disposal of produce in terms of s.7. Manure produced on the holding, not being disposable by the tenant, is not covered by this definition.

Tenant. See Gill, para. 38 *et seq.* Like *landlord*, *supra*, this term is widely defined but while parties such as curators or guardians have the same position as they would have in relation to the landlord's interest, the rights of executors, even if duly confirmed in respect of the tenancy interest, are limited by the rules requiring them, within the time prescribed, to divest themselves in favour of a successor of the late tenant who does not himself become a tenant unless due intimation has been made to the landlord whose objections, if any, have failed (see s.12). Again, where the tenant has been entitled to and has bequeathed his lease, the legatee does not attain the status of tenant until due intimation has been made to the landlord whose objections, if any, have failed (see s.11). In *inter vivos* transmission the assignee or disponee of an agriculture tenant is by implication, even if not expressly, excluded unless the landlord chooses to accept him. The common law position of the trustee in bankruptcy is the same in relation to a tenancy interest as it is in relation to a right of ownership. Thus a lease is not automatically annulled by the tenant's sequestration but the provisions of s.21(6) or of s.22(2)(f) are likely to result in the trustee's tenure of the lease being of limited duration.

Where there are joint tenants all tenants come within the statutory definition and must as a general rule be parties to any action affecting the tenancy, such as notices and counter-notices given to or received from the landlord.

It may be noted that the definitions of "Whitsunday" and "Martinmas," as contained in s.93(1) of the 1949 Act, have been omitted here, this matter now being regulated by the Term and Quarter Days (Scotland) Act 1990 which, *inter alia*, confirms the meaning of these terms as the 28th day of the month in each case.

Subs. (2)

It may be thought surprising that the Schedules to the 1948 Act have not been incorporated in the consolidation but theoretically at least they may still have significance for certain powers of the authorities based on provisions of the 1948 Act such as s.35 which remain in force.

Subs. (3)

Such references are to be found, *e.g.* in ss.44 and 76.

Subs. (4)

See Gill, paras. 102 and 103.

Custom cannot override the express terms of the lease or agreement but evidence of custom may be invoked to determine the rights and duties of the parties so far as not specifically defined in the relevant documents. The application of the principles of good husbandry will be determined in each case by reference to the situation and character of the holding and the custom of the district (see *Mackenzie* v. *McGillivray*, 1921 S.C. 722, *per* Lord President Clyde at p. 731).

Subs. (5)

This has the effect that any notices may be served by or on the agents of the parties. It is advisable, although perhaps not essential, that the agency should be disclosed in a notice given by an agent (see Gill, paras. 290 and 306).

Construction of references in other Acts to holdings as defined by earlier Acts

86. References, in whatever terms, in any enactment, other than an enactment contained in—

> this Act,
>
> the Agricultural Holdings (Scotland) Acts 1923 and 1931, or,
>
> Part I of the Agriculture (Scotland) Act 1948

to a holding within the meaning of the Agricultural Holdings (Scotland) Act 1923 or of the Agricultural Holdings (Scotland) Acts 1923 to 1948 shall be construed as references to an agricultural holding within the meaning of this Act.

DEFINITIONS

"agricultural holding": s.1(1).

DERIVATIONS
    Agricultural Holdings (Scotland) Act 1949, s.95.

Savings

87. Schedule 12 to this Act, which exempts from the operation of this Act certain cases current at the commencement of this Act and contains other transitional provisions and savings shall have effect.

DERIVATIONS
    Agricultural Holdings (Scotland) Act 1949, s.99.

Consequential amendments and repeals

Consequential amendments and repeals

88.—(1) The enactments specified in Schedule 11 to this Act shall be amended in accordance with that Schedule.

(2) The enactments specified in Schedule 13 to this Act are repealed to the extent there specified.

DERIVATIONS
    Agricultural Holdings (Scotland) Act 1949, s.97.

Citation, commencement and extent

Citation, commencement and extent

89.—(1) This Act may be cited as the Agricultural Holdings (Scotland) Act 1991.

(2) This Act shall come into force at the end of the period of 2 months beginning with the date on which it is passed.

(3) This Act shall extend to Scotland only, except for those provisions in Schedule 11 which amend enactments which extend to England and Wales or to Northern Ireland.

DERIVATIONS
    Agricultural Holdings (Scotland) Act 1949, s.101.

GENERAL NOTE
    The Act received Royal Assent on July 25, 1991.

SCHEDULES

Section 4   SCHEDULE 1

PROVISIONS REQUIRED IN LEASES

1. The names of the parties.
2. Particulars of the holding with sufficient description, by reference to a map or plan, of the fields and other parcels of land comprised therein to identify the extent of the holding.
3. The term or terms for which the holding or different parts thereof is or are agreed to be let.
4. The rent and the dates on which it is payable.
5. An undertaking by the landlord in the event of damage by fire to any building comprised in the holding to reinstate or replace the building if its reinstatement or replacement is required for the fulfilment of his responsibilities to manage the holding in accordance with the rules of good estate management, and (except where the interest of the landlord is held for the purposes of a government department or a person representing Her Majesty under section 79 of this Act is deemed to be the landlord, or where the landlord has made provision approved by the Secretary of State for defraying the cost of any such reinstatement or replacement) an undertaking by the landlord to insure to their full value all such buildings against damage by fire.
6. An undertaking by the tenant, in the event of the destruction by fire of harvested crops grown on the holding for consumption thereon, to return to the holding the full equivalent

manurial value of the crops destroyed, in so far as the return thereof is required for the fulfilment of his responsibilities to farm in accordance with the rules of good husbandry, and (except where the interest of the tenant is held for the purposes of a government department or where the tenant has made provision approved by the Secretary of State in lieu of such insurance) an undertaking by the tenant to insure to their full value all dead stock on the holding and all such harvested crops against damage by fire.

DEFINITIONS
"landlord": s.85(1).
"rules of good estate management": s.85(2); Agriculture (Scotland) Act 1948, Scheds. 5, 6.
"rules of good husbandry": s.85(2); Agriculture (Scotland) Act 1948, Scheds. 5, 6.

DERIVATIONS
Agricultural Holdings (Scotland) Act 1949, Sched. 5.

GENERAL NOTE
See Gill, paras. 93–95. (For the corresponding English provision see the Agricultural Holdings Act 1986, Sched. 1).
Reference should be made to s.4 and the notes on that section. The following notes refer to the paragraphs of the Schedule indicated by their numbers.

Para. 2
This requirement can be and often is conveniently met by using as the plan the appropriate sheet or sheets of a large-scale Ordnance Survey Map on which the fields or enclosures comprised in the farm will be identified by numbers and their areas indicated.

Paras. 5 and 6
It is practically unknown for a landlord or tenant to make provision approved by the Secretary of State in lieu of insurance.

Para. 6
The terms of this paragraph are consistent with those of s.7 under which the tenant's right to dispose of the produce of the holding is qualified by an undertaking to return to the holding the manurial value of crops sold off the holding. There is no statutory definition of "dead stock" but in relation to a farm the term is generally regarded as covering such items belonging to the tenant as stored materials, farming implements, machinery and vehicles.

Section 25   SCHEDULE 2

GROUNDS FOR CONSENT TO OPERATION OF NOTICES TO QUIT A TENANCY WHERE SECTION 25(3) APPLIES

PART I

GROUNDS FOR CONSENT TO OPERATION OF NOTICE TO QUIT A TENANCY LET BEFORE JANUARY 1, 1984

Case 1
The tenant has neither sufficient training in agriculture nor sufficient experience in the farming of land to enable him to farm the holding with reasonable efficiency.

Case 2
(a) The holding or any agricultural unit of which it forms part is not a two-man unit;
(b) the landlord intends to use the holding for the purpose of effecting an amalgamation within 2 years after the termination of the tenancy; and
(c) the notice specifies the land with which the holding is to be amalgamated.

Case 3
The tenant is the occupier (either as owner or tenant) of agricultural land which—
(a) is a two-man unit;
(b) is distinct from the holding and from any agricultural unit of which the holding forms part; and
(c) has been occupied by him since before the death of the person from whom he acquired right to the lease of the holding;
and the notice specifies the agricultural land.

Part II

Grounds for Consent to Operation of Notice to Quit a Tenancy Let on or After January 1, 1984

Case 4

The tenant does not have sufficient financial resources to enable him to farm the holding with reasonable efficiency.

Case 5

The tenant has neither sufficient training in agriculture nor sufficient experience in the farming of land to enable him to farm the holding with reasonable efficiency:

Provided that this Case shall not apply where the tenant has been engaged, throughout the period from the date of death of the person from whom he acquired right to the lease, in a course of relevant training in agriculture which he is expected to complete satisfactorily within 4 years from the said date, and has made arrangements to secure that the holding will be farmed with reasonable efficiency until he completes that course.

Case 6

(a) The holding or any agricultural unit of which it forms part is not a two-man unit;

(b) the landlord intends to use the holding for the purpose of effecting an amalgamation within 2 years after the termination of the tenancy; and

(c) the notice specifies the land with which the holding is to be amalgamated.

Case 7

The tenant is the occupier (either as owner or tenant) of agricultural land which—

(a) is a two-man unit;

(b) is distinct from the holding; and

(c) has been occupied by him throughout the period from the date of giving of the notice; and the notice specifies the land.

Part III

Supplementary

1. For the purposes of section 25 of this Act and this Schedule—
   "amalgamation" means a transaction for securing that agricultural land which is comprised in a holding to which a notice to quit relates and which together with other agricultural land could form an agricultural unit, shall be owned and occupied in conjunction with that other land (and cognate expressions shall be construed accordingly);
   "near relative" in relation to a deceased tenant of an agricultural holding means a surviving spouse or child of that tenant, including a child adopted by him in pursuance of an adoption order (as defined in section 23(5) of the Succession (Scotland) Act 1964); and
   "two-man unit" means an agricultural unit which in the opinion of the Land Court is capable of providing full-time employment for an individual occupying it and at least one other man.

2. For the purposes of determining whether land is a two-man unit, in assessing the capability of the unit of providing employment it shall be assumed that the unit is farmed under reasonably skilled management, that a system of husbandry suitable for the district is followed and that the greater part of the feeding stuffs required by any livestock kept on the unit is grown there.

3. For the purposes of Case 7 of this Schedule, occupation of agricultural land—
   (a) by a company which is controlled by the tenant shall be treated as occupation by the tenant; and
   (b) by a Scottish partnership shall, notwithstanding section 4(2) of the Partnership Act 1890, be treated as occupation by each of its partners.

Definitions
   "agricultural land": s.1(2).
   "agricultural unit": s.85(1).
   "agriculture": s.85(1).

"farming of land": s.85(3).
"landlord": s.85(1).
"tenant": s.85(1).

DERIVATIONS
Agricultural Holdings (Amendment) (Scotland) Act 1983, Sched. 1.

GENERAL NOTE
Part I of the Schedule, containing Cases 1–3, originates in the 1968 Act and applies to tenancies let before the 1983 Act came into force on January 1, 1984. Part II, containing cases 4–7 as introduced by that Act, applies to tenancies let on or after that date. The following comments applying to the particular cases should be read along with s.25 and the notes thereon.

Case 1
The landlord must prove the tenant's inadequacy in both respects but it is the tenant's personal capacity which will be in issue and he will not be entitled to plead that he has access to skilled advice or has available the service of a competent manager, as has sometimes been permitted in the case of objections to a successor under the provisions now contained in ss.11 and 12. Here the only issue is the tenant's own personal training and experience. Training in agriculture envisages a formal course of instruction, but in its absence adequate farming experience may suffice (see on this matter generally *Macdonald* v. *Macrae*, 1987 S.L.C.R. 72). In opposing an application for consent involving this Case the tenant may invoke the "fair and reasonable landlord" plea (see s.25(3)) but the prospects of its success would seem to be at best doubtful.

Case 2
To succeed under this Case the landlord must discharge the onus of proving that the holding or any agricultural unit of which it forms part is not a two-man unit. In *Jenners Princes Street Edinburgh* v. *Howe*, 1990 S.L.T. (Land Ct.) 26 it was held that any land actually occupied for agricultural purposes by the tenant, whether formally or informally, as a single unit was included in the agricultural unit, the wording in this Case being significantly different from that of Case 3, which requires that the tenant be occupier ("either as owner or tenant") of the land comprising the unit in question. The landlord must also show that he has a genuine proposal for the amalgamation of the holding with specific land, to take place within two years of the termination of the tenancy. The cases of *Mackenzie* v. *Lyon*, 1984 S.L.T. (Land Ct.) 30 and *Earl of Seafield* v. *Currie*, 1980 S.L.T. (Land Ct.) 10 illustrate the problems of proof which may arise under this Case.

"Two-man unit" and "amalgamation," as referred to here and in other parts of this Schedule, are defined in Pt. III of the Schedule (see below). In terms of s.25(3) the "fair and reasonable landlord" plea is available to the tenant in this case. It was successfully invoked, although in somewhat special circumstances, in *Altyre Estates* v. *McLay*, 1975 S.L.T. (Land Ct.) 12) and the Land Court in *Earl of Seafield* v. *Currie* (above) indicated that they would have sustained the plea as taken by the tenant, had the landlord satisfied them on the grounds of his application for consent.

Case 3
The two-man unit must be distinct from the holding and from any agricultural unit of which the holding forms part. The latter requirement is dispensed with in Case 7, which applies to tenancies originating on or after January 1, 1984. Actual occupation by the tenant of the land in question must be proved. Ownership of tenanted subjects will not suffice. Again, the occupation must be as owner or tenant. Informal occupation, as meeting the requirements of Case 2, is not sufficient for the land in question to be regarded as existing or alternative source of livelihood for the tenant (see *Jenners Princes Street Edinburgh* v. *Howe*, above, p. 28).

In terms of this case, as appearing in the 1968 Act, it has been held that occupation of the other land by a firm of which the tenant is a partner is not relevant (*Haddo House Estate Trs.* v. *Davidson*, 1982 S.L.T. (Land Ct.) 14), but in this respect again the position is changed in Case 7. Similar provisions in force in England were held by the House of Lords not to require sole occupancy of the other ground (see *Jackson* v. *Hall*; *Williamson* v. *Thompson* [1980] A.C. 854 concerning a provision now represented by the 1986 Act, s.36(3)(b)), a ruling which would seem to be unfair if joint occupancy is not providing the tenant with a livelihood.

Two questions not resolved by the wording of Case 3 or of Case 7 or by any reported case are raised by Gill (para. 395). Firstly, must the other agricultural land in the tenant's occupation be in Scotland? This is an important question in border districts where farming enterprises may embrace land in both countries. It is suggested that no such limitation should be regarded as implied. Secondly, does the tenant's occupation of the land in question have to be as a tenant with security of tenure under the Act if not as owner? Here again it is suggested that no such restriction can be inferred, although this seems inconsistent with the apparent intention of the legislation that the tenant should have secure possession of the land in question, making retention of the holding to which he has succeeded unnecessary for his livelihood.

The requirement that the other agricultural land should have been occupied by the successor tenant since before the late tenant's death can be unfair to the landlord in certain circumstances, *e.g.* where the death results in the tenant inheriting land owned by the late tenant. Again Case 7 contains an alteration in this respect. Section 25(3) makes the "fair and reasonable landlord" plea available to the tenant under Case 3, and, while there are no reported instances of its being invoked, it would appear that in certain circumstances it might succeed.

Case 4

This ground of consent was introduced by the 1983 Act. While there is as yet no reported instance of the Case being invoked the question of a successor tenant's financial standing has on occasion arisen under the provisions now contained in ss.11 and 12. In *Reid* v. *Duffus Estates*, 1953 S.L.C.R. 13, an objection to a legatee as tenant because he required a bank overdraft to provide necessary working capital was unsuccessful, the Land Court taking the view that a guarantee of solvency could not be required of a tenant. The onus there was on the landlord to substantiate his objection but here the position is reversed in terms of s.25(3), requiring the tenant to satisfy the court that the circumstances are not as specified in this case. Section 25(3) also means that the "fair and reasonable landlord" plea is not available to the tenant.

Case 5

See note to Case 1, the requirement of this case being basically the same but in terms of s.25(3) the onus is on the tenant and the "fair and reasonable landlord" plea does not apply. A proviso, however, gives the youthful successor or novice a chance to meet the charge of inadequate training or experience by having been from the date of the late tenant's death engaged in a suitable course of training which he is expected to complete satisfactorily within four years of that date and having made arrangements for the efficient farming of the holding till completion of the course. It should be noted that the proviso will not benefit a tenant who takes up a course of training after his acquisition of the tenancy, which acquisition may, under the provisions of s.16 of the 1964 Act, take place a considerable time after the late tenant's death.

Case 6

The terms of this case are identical with those of Case 2. As under that Case, s.25(3) has the result that the onus is on the landlord, and the "fair and reasonable landlord" plea is available to the tenant.

Case 7

Basically, this involves the same requirements as Case 3, with the "fair and reasonable landlord" plea available to the tenant in terms of s.25(3). There are, however, significant differences. In the first place, the onus in terms of s.25(3) is on the tenant, although he is not to be required to prove that he is not the owner of any land. Secondly, while the other agricultural land occupied by the tenant must be distinct from the holding, it need not be outwith any agricultural unit of which the holding forms part. Again, occupation of the other agricultural land from the date of giving of the notice to quit is substituted for occupation since before the late tenant's death as required in Case 3. This results that where after succeeding to a tenancy a party obtains occupation of other agricultural land the landlord in the tenancy to which he has succeeded may be able to serve a notice to quit based on this case, complying with the requirement of s.25(2)(b) as regards its effective date. Other provisions affecting Case 7 but not Case 3 are contained in para. 3 of Pt. III of the Schedule.

Para. 1

As to the nature of amalgamation, see *Mackenzie* v. *Lyon*, 1984 S.L.T. (Land Ct.) 30. The ownership and occupation of the resulting agricultural unit need not coincide. The landlord's intention may be to let the unit to a tenant. It is, however, necessary that the landlord own the land with which the holding is to be amalgamated and that the resulting unit is to be in single occupation (*Mackenzie* v. *Lyon*).

Reference has been made to the definition of a near relative in connection with s.25.

Paragraph 2 should be read along with the definition of a two-man unit as referred to in Cases 2, 3, 6 and 7. That paragraph specifies certain assumptions which the Land Court are to make in deciding whether or not they are dealing with a "two-man" unit. They involve that the matter be dealt with on an objective basis irrespective of the standard of farming achieved by the tenant, normal commercial criteria applying to the results of the farming operations. The Land Court have considered this matter in the cases of *Poett* v. *Henderson*, 1979 Central RN 11 and *Earl of Seafield* v. *Currie*, 1980 S.L.T. (Land Ct.) 10, and more recently in *Jenners Princes Street Edinburgh* v. *Howe*, 1990 S.L.T. (Land Ct.) 26, at pp. 28–29, where it was remarked that "full-time" employment must be taken to mean what it says and cannot be applied to casual workers such as raspberry pickers.

Para. (3)

It would seem to be right that in the matter of occupation of other agricultural land under Case 7 the successor tenant should be identified with a company in which he has a controlling interest. A question might be said to arise as to the fairness of this ruling in the case of companies in which the proprietor of the ground as landlord is empowered by liquidating the company or by other means to bring the tenancy to an end. Such arrangements for the avoidance of the agricultural tenant's security of tenure are, however, uncommon now, the lease to a limited partnership involving tenant and landlord or tenant and landlord's nominee having become the standard format.

In discarding for the purposes of Case 7 the rule confirmed by statute that a Scottish firm is a legal person as distinct from its partners, this paragraph not only reverses the ruling of the Land Court in *Haddo House Estate Trust* v. *Davidson*, in which a firm, of which the successor tenant was a member, owned and occupied a number of agricultural units. It also has the result, unfortunately perhaps, that a successor tenant will be treated as occupying other agricultural land let to a partnership (probably in limited form) between himself and the landlord or his nominee, where security of tenure is conditional on the continued existence of the firm.

Section 33   SCHEDULE 3

1923 ACT IMPROVEMENTS FOR WHICH COMPENSATION MAY BE PAYABLE

PART I

IMPROVEMENTS FOR WHICH CONSENTS REQUIRED

1. Erection, alteration, or enlargement of buildings.
2. Formation of silos.
3. Laying down of permanent pasture.
4. Making and planting of osier beds.
5. Making of water meadows or works of irrigation.
6. Making of gardens.
7. Making or improvement of roads or bridges.
8. Making or improvement of watercourses, ponds, wells, or reservoirs, or of works for the application of water power or for supply of water for agricultural or domestic purposes.
9. Making or removal of permanent fences.
10. Planting of hops.
11. Planting of orchards or fruit bushes.
12. Protecting young fruit trees.
13. Reclaiming of waste land.
14. Warping or weiring of land.
15. Embankments and sluices against floods.
16. Erection of wirework in hop gardens.
17. Provision of permanent sheep dipping accommodation.
18. In the case of arable land, the removal of bracken, gorse, tree roots, boulders, or other like obstructions to cultivation.

PART II

IMPROVEMENTS FOR WHICH NOTICE REQUIRED

19. Drainage.

PART III

IMPROVEMENTS FOR WHICH NO CONSENTS OR NOTICE REQUIRED

20. Chalking of land.

21. Clay-burning.

22. Claying of land or spreading blaes upon land.

23. Liming of land.

24. Marling of land.

25. Application to land of purchased artificial or other manure.

26. Consumption on the holding by cattle, sheep, or pigs, or by horses other than those regularly employed on the holding, of corn, cake, or other feeding stuff not produced on the holding.

27. Consumption on the holding by cattle, sheep, or pigs, or by horses other than those regularly employed on the holding, of corn proved by satisfactory evidence to have been produced and consumed on the holding.

28. Laying down temporary pasture with clover, grass, lucerne, sainfoin, or other seeds, sown more than 2 years prior to the termination of the tenancy, in so far as the value of the temporary pasture on the holding at the time of quitting exceeds the value of the temporary pasture on the holding at the commencement of the tenancy for which the tenant did not pay compensation.

29. Repairs to buildings, being buildings necessary for the proper cultivation or working of the holding, other than repairs which the tenant is himself under an obligation to execute.

DERIVATIONS

Agricultural Holdings (Scotland) Act 1949, Sched. 2. This Schedule lists old improvements in the 1923 category for which compensation may be claimed. The relevant provisions of the Act are to be found in ss.33, 34, 36, 38, 40, 51 and 79.

GENERAL NOTE

For the corresponding English provision see the Agricultural Holdings Act 1986, Sched. 9, Pt. II, applying to this Schedule and Sched. 4.

Section 33 SCHEDULE 4

1931 ACT IMPROVEMENTS FOR WHICH COMPENSATION MAY BE PAYABLE

PART I

IMPROVEMENTS FOR WHICH CONSENT REQUIRED

1. Erection, alteration, or enlargement of buildings.

2. Laying down of permanent pasture.

3. Making and planting of osier beds.

4. Making of water meadows or works of irrigation.

5. Making of gardens.

6. Planting of orchards or fruit bushes.

7. Protecting young fruit trees.

8. Warping or weiring of land.

9. Making of embankments and sluices against floods.

PART II

IMPROVEMENTS OF WHICH NOTICE REQUIRED

10. Drainage.

11. Formation of silos.

12. Making or improvement of roads or bridges.

13. Making or improvement of watercourses, ponds or wells, or of works for the application of water power or for the supply of water for agricultural or domestic purposes.

14. Making or removal of permanent fences.

15. Reclaiming of waste land.

16. Repairing or renewal of embankments and sluices against floods.

17. Provision of sheep dipping accommodation.

18. Provision of electrical equipment other than moveable fittings and appliances.

PART III

IMPROVEMENTS FOR WHICH NO CONSENT OR NOTICE REQUIRED

19. Chalking of land.

20. Clay-burning.
21. Claying of land or spreading blaes upon land.
22. Liming of land.
23. Marling of land.
24. Eradication of bracken, whins, or gorse growing on the holding at the commencement of a tenancy and in the case of arable land the removal of tree roots, boulders, stones or other like obstacles to cultivation.
25. Application to land of purchased artificial or other manure.
26. Consumption on the holding by cattle, sheep, or pigs, or by horses other than those regularly employed on the holding, of corn, cake, or other feeding stuff not produced on the holding.
27. Consumption on the holding by cattle, sheep, or pigs, or by horses other than those regularly employed on the holding, of corn proved by satisfactory evidence to have been produced and consumed on the holding.
28. Laying down temporary pasture with clover, grass, lucerne, sainfoin, or other seeds, sown more than 2 years prior to the termination of the tenancy, in so far as the value of the temporary pasture on the holding at the time of quitting exceeds the value of the temporary pasture on the holding at the commencement of the tenancy for which the tenant did not pay compensation.
29. Repairs to buildings, being buildings necessary for the proper cultivation or working of the holding, other than repairs which the tenant is himself under an obligation to execute.

DERIVATIONS
   Agricultural Holdings (Scotland) Act 1949, Sched. 3.
   This schedule lists old improvements in the 1931 category for which compensation may be claimed. The relevant provisions of the Act are to be found in ss.33, 34, 36, 38, 40, 51 and 79.

Section 33   SCHEDULE 5

NEW IMPROVEMENTS FOR WHICH COMPENSATION MAY BE PAYABLE

PART I

IMPROVEMENTS FOR WHICH CONSENT IS REQUIRED

1. Laying down of permanent pasture.
2. Making of water-meadows or works of irrigation.
3. Making of gardens.
4. Planting of orchards or fruit bushes.
5. Warping or weiring of land.
6. Making of embankments and sluices against floods.
7. Making or planting of osier beds.
8. Haulage or other work done by the tenant in aid of the carrying out of any improvement made by the landlord for which the tenant is liable to pay increased rent.

PART II

IMPROVEMENTS FOR WHICH NOTICE IS REQUIRED

9. Land drainage.
10. Construction of silos.
11. Making or improvement of farm access or service roads, bridges and fords.
12. Making or improvement of watercourses, ponds or wells, or of works for the application of water power for agricultural or domestic purposes or for the supply of water for such purposes.
13. Making or removal of permanent fences, including hedges, stone dykes and gates.
14. Reclaiming of waste land.
15. Renewal of embankments and sluices against floods.
16. Provision of stells, fanks, folds, dippers, pens and bughts necessary for the proper conduct of the holding.
17. Provision or laying on of electric light or power, including the provision of generating plant, fixed motors, wiring systems, switches and plug sockets.
18. Erection, alteration or enlargement of buildings, making or improvement of permanent yards, loading banks and stocks and works of a kind referred to in paragraph 13(2) of Schedule 8 to the Housing (Scotland) Act 1987 (subject to the restrictions mentioned in that subsection).

19. Erection of hay or sheaf sheds, sheaf or grain drying racks, and implement sheds.

20. Provision of fixed threshing mills, barn machinery and fixed dairying plant.

21. Improvement of permanent pasture by cultivation and re-seeding.

22. Provision of means of sewage disposal.

23. Repairs to fixed equipment, being equipment reasonably required for the efficient farming of the holding, other than repairs which the tenant is under an obligation to carry out.

Part III

Improvements For Which No Consent Or Notice Required

24. Protecting fruit trees against animals.

25. Clay burning.

26. Claying of land.

27. Liming (including chalking) of land.

28. Marling of land.

29. Eradication of bracken, whins or broom growing on the holding at the commencement of the tenancy and, in the case of arable land, removal of tree roots, boulders, stones or other like obstacles to cultivation.

30. Application to land of purchased manure and fertiliser, whether organic or inorganic.

31. Consumption on the holding of corn (whether produced on the holding or not) or of cake or other feeding stuff not produced on the holding by horses, cattle, sheep, pigs or poultry.

32. Laying down temporary pasture with clover, grass, lucerne, sainfoin, or other seeds, sown more than 2 years prior to the termination of the tenancy, in so far as the value of the temporary pasture on the holding at the time of quitting exceeds the value of the temporary pasture on the holding at the commencement of the tenancy for which the tenant did not pay compensation.

DERIVATIONS

Agricultural Holdings (Scotland) Act 1949, Sched. 1.

GENERAL NOTE

See Gill, para. 569. (For the corresponding English provision see the Agricultural Holdings Act 1986, Scheds. 7 and 8, Pt. I).

This Schedule lists new improvements for which compensation can be claimed. The relevant provisions of the Act are to be found in ss.33–40, 51, 73, 75 and 79.

Section 40   SCHEDULE 6

Market Garden Improvements

1. Planting of fruit trees or bushes permanently set out.

2. Planting of strawberry plants.

3. Planting of asparagus, rhubarb, and other vegetable crops which continue productive for 2 or more years.

4. Erection, alteration or enlargement of buildings for the purpose of the trade or business of a market gardener.

DERIVATIONS

Agricultural Holdings (Scotland) Act 1949, Sched. 4.

GENERAL NOTE

See Gill, para. 548. (For the corresponding English provision see the Agricultural Holdings Act 1986, Sched. 10).

The Schedule lists market garden improvements for which compensation may be claimed. The relevant provisions of the Act are to be found in ss.40, 41, 73 and 79.

Section 61   SCHEDULE 7

Arbitrations

Appointment of Arbiters

1. A person agreed upon between the parties or, in default of agreement, appointed on the

application in writing of either of the parties by the Secretary of State from among the members of the panel constituted under this Act for the purpose, shall be appointed arbiter.

2. If a person appointed arbiter dies, or is incapable of acting, or for 7 days after notice from either party requiring him to act fails to act, a new arbiter may be appointed as if no arbiter had been appointed.

3. Neither party shall have the power to revoke the appointment of the arbiter without the consent of the other party.

4. An appointment, notice, revocation and consent of a kind referred to in any of paragraphs 1 to 3 of this Schedule must be in writing.

PARTICULARS OF CLAIM

5. Each of the parties to the arbitration shall, within 28 days from the appointment of the arbiter, deliver to him a statement of that party's case with all necessary particulars; and—
   (a) no amendment or addition to the statement or particulars delivered shall be allowed after the expiration of the said 28 days except with the consent of the arbiter;
   (b) a party to the arbitration shall be confined at the hearing to the matters alleged in the statement and particulars so delivered and any amendment thereof or addition thereto duly made.

EVIDENCE

6. The parties to the arbitration, and all persons claiming through them respectively, shall, subject to any legal objection—
   (a) submit to be examined by the arbiter on oath or affirmation in relation to the matters in dispute; and
   (b) produce before the arbiter;
all samples, books, deeds, papers, accounts, writings, and documents, within their possession or power respectively which may be required or called for, and do all other things which during the proceedings the arbiter may require.

7. The arbiter shall have power to administer oaths, and to take the affirmation of parties and witnesses appearing, and witnesses shall, if the arbiter thinks fit, be examined on oath or affirmation.

AWARD

8. The arbiter shall make and sign his award within 3 months of his appointment or within such longer period as may, either before or after the expiry of the aforesaid period be agreed to in writing by the parties, or be fixed by the Secretary of State.

9. The arbiter may, if he thinks fit, make an interim award for the payment of any sum on account of the sum to be finally awarded.

10. An arbiter appointed by the Secretary of State or the Land Court in an arbitration under section 13(1) of this Act shall, in making his award, state in writing his findings of fact and the reasons for his decision and shall make that statement available to the Secretary of State and to the parties.

11. The award and any statement made under paragraph 10 of this Schedule shall be in such form as may be specified by statutory instrument made by the Secretary of State.

12. The arbiter shall—
   (a) state separately in his award the amounts awarded in respect of the several claims referred to him; and
   (b) on the application of either party, specify the amount awarded in respect of any particular improvement or any particular matter which is the subject of the award.

13. Where by virtue of this Act compensation under an agreement is to be substituted for compensation under this Act for improvements, the arbiter shall award compensation in accordance with the agreement instead of in accordance with this Act.

14. The award shall fix a day not later than one month after delivery of the award for the payment of the money awarded as compensation, expenses or otherwise.

15. Subject to section 61(2) of this Act, the award shall be final and binding on the parties and the persons claiming under them respectively.

16. The arbiter may correct in an award any clerical mistake or error arising from any accidental slip or omission.

EXPENSES

17. The expenses of and incidental to the arbitration and award shall be in the discretion of the arbiter, who may direct to and by whom and in what manner those expenses or any part

thereof are to be paid, and the expenses shall be subject to taxation by the auditor of the sheriff court on the application of either party, but that taxation shall be subject to review by the sheriff.

18. The arbiter shall, in awarding expenses, take into consideration the reasonableness or unreasonableness of the claim of either party whether in respect of amount or otherwise, and any unreasonable demand for particulars or refusal to supply particulars, and generally all the circumstances of the case, and may disallow the expenses of any witness whom he considers to have been called unnecessarily and any other expenses which he considers to have been incurred unnecessarily.

19. It shall not be lawful to include in the expenses of and incidental to the arbitration and award, or to charge against any of the parties, any sum payable in respect of remuneration or expenses to any person appointed by the arbiter to act as clerk or otherwise to assist him in the arbitration unless such appointment was made after submission of the claim and answers to the arbiter and with either the consent of the parties to the arbitration or the sanction of the sheriff.

STATEMENT OF CASE

20. Subject to paragraph 22 of this Schedule, the arbiter may at any stage of the proceedings, and shall, if so directed by the sheriff (which direction may be given on the application of either party), state a case for the opinion of the sheriff on any question of law arising in the course of the arbitration.

21. Subject to paragraph 22 of this Schedule, the opinion of the sheriff on any case stated under the last foregoing paragraph shall be final unless, within such time and in accordance with such conditions as may be specified by act of sederunt, either party appeals to the Court of Session, from whose decision no appeal shall lie.

22. Where the arbiter in any arbitration under section 13(1) of this Act has been appointed by the Secretary of State or by the Land Court, paragraphs 20 and 21 of this Schedule shall not apply, and instead the arbiter may at any stage of the proceedings state a case (whether at the request of either party or on his own initiative) on any question of law arising in the course of the arbitration, for the opinion of the Land Court, whose decision shall be final.

REMOVAL OF ARBITER AND SETTING ASIDE OF AWARD

23. Where an arbiter has misconducted himself the sheriff may remove him.

24. When an arbiter has misconducted himself, or an arbitration or award has been improperly procured, the sheriff may set the award aside.

FORMS

25. Any forms for proceedings in arbitrations under this Act which may be specified by statutory instrument made by the Secretary of State shall, if used, be sufficient.

DERIVATIONS
Agricultural Holdings (Scotland) Act 1949, Sched. 6.
Agriculture Holdings (Amendment) (Scotland) Act 1983, s.5(2).

GENERAL NOTE
See Gill, paras. 617–657. (For the corresponding English provision see the Agricultural Holdings Act 1986, s.5(2)).
Reference should be made to s.61 and the notes on that section. The following notes refer to the paragraphs of the Schedule indicated by their numbers.

Para. 1
This provides the parties with the alternative of an arbiter whom they agree to nominate and an arbiter appointed by the Secretary of State. Gill (paras. 619–620) explains the various points of distinction between the private arbiter, as the appointee of the parties is sometimes called, and the statutory arbiter. The latter, but not the former, requires to be a member of the official panel of arbiters (see s.63(1)(2)) and is affected by the provisions of the Tribunals and Inquiries Act 1971.

The appointment of a private arbiter will normally be effected by a joint document of submission on the lines exemplified in Connell (*op. cit.* pp. 253–254). To have a statutory arbiter appointed, application requires to be made to the Secretary of State in a form prescribed in Sched. 2 to the Agricultural Holdings (Specification of Forms) (Scotland) Order 1983 (S.I. 1983 No. 1073), in which Form A applies to cases other than rent variations and Form B to rent variations. The document of submission to a private arbiter will make clear the nature and scope of the reference. In making application to the Secretary of State for an appointment, the questions or differences at issue should be precisely stated, as the content of the application in this respect will be reproduced verbatim in the instrument of appointment. While either party to a dispute can submit the application, it is appropriate that the application should be a joint one if each of the parties has claims against the other, *e.g.* landlord and outgoing tenant, it not being competent to present a counterclaim in the arbitration proceedings (see *Chalmers Property Investment Co.* v. *Bowman*, 1953 S.L.T. (Sh. Ct.) 38 and Gill, para. 623).

Para. 2
The words "incapable of acting" cover incapacity from any cause, including removal from office under para. 23 (*Dundee Corporation* v. *Guthrie*, 1969 S.L.T. 93).

Para. 3
It appears that an appointment by the Secretary of State may be revoked by consent (*Dundee Corporation* v. *Guthrie*, above, at p. 98).

Para. 5
The date of appointment of the arbiter, from which date the period of 28 days runs, is, in the case of a private arbiter, the date of the submission and not that of the arbiter's acceptance. In a statutory arbitration it is the date of the instrument of appointment (see Gill, para. 622). The arbiter cannot extend this time limit (*Stewart* v. *Brims*, 1969 S.L.T. (Sh. Ct.) 2) but may allow late delivery of the party's statement of case if the other party consents (*Suggett* v. *Shaw*, 1987 S.L.T. (Land Ct.) 5). As to the result of a party's failure to lodge a statement of case, see Gill, para. 628 and the cases of *Jamieson* v. *Clark* (1951) 67 Sh.Ct.Rep. 17 and *Collett* v. *Deeley*, 1949 100 L.J. 108. Briefly stated, he is precluded from setting up a case and leading evidence at the hearing, so that if he is a respondent he is limited to attacking his opponent's case by cross-examination of witnesses and if he is a claimant carrying the onus of proof he will have his claim rejected *de plano*. It appears that the statement of case and particulars may, if desired, be contained in one document. Whatever form they take, they must give fair notice of the basis or nature of the claim, quantifying it if it is a pecuniary one. It will be appreciated that, as affecting matters such as outgoing claims, much more detail and precision is required here than under the provisions of s.62(2)(3).
Sub-para. (a) has the result that some amendment or adjustment of the parties' statement of case may be allowed, this being desirable as neither party has the right to see its opponent's statement of case before it is lodged with the arbiter. In this way an "amendment or addition" to a party's statement of case as referred to in sub-para. (b) may be allowed, but if the document originally lodged by a party does not constitute a statement of case, the defect cannot be cured in this way (*Robertson Trs.* v. *Cunningham*, 1951 S.L.T. (Sh. Ct.) 89). Sub-para. (b) has been held to be peremptory in effect and incapable of being waived, even of consent (*Stewart* v. *Brims*, 1969 S.L.T. (Sh. Ct.) 2 at pp. 6–7).

Para. 6
The duties incumbent on the parties will include giving access facilities in any case where an inspection by an arbiter is required. Legal objections such as confidentiality may, however, be invoked as regards the giving of evidence or production of documents. In practice, parties will usually be required by the arbiter to lodge any documents on which they are founding, including of course any written lease there may be, by a date some time before the hearing.

Para. 7
In general, the arbiter has a wide discretion in the conduct of proceedings in which there may be a degree of informality which would not be acceptable in court (*Paterson* v. *Glasgow Corporation*, 1901 3F H.L. 34, *per* Lord Robertson at p. 40). For the basic principles applicable and the practice in the arbitration procedure, see Gill, paras. 631–636).

Para. 8
Gill (para. 637) explains the practice of issuing proposed findings before the issue of an award. The three-month time limit for issue of the award running from the date of appointment as explained in respect of para. 5 is peremptory, disregard of it constituting misconduct on the part of the arbiter (*Halliday* v. *Semple*, 1960 S.L.T. (Sh. Ct.) 11). There are, however, provisions for extension of the time limit which is often found necessary in the more difficult cases. The agreement of the parties to an extension must be in written form delivered to the arbiter. An application to the Secretary of State for extension can be made even after the expiry of the statutory time limit (*Dundee Corporation* v. *Guthrie*, above). It should conform to Form C in Sched. 2 to the Agricultural Holdings (Specification of Forms) (Scotland) Order 1983 (S.I. 1983 No. 1073).

Para. 9
   Cf. s.69(3), which provides for interim awards in sheep stock valuation cases but only where the outcome of an appeal to the Sheriff by way of stated case is awaited.

Para. 10
   This provision, applying only to rent arbitrations, was introduced by the 1983 Act, along with the directions to arbiters now incorporated in s.13(4). In other arbitrations a private arbiter cannot be required to give reasons for his decision but a statutory arbiter must do so at the request of either party, the statement of reasons forming part of his decision and being incorporated in his award (Tribunals and Inquiries Act 1971, s.12).
   In accordance with s.64, the appointment of the arbiter will be made by the Land Court in cases where the Secretary of State, through the appropriate department, is in the position of landlord or tenant. Where the appointment has been made by the Secretary of State, by whom the arbiter's remuneration will fall to be fixed in terms of s.63(3)(a), it may be found convenient to submit to the Department, along with the application to have the arbiter's remuneration fixed, the findings in fact and statement of reasons.

Para. 11
   The prescribed form is in Sched. 1 to the 1983 Order, referred to under para. 8. It requires to be attested.

Para. 12
   Adherence to the form provided should in most cases result in these requirements being met (see under para. 24).

Para. 13
   This accords with provisions of the Act such as s.37 dealing with substituted compensation.

Para. 14
   In arbitrations on milk quota compensation the period is three months after delivery of the award (1986 Act, Sched. 2, para. 11(4), as amended in terms of Sched. 11, para. 2(b)).

Para. 15
   The exception occurs in rent arbitrations where in terms of s.61(2)(3) an appeal to the Land Court against the award of a statutory arbiter on any question of law or fact (including the amount of the award) may be brought within two months of the date of issue of the award.

Para. 16
   The correction may be made at any time after the delivery of the award.

Para. 17
   The rule generally applied in the courts whereby expenses follow success is applicable to arbitrations but in rent arbitrations or other arbitrations concerning matters of valuation it is usual for each party to be required to bear his own expenses.
   Where there is an appeal from the arbiter to the Land Court the arbiter's ruling on expenses is unlikely to be altered (*MacGregor* v. *Glencruitten Trust*, 1985 S.L.C.R. 77).
   As mentioned in connection with s.61(4) the power given to the Secretary of State by that subsection to make regulations for expediting or reducing the expense of proceedings on arbitrations under this Act has not yet been exercised.

Para. 18
   In complying with this paragraph the arbiter will again be following the usual practice of the courts.

Para. 19
   As to the appointment and functions of a clerk, usually a legally qualified person, see Gill (626). In arbitrations of any size or complexity, appointment of consent is normal.

Paras. 20 and 21
   Paragraph 22 deals with appeals in rent arbitrations. In all other arbitrations under the Act the appeal procedure is by Stated Case, the content of these paras. 20 and 21 covering the whole course of procedure (*Forsyth Grant* v. *Salmon*, 1961 S.C. 54, *per* Lord Mackintosh at p. 58). The case can be stated at any time before the issue of the final award and is dealt with by the Sheriff in whose jurisdiction the holding lies. It has been held that the expenses of the States

Case in the Sheriff Court fall to be determined by the Sheriff and not by the arbiter (*Thomson* v. *Earl of Galloway*, 1919 S.C. 611; *Jamieson* v. *Clark* (1951) 67 Sh.Ct.Rep. 17 at p. 21), although the arbiter deals with the expenses of preparation of the Stated Case. (As to procedure and practice in this matter see Gill, 649 and 650.) An appeal from the Sheriff to the Court of Session, the decision of which is final, can be taken following the procedure prescribed in paras. 262–263 of the Court of Session Rules of Court. While the case is said to be stated "for the opinion" of the Sheriff, his ruling, or that of the Court of Session on appeal, is binding on and must be implemented by the arbiter (*Mitchell Gill* v. *Buchan*, 1921 S.C. 390).

Para. 22

This paragraph prescribes the procedure for appeal by Stated Case in rent arbitrations conducted by a statutory arbiter, these being excluded from the application of paras. 20 and 21. The appeal here, which is on any question of law arising, is to the Land Court, the decision of which is final, but there is no provision as there is in para. 20 for the arbiter being directed to state a case. It should be noted that this right of appeal is distinct from and in addition to the appeal to the Land Court on any question of law or fact against the decision of a statutory arbiter under s.61(2)(3).

Para. 23

"Misconduct" in this context can signify any fault or mistake by the arbiter in the conduct of the arbitration (*Paterson* v. *Glasgow Corporation*, 1901 3F H.L. 34, *per* Lord Chancellor Halsbury at p. 38). Thus it will include not only failures to comply with the directions of this Schedule, *e.g.* by issuing an award out of time (*Halliday* v. *Semple*, 1960 S.L.T. (Sh. Ct.) 11) but also anything inconsistent with justice having been done (see *Mitchell Gill* v. *Buchan*, above). But it need not involve any impropriety, nor any wilful or malicious conduct by the arbiter (*Mitchell Gill* v. *Buchan*). Specific averments are required from a party seeking to have an arbiter removed for misconduct (*MacLean* v. *Chalmers Property Investment Co.*, 1951 S.L.T. (Sh. Ct.) 71). The objection to the arbiter's action should be taken when it occurs but failure to do so then does not validate the objectionable action (*MacLean*, at p. 72).

On removal of the arbiter and reduction of any award he has made, a new arbiter may be appointed (*Dundee Corporation* v. *Guthrie*, 1969 S.L.T. 93).

Para. 24

It appears that the aggrieved party may have the alternative of reduction proceedings in the Court of Session (see *Dunlop* v. *Mundell*, 1943 S.L.T. 286—a decision on the similar wording in s.1(2) of the Sheep Stocks Valuation (Scotland) Act 1937).

Para. 25

As to forms in use under the Agricultural Holdings (Specification of Forms) (Scotland) Order 1983 (S.I. 1983 No. 1073) see under paras. 8 and 11.

Section 57   SCHEDULE 8

SUPPLEMENTARY PROVISIONS WITH RESPECT TO PAYMENTS UNDER SECTION 56

1. Subject to paragraph 4 of this Schedule, any dispute with respect to any sum which may be or become payable by virtue of section 56(1) of this Act shall be referred to and determined by the Lands Tribunal for Scotland.

2. If in any case the sum to be paid by virtue of the said section 56(1) to the tenant of an agricultural holding or to a statutory small tenant by an acquiring authority would, apart from this paragraph and paragraph 3 of this Schedule, fall to be ascertained in pursuance of section 54(2) of this Act by reference to the rent of the holding at a rate which was not—

   (a) determined by arbitration under section 13 or 15 of this Act;

   (b) determined by the Land Court in pursuance of section 61(2) of this Act; or

   (c) in the case of a statutory small tenant, fixed by the Scottish Land Court in pursuance of section 32(7) and (8) of the 1911 Act;

and which the authority consider is unduly high, the authority may make an application to the Lands Tribunal for Scotland for the rent to be considered by the tribunal;

3. Where, on an application under paragraph 2 above, the tribunal are satisfied that—

   (a) the rent to which the application relates is not substantially higher than the rent which in their opinion would be determined for the holding in question on a reference to arbitration duly made in pursuance of—

      (i) section 13 of this Act; or

      (ii) in the case of a statutory small tenancy, the equitable rent which in their opinion would be fixed by the Land Court under section 32(7) and (8) of the 1911 Act;

(hereafter in this paragraph referred to as "the appropriate rent"); or

(b) the rent to which the application relates is substantially higher than the appropriate rent but was not fixed by the parties to the relevant lease with a view to increasing the amount of any compensation payable, or of any sum to be paid by virtue of section 56(1) of this Act, in consequence of the compulsory acquisition or taking of possession of any land included in the holding,

they shall dismiss the application; and if the tribunal do not dismiss the application in pursuance of the foregoing provisions of this paragraph they shall determine that, in the case to which the application relates, the sum to be paid by virtue of section 56(1) of this Act shall be ascertained in pursuance of the said section 13 by reference to the appropriate rent instead of by reference to the rent to which the application relates.

4. For the purposes of paragraph 3(a) above, section 13(1) of this Act shall have effect as if for the reference therein to the next ensuing day there were substituted a reference to the date of the application referred to in paragraph 3(a) above.

5. The enactments mentioned in paragraph 6 of this Schedule shall, subject to any necessary modifications, have effect in their application to such an acquiring of an interest or taking of possession as is referred in section 56(1) of this Act (hereafter in this paragraph referred to as "the relevant event")—

(a) in so far as those enactments make provision for the doing, before the relevant event, of any thing connected with compensation (including in particular provision for determining the amount of the liability to pay compensation or for the deposit of it in a Scottish bank or otherwise), as if references to compensation, except compensation for damage or injurious affection, included references to any sum which will become payable by virtue of section 56 of this Act in consequence of the relevant event; and

(b) subject to sub-paragraph (a) above, as if references to compensation (except compensation for damage or injurious affection) included references to sums payable or, as the context may require, to sums paid by virtue of section 56 of this Act in the consequence of the relevant event.

6. The enactments aforesaid are—

(a) sections 56 to 60, 62, 63 to 65, 67 to 70, 72, 74 to 79, 83 to 87, 114, 115 and 117 of the Lands Clauses (Scotland) Act 1845;

(b) paragraph 3 of Schedule 2 to the Acquisition of Land (Authorisation Procedure) (Scotland) Act 1947;

(c) Parts I and II and section 40 of the Land Compensation (Scotland) Act 1963;

(d) paragraph 4 of Schedule 6 to the New Towns (Scotland) Act 1968;

(e) any provision in any local or private Act, in any instrument having effect by virtue of an enactment, or in any order or scheme confirmed by Parliament or brought into operation in accordance with special parliamentary procedure, corresponding to a provision mentioned in sub-paragraph (a), (b) or (d) above.

DEFINITIONS

"agricultural holding": s.1(1).
"statutory small tenant": s.54(1).

DERIVATIONS

Agriculture (Miscellaneous Provisions) Act 1968, Scheds. 4 and 5, paras. 6 and 7.

GENERAL NOTE

For the corresponding English provision see the Agriculture (Miscellaneous Provisions) Act 1968, Sched. 3.

The provisions of this Schedule are intended to prevent excessive amounts being claimed from the acquiring authority under s.56 by tenants of subjects which are being acquired compulsorily. Claims for additional payments under s.56 being based on the rental of the subjects acquired, a collusive arrangement between landlord and tenant could result in an unduly high rent being payable at the relevant time. This possibility does not exist if the rent payable has been determined by arbitration or by the Land Court under the relevant statutory provisions, but where that is not so the acquiring authority is empowered to have the rent reviewed by the Lands Tribunal for Scotland as the tribunal dealing with questions of compensation in compulsory acquisition. The Tribunal has a discretion to substitute "an appropriate rent" for the rent payable as the measure of the acquiring authority's liability. They are not to do so, however, if they consider that the rent payable is not substantially higher than the appropriate rent, *i.e.* the rent which could be expected to be determined by an arbiter or by the Land Court under the relevant statutory provisions or if in the Tribunal's view the rent, even although substantially higher than such appropriate rent, has not been fixed by the parties with a view to increasing the compensation payable.

                  SCHEDULE 9

VALUATION OF SHEEP STOCK IN SCOTLAND IN RESPECT OF OLD LEASES

PART I

VALUATION MADE IN RESPECT OF A TENANCY TERMINATING AT WHITSUNDAY

1. The Land Court or the arbiter (in Part I and Part II of this Schedule referred to as "the valuer") shall ascertain the number of, and the prices realised for, the ewes and the lambs sold off the hill from the stock under valuation at the autumn sales in each of the 3 preceding years, and shall determine by inspection the number of shotts present in the stock at that time of the valuation.

2. The valuer shall calculate an average price per ewe, and an average price per lamb, for the ewes and lambs sold as aforesaid for each of the 3 preceding years. In calculating the average price for any year the valuer shall disregard such number of ewes and lambs so sold in that year, being the ewes or lambs sold at the lowest prices, as bears the same proportion to the total number of ewes or lambs so sold in that year as the number of shotts as determined bears to the total number of ewes or lambs in the stock under valuation.

3. The valuer shall then ascertain the mean of the average prices so calculated for the 3 preceding years for ewes and for lambs, respectively. The figures so ascertained or ascertained, in a case to which paragraph 4 below applies, in accordance with that paragraph, are in this Part of this Schedule referred to as the "3-year average price for ewes" and the "3-year average price for lambs."

4. In the case of any sheep stock in which the number of ewes or the number of lambs sold off the hill at the autumn sales during the preceding 3 years has been less than half the total number of ewes or of lambs sold, the 3-year average price for ewes or the 3-year average price for lambs, as the case may be, shall, in lieu of being ascertained by the valuer as aforesaid, be determined by the Land Court on the application of the parties; and the Land Court shall determine such prices by reference to the prices realised at such sales for ewes and for lambs respectively from similar stocks kept in the same district and under similar conditions.

5. The 3-year average price for ewes shall be subject to adjustment by the valuer within the limits of 20 per cent. (in the case of leases entered into before May 15, 1963, 50 pence) upwards or downwards as he may think proper having regard to the general condition of the stock under valuation and to the profit which the purchaser may reasonably expect it to earn. The resultant figure shall be the basis of the valuation of the ewes, and is in this Part of this Schedule referred to as the "basic ewe value."

The valuer shall similarly adjust the 3 year average price for lambs, and the resultant figure shall be the basis for the valuation of the lambs and is in this Part of this Schedule referred to as the "basic lamb value."

6. In making his award the valuer shall value the respective classes of stock in accordance with the following rules, that is to say—

    (a) ewes of all ages (including gimmers) shall be valued at the basic ewe value with the addition of 30 per cent. (in the case of leases entered into before May 15, 1963, 75 pence) of such value per head;

    (b) lambs shall be valued at the basic lamb value; so however that twin lambs shall be valued at such price as the valuer thinks proper;

    (c) ewe hoggs shall be valued at two-thirds of the combined basic values of a ewe and a lamb subject to adjustment by the valuer within the limits of 10 per cent. (in the case of leases entered into before May 15, 1963, 25 pence) per head upwards or downwards as he may think proper, having regard to their quality and condition;

    (d) tups shall be valued at such price as in the opinion of the valuer represents their value on the farm having regard to acclimatisation or any other factor for which he thinks it proper to make allowance;

    (e) eild sheep shall be valued at the value put upon the ewes subject to such adjustment as the valuer may think proper having regard to their quality and condition; and

    (f) shotts shall be valued at such value not exceeding two-thirds of the value put upon good sheep of the like age and class on the farm as the valuer may think proper.

PART II

VALUATION MADE IN RESPECT OF A TENANCY TERMINATING AT MARTINMAS

7. The valuer shall ascertain the number of, and the prices realised for, the ewes sold off the hill from the stock under valuation at the autumn sales in the current year and in each of the 2 preceding years, and shall calculate an average price per ewe so sold for each of the said years. In calculating the average price for any year the valuer shall disregard one-tenth of the total number of ewes so sold in that year being the ewes sold at the lowest price.

8. The mean of the average prices so calculated shall be subject to adjustment by the valuer within the limits of 10 per cent. (in the case of leases entered into before May 15, 1963, 25 pence) upward or downwards as he may think proper having regard to the general condition of the stock under valuation and to the profit which the purchaser may reasonably expect it to earn. The resultant figure shall be the basis of the valuation of the ewes and is in this Part of this Schedule referred to as the "basic ewe value."

9. In making his award the valuer shall assess the respective classes of stock in accordance with the following rules, that is to say—

   (a) ewes of all ages (including gimmers) shall be valued at the basic ewe value with the addition of 30 per cent. (in the case of leases entered into before May 15, 1963, 75 pence) of such value per head;

   (b) ewe lambs shall be valued at the basic ewe value subject to adjustment by the valuer within the limits of 10 per cent. (in the case of leases entered into before May 15, 1963, 25 pence) per head upwards or downwards as he may think proper having regard to their quality and condition; and

   (c) tups shall be valued at such price as in the opinion of the valuer represents their value on the farm having regard to acclimatisation or any other factor for which he thinks it proper to make allowance.

PART III

PARTICULARS TO BE SHOWN IN AN ARBITER'S AWARD

10. The 3-year average price for ewes and the 3-year average price for lambs ascertained under Part I, or the mean of the average prices calculated under Part II, of this Schedule, as the case may be.

11. Any amount added or taken away by way of adjustment for the purpose of fixing the basic ewe value or the basic lamb value, and the grounds on which such adjustment was made.

12. The number of each class of stock valued (ewes and gimmers of all ages with lambs being taken as one class, and eild ewes and eild gimmers being taken as separate classes at a Whitsunday valuation, and ewes and gimmers of all ages being taken as one class at a Martinmas valuation) and the value placed on each class.

13. Any amount added to or taken away by way of adjustment in fixing the value of ewe hoggs at a Whitsunday valuation, or the value of ewe lambs at a Martinmas valuation, and the grounds on which such adjustment was made.

PART IV

INTERPRETATION

14. In this Schedule the expressions "ewe," "gimmer," "eild ewe," "eild gimmer," "lamb," "ewe hogg," "eild sheep" and "tup" shall be construed as meaning respectively sheep of the classes customarily known by those designations in the locality in which the flock under valuation is maintained.

DERIVATION

Hill Farming Act 1946, Sched. 2.
Agriculture (Miscellaneous Provisions) Act 1963, s.21.

GENERAL NOTE

This Schedule contains the directions for valuations of sheep stocks by an arbiter or by the Land Court. These are based on average prices obtained at the autumn sales for ewes and lambs sold off the hill in the case of a Whitsunday outgoing in each of the three preceding years and in the case of a Martinmas outgoing for ewes sold in the current and each of the two preceding years. These directions apply to tenancies under what are termed old leases, *i.e.* leases entered into after November 6, 1946, but before December 1, 1986. Within its terms, however, the

Schedule distinguishes between leases entered into before May 15, 1963 and leases entered into on or after that date, certain additions permitted to be made to basic prices of stock being limited to fixed cash amounts in the former case but based on percentages of the prices in the latter. The resulting difference can be substantial. See also s.68 and notes thereon.

Section 70   SCHEDULE 10

VALUATION OF SHEEP STOCK IN SCOTLAND IN RESPECT OF LEASES ENTERED INTO AFTER DECEMBER 1, 1986

PART I

VALUATION MADE IN RESPECT OF A TENANCY TERMINATING AT WHITSUNDAY

1. The Land Court or the arbiter (in Part I and Part II of this Schedule referred to as "the valuer") shall ascertain the number of, and the prices realised for, the regular cast ewes and the lambs sold off the hill from the stock under valuation at the autumn sales in each of the 3 preceding years, and shall determine by inspection the number of shotts present in the stock at that time of the valuation.

2. The valuer shall calculate an average price per ewe, and an average price per lamb, for the regular cast ewes and lambs sold as aforesaid for each of the 3 preceding years. In calculating the average price for any year the valuer shall disregard such number of regular cast ewes and lambs so sold in that year, being the ewes or lambs sold at the lowest prices, as bears the same proportion to the total number of regular cast ewes or lambs so sold in that year as the number of shotts as determined bears to the total number of ewes or lambs in the stock under valuation.

3. The valuer shall then ascertain the mean of the average prices so calculated for the 3 preceding years for regular cast ewes and for lambs, respectively. The figures so ascertained or ascertained, in a case to which paragraph 4 below applies, in accordance with that paragraph, are in this Part of this Schedule referred to as the "3-year average price for regular cast ewes" and the "3-year average price for lambs."

4. In the case of any sheep stock in which the number of regular cast ewes or the number of lambs sold off the hill at the autumn sales during the preceding 3 years has been less than half the total number of regular cast ewes or of lambs sold, the 3-year average price for regular cast ewes or the 3-year average price for lambs, as the case may be shall, in lieu of being ascertained by the valuer as aforesaid, be determined by the Land Court on the application of the parties; and the Land Court shall determine such prices by reference to the prices realised at such sales for regular cast ewes and for lambs respectively from similar stocks kept in the same district and under similar conditions.

5. The 3-year average price for regular cast ewes shall be subject to adjustment by the valuer within the limits of 30 per cent. upwards or downwards as he may think proper having regard to the general condition of the stock under valuation and to the profit which the purchaser may reasonably expect it to earn. The resultant figure shall be the basis of the valuation of the ewes, and is in this Part of this Schedule referred to as the "basic ewe value."

The valuer shall adjust the 3 year average price for lambs within the limits of 20 per cent. upwards or downwards as he may think proper having regard to their quality and condition. The resultant figure shall be the basis for the valuation of the lambs and is in this Part of this Schedule referred to as the "basic lamb value."

6. In making his award the valuer shall value the respective classes of stock in accordance with the following rules, that is to say—

(a) ewes of all ages (including gimmers) shall be valued at the basic ewe value with the addition of 30 per cent. of such value per head;

(b) lambs shall be valued at the basic lamb value but twin lambs shall be valued at such price as the valuer thinks proper;

(c) ewe hoggs shall be valued at three quarters of the combined basic values of a ewe and a lamb subject to adjustment by the valuer within the limits of 25 per cent. per head upwards or downwards as he may think proper, having regard to their quality and condition;

(d) tups shall be valued at such price as in the opinion of the valuer represents their value on the farm having regard to acclimatisation or any other factor for which he thinks it proper to make allowance;

(e) eild sheep shall be valued at the value put upon the ewes subject to such adjustment as the valuer may think proper having regard to their quality and condition; and

(f) shotts shall be valued at such value not exceeding two-thirds of the value put upon good sheep of the like age and class on the farm as the valuer may think proper.

PART II

VALUATION MADE IN RESPECT OF A TENANCY TERMINATING AT MARTINMAS

7. The valuer shall ascertain the number of, and the prices realised for, the regular cast ewes sold off the hill from the stock under valuation at the autumn sales in the current year and in each of the 2 preceding years, and shall calculate an average price per ewe so sold for each of the said years. In calculating the average price for any year the valuer shall disregard one-fifth of the total number of regular cast ewes so sold in that year being the ewes sold at the lowest price.

8. The mean of the average prices so calculated shall be subject to adjustment by the valuer within the limits of 30 per cent. upward or downwards as he may think proper having regard to the general condition of the stock under valuation and to the profit which the purchaser may reasonably expect it to earn. The resultant figure shall be the basis of the valuation of the ewes and is in this Part of this Schedule referred to as the "basic ewe value."

9. In making his award the valuer shall assess the respective classes of stock in accordance with the following rules, that is to say—

(a) ewes of all ages (including gimmers) shall be valued at the basic ewe value with the addition of 30 per cent. of such value per head;

(b) ewe lambs shall be valued at the basic ewe value subject to adjustment by the valuer within the limits of 20 per cent. per head upwards or downwards as he may think proper having regard to their quality and condition; and

(c) tups shall be valued at such price as in the opinion of the valuer represents their value on the farm having regard to acclimatisation or any other factor for which he thinks it proper to make allowance.

PART III

PARTICULARS TO BE SHOWN IN AN ARBITER'S AWARD

10. The 3-year average price for regular cast ewes and the 3-year average price for lambs ascertained under Part I, or the mean of the average prices calculated under Part II, of this Schedule, as the case may be.

11. Any amount added or taken away by way of adjustment for the purpose of fixing the basic ewe value or the basic lamb value, and the grounds on which such adjustment was made.

12. The number of each class of stock valued (ewes and gimmers of all ages with lambs being taken as one class, and eild ewes and eild gimmers being taken as separate classes at a Whitsunday valuation, and ewes and gimmers of all ages being taken as one class at a Martinmas valuation) and the value placed on each class.

13. Any amount added to or taken away by way of adjustment in fixing the value of ewe hoggs at a Whitsunday valuation, or the value of ewe lambs at a Martinmas valuation, and the grounds on which such adjustment was made.

PART IV

INTERPRETATION

14. In this Schedule the expressions "regular cast ewes," "ewe," "gimmer," "eild ewe," "eild gimmer," "lamb," "ewe hogg," "eild sheep" and "tup" shall be construed as meaning respectively sheep of the classes customarily known by those designations in the locality in which the flock under valuation is maintained.

DERIVATIONS

Hill Farming Act 1946, Sched. 2.

Hill Farming Act 1946 (Variation of Second Schedule) (Scotland) Order 1986 (S.I. 1986 No. 1823).

GENERAL NOTE

This Schedule, applying to tenancies under leases entered into on or after December 1, 1986, contains directions for the valuation of sheep stocks by an arbiter or by the Land Court based on average prices obtained in the case of a Whitsunday outgoing, for regular cast ewes and lambs sold off the hill at the Autumn Sales of the three preceding years and in the case of a Martinmas outgoing for regular case ewes sold off the hill at the Autumn Sales of the current year and the two preceding years.

In general, the terms of the Schedule reproduce those of Sched. 9 but are adjusted to incorporate the changes made by the Statutory Instrument of 1986.

See also s.68 and notes thereon.

SCHEDULE 11

CONSEQUENTIAL AMENDMENTS OF ENACTMENTS

Hill Farming Act 1946 (c. 73)

1. In section 9, as substituted by the Seventh Schedule to the 1949 Act,—
(a) in subsection (1), for "Agricultural Holdings (Scotland) Act 1949" substitute "Agricultural Holdings (Scotland) Act 1991, referred to in subsections (2) and (4) below as "the 1991 Act";
(b) in subsections (2) and (4), for "the said Act of 1949" substitute "the 1991 Act";
(c) in subsection (2)—
(i) for "Part I or Part II of the First Schedule" substitute "Part I or II of Schedule 5,";
(ii) in paragraph (a), for "section fifty of that Act" substitute "section 37 of the 1991 Act";
(iii) in paragraph (b), for "section fifty-one of that Act" substitute "section 38 of the 1991 Act";
(iv) in paragraph (b), for "section fifty-two of that Act" substitute "section 39 of the 1991 Act,";
(v) for "the said section fifty or the said fifty-one" substitute "section 37 or 38 of the 1991 Act";
(d) in subsection (3), for "section eight of the Agricultural Holdings (Scotland) Act 1949" substitute "section 15 of the 1991 Act."

Reserve and Auxiliary forces (Protection of Civil Interests) Act 1951 (c. 65)

2. In section 21—
(a) in subsection (2) for "Subsection (1) of section twenty-five of the Agricultural Holdings (Scotland) Act 1949" substitute "section 22 of the Agricultural Holdings (Scotland) Act 1991," and for "section twenty-six of that Act" substitute "section 24 of that Act,";
(b) in subsection (3) for "section twenty-five" in both places where it occurs substitute "section 22," and for "section twenty-six" substitute "section 24";
(c) in subsection (8) for "the said Act of 1949" substitute "the Agricultural Holdings (Scotland) Act 1991."
3. In section 22(4)(a), for "subsection (1) of section twenty five of the Agricultural Holdings (Scotland) Act 1949" substitute "section 22(1) of the Agricultural Holdings (Scotland) Act 1991."
4. In section 38(6)(a)(i), for "Agricultural Holdings (Scotland) Act 1949" substitute "Agricultural Holdings (Scotland) Act 1991."

Crofters (Scotland) Act 1955 (c. 21)

5. In section 14(10), for "Agricultural Holdings (Scotland) Act 1949" substitute "Agricultural Holdings (Scotland) Act 1991."
6. In section 37(1), in the definition of "fixed equipment," for "Agricultural Holdings (Scotland) Act 1949" substitute "Agricultural Holdings (Scotland) Act 1991."
7. In Schedule 2, paragraph 10, for "section 15 of the Agricultural Holdings (Scotland) Act 1949" substitute "section 52 of the Agricultural Holdings (Scotland) Act 1991."

Agriculture (Safety, Health and Welfare Provisions) Act 1956 (c. 49)

8. In section 25(4), for the words from "the provisions" to "section eighteen" substitute "section 5(2), (3) and (5) of the Agricultural Holdings (Scotland) Act 1991 (liabilities of landlord and tenant of agricultural holding regarding fixed equipment) and section 10."
9. In section 25(5), for "section eight of the Agricultural Holdings (Scotland) Act 1949" substitute "section 15 of the Agricultural Holdings (Scotland) Act 1991."
10. In section 25(10), in the definition of "agricultural holding," "fixed equipment" and "landlord," for "the Agricultural Holdings (Scotland) Act, 1949" substitute "the Agricultural Holdings (Scotland) Act 1991."

Coal Mining (Subsidence) Act 1957 (c. 59)

11. In section 10(1)(a), for "Agricultural Holdings (Scotland) Act 1949" substitute "Agricultural Holdings (Scotland) Act 1991."

Opencast Coal Act 1958 (c. 69)

12. In section 14A—
(a) in subsection (3), for the words "Agricultural Holdings (Scotland) Act 1949 in this Act referred to as the Scottish Act of 1949" substitute "the Scottish Act of 1991,";
(b) in subsection (4), for "the Scottish Act of 1949" substitute "the Scottish Act of 1991";
(c) in subsection (5), for "the Scottish Act of 1949" substitute "the Scottish Act of 1991";
(d) in subsection (6)—
　　(i) for "section 25(2) of the Scottish Act of 1949" substitute "section 22(2) of the Scottish Act of 1991"; and
　　(ii) for "(c)" substitute "(b)";
(e) in subsection (7), for the words from "For the purposes" to "paragraph (e) of subsection (1)" substitute "The condition specified in section 24(1)(e) of the Scottish Act of 1991 (consent of Land Court to notice to quit where land to be used for purposes other than agriculture)";
(f) in subsection (8), for "section 7 of the Scottish Act of 1949" substitute "section 13 of the Scottish Act of 1991";
(g) in subsection (9), for "section 8 of the Scottish Act of 1949" substitute "section 15 of the Scottish Act of 1991."

13. For section 24(10) substitute—
"(10) In the application of this section to Scotland, for references—
(a) to the Act of 1986 and to sections 70 and 83(4) of that Act there shall be substituted respectively references to the Scottish Act of 1991 and to sections 44 and 62(3) of that Act;
(b) to subsections (1), (2) and (3) of section 69 of the Act of 1986 there shall be substituted respectively references to sections 34(5) and 35(4) and (5) of the Scottish Act of 1991 (as they apply to new improvements);
(c) to Parts I and II of Schedule 7 to the Act of 1986 and to the first day of March 1948 there shall be substituted respectively references to Parts I and II of Schedule 5 to the Scottish Act of 1991 and to the first day of November 1948; and
(d) to sub-paragraphs (1) and (2) of paragraph 5 of Part I of Schedule 9 to the 1986 Act there shall be substituted respectively references to sections 34(5) and 35(4) of the Scottish Act of 1991 (as they apply to old improvements).".

14. For section 25(3) substitute—
"(3) In the application of this section to Scotland, for paragraphs (a) and (b) of subsection (1) above there shall be substituted the words "under section 45 of the Scottish Act of 1991 (which relates to compensation for deterioration of a holding or part thereof for which a tenant is responsible).".

15. In section 26(6) after "Scotland" insert "(a)" and for the words from "in subsection (3)" to the end substitute—
"(b) in subsection (3) of this section for the reference to the Act of 1986 there shall be substituted a reference to the Scottish Act of 1991; and
(c) in subsection (5) of this section there shall be substituted—
　　(i) for the reference to section 91 of the Act of 1986 a reference to section 73 of the Scottish Act of 1991;
　　(ii) for the reference to Schedule 8 to the Act of 1986 a reference to Part III of Schedule 5 to the Scottish Act of 1991;
　　(iii) for the reference to Parts I, II and III of the Fourth Schedule to this Act a reference to Parts IV and V of that Schedule.".

16. In section 27(4), for "section fourteen of the Scottish Act of 1949" substitute "section 18 of the Scottish Act of 1991."

17. In section 28(6)—
(a) for "to section sixty-five of the Scottish Act of 1949 and to paragraph (b) of subsection (1) of that section" substitute "section 40 of the Scottish Act of 1991 and to subsection (4)(a) of that section";
(b) for "to subsection (1) of section sixty-six of the Scottish Act of 1949 and to section 14 of that Act" substitute "to section 41(1) and to section 18 of the Scottish Act of 1991";
(c) for "to section seventy-nine of the Scottish Act of 1949 and to the Fourth Schedule to that Act" substitute "to section 73 of the Scottish Act of 1991 and to Schedule 6 thereto."

18. In section 52(2)—

(a) in the definition of "agricultural holding," for "1949" substitute "1991";
(b) for the definition of "the Scottish Act of 1949" substitute " "the Scottish Act of 1991" means the Agricultural Holdings (Scotland) Act 1991;".
19. In section 52(5)(a)—
(a) for "the Scottish Act of 1949" where it first occurs substitute "the Scottish Act of 1991"; and
(b) for "sections fifty-seven and fifty-eight of the Scottish Act of 1949" substitute "section 45 of the Scottish Act of 1991."
20. In Schedule 6, paragraph 31, for "section 2(1) of the Scottish Act of 1949" substitute "section 2 of the Scottish Act of 1991."
21. For Schedule 7, paragraph 25(a) substitute—
"(a) for references—
(i) to the Act of 1986 and to sections 12, 13, 23 and 84 of that Act there shall be substituted respectively references to the Scottish Act of 1991 and to sections 13, 15, 10 and 61 of that Act;
(ii) to section 10 of the Act of 1986 and to subsections (3) and (4) of that section there shall be substituted respectively references to section 18 of the Scottish Act of 1991 and to subsections (2) and (3) of that section; and
(iii) to subsection (3) of section 79 of the Act of 1986 there shall be substituted references to section 40(4)(a) of the Scottish Act of 1991.".

Horticulture Act 1960 (c. 22)

22. In section 1(1)(b), for "Agricultural Holdings (Scotland) Act 1949" substitute "Agricultural Holdings (Scotland) Act 1991."

Crofters (Scotland) Act 1961 (c. 58)

23. In section 13(1), for "the Agricultural Holdings (Scotland) Act 1949" substitute "the Agricultural Holdings (Scotland) Act 1991."

Succession (Scotland) Act 1964 (c. 41)

24. In section 16—
(a) in subsections (2)(c) and (3)(b)(i), for "section 20 of the Act of 1949" substitute "section 11 of the 1991 Act";
(b) in subsection (6)(b), for "section 27(2) of the Act of 1949" substitute "section 23(2) and (3) of the 1991 Act" and for "section 25(2)(f)" substitute "section 22(2)(e)";
(c) in subsection (8), for "subsections (2) to (7) of section 20 of the Act of 1949" substitute "section 11(2) to (8) of the 1991 Act";
(d) in subsection 9—
(i) in the definition of "agricultural lease," for "the Act of 1949" substitute "the 1991 Act";
(ii) for the definition of "the Act of 1949" substitute "the 1991 Act" means the Agricultural Holdings (Scotland) Act 1991;".
25. In section 29(2), for "section 20 of the Agricultural Holdings (Scotland) Act 1949" substitute "section 11 of the Agricultural Holdings (Scotland) Act 1991."

Agriculture Act 1967 (c. 22)

26. In section 26(1), for "the Agricultural Holdings (Scotland) Act 1949" substitute "the Agricultural Holdings (Scotland) Act 1991."
27. In section 27(5B), for "the Agricultural Holdings (Scotland) Act 1949" substitute "the Agricultural Holdings (Scotland) Act 1991."
28. In section 28(1)(a), for "section 35 of the Agricultural Holdings (Scotland) Act 1949" substitute "section 43 of the Agricultural Holdings (Scotland) Act 1991."
29. In section 29—
(a) in subsection (3)(a), for "section 35 of the Agricultural Holdings (Scotland) Act 1949" substitute "section 43 of the Agricultural Holdings (Scotland) Act 1991"; and
(b) in subsection (4), for "section 25(1) of the Agricultural Holdings (Scotland) Act 1949" substitute "section 22(1) of the Agricultural Holdings (Scotland) Act 1991."
30. In section 48(2)(a), for "section 35 of the Agricultural Holdings (Scotland) Act 1949" substitute "section 43 of the Agricultural Holdings (Scotland) Act 1991."
31. In Schedule 3, paragraph 7(5)—
(a) for "sections 75 and 77 of the Agricultural Holdings (Scotland) Act 1949" substitute "sections 61 and 64 of the Agricultural Holdings (Scotland) Act 1991"; and
(b) for "sections 78 and 87(2)" substitute "sections 60(2) and 80(2)."

Conveyancing and Feudal Reform (Scotland) Act 1970 (c. 35)

32. In Schedule 1 in paragraph 5(a), for "Agricultural Holdings (Scotland) Act 1949" substitute "Agricultural Holdings (Scotland) Act 1991."

Land Compensation (Scotland) Act 1973 (c. 56)

33. In section 31(3)(c) for "Agricultural Holdings (Scotland) Act 1949" substitute "Agricultural Holdings (Scotland) Act 1991."

34. In section 44—
(a) in subsection (2)(a)(i) for "section 25(2)(c) of the Agricultural Holdings (Scotland) Act 1949" substitute "section 22(2)(b) of the Agricultural Holdings (Scotland) Act 1991";
(b) in subsection (2)(a)(ii)—
     (i) for "section 26(1)(e)" substitute "section 24(1)(e)"; and
     (ii) for "section 25(2)(c)" substitute "section 22(2)(b)";
(c) in subsection (3)(a) for "sections 25(2)(c) and 26(1)(e)" substitute "sections 22(2)(b) and 24(1)(e)";
(d) in subsection (4), for "section 12 of the Agricultural (Miscellaneous Provisions) Act 1968" substitute "section 56 of the Agricultural Holdings (Scotland) Act 1991."

35. In section 52—
(a) in subsection (3)(d) for "Agricultural Holdings (Scotland) Act 1949" substitute "Agricultural Holdings (Scotland) Act 1991"; and
(b) in subsection (4) for "section 59(1) of the Agricultural Holdings (Scotland) Act 1949" substitute "section 47(1) of the Agricultural Holdings (Scotland) Act 1991" and for "the said section 59(1)" substitute "the said section 47(1)."

36. In section 55—
(a) for subsection (1)(b) substitute—
    "(b) either—
        (i) section 22(1) of the Agricultural Holdings (Scotland) Act 1991 does not apply by virtue of subsection (2)(b) of that section; or
        (ii) the Scottish Land Court have consented to the notice on the ground set out in section 24(1)(e) of that Act.";
(b) in subsection (2)(a), for "section 12 of the Agriculture (Miscellaneous Provisions) Act 1968" substitute "section 56 of the Agricultural Holdings (Scotland) Act 1991";
(c) in subsection (2)(b) for "Agricultural Holdings (Scotland) Act 1949" substitute "Agricultural Holdings (Scotland) Act 1991," and for "sections 9 and 15(3) of the Agriculture (Miscellaneous Provisions) Act 1968" substitute "sections 54 and 58(1) and (2) of that Act";
(d) in subsection (6) for "section 33 of the Agricultural Holdings (Scotland) Act 1949" substitute "section 30 of the Agricultural Holdings (Scotland) Act 1991."

37. In section 80(1), in the definitions of "agricultural holding" and "holding" for "Agricultural Holdings (Scotland) Act 1949" substitute "Agricultural Holdings (Scotland) Act 1991."

Land Tenure Reform (Scotland) Act 1974 (c. 38)

38. In section 8(5)(a), for "Agricultural Holdings (Scotland) Act 1949" substitute "Agricultural Holdings (Scotland) Act 1991."

Control of Pollution Act 1974 (c. 40)

39. In section 31(B)(2)(a), for the words "an absolute owner (within the meaning of section 93 of the Agricultural Holdings (Scotland) Act 1949)" substitute "the owner of the dominium utile."

Matrimonial Homes (Family Protection) (Scotland) Act 1981 (c. 59)

40. In section 13(8), in the definition of "agricultural holding," for "Agricultural Holdings (Scotland) Act 1949" substitute "Agricultural Holdings (Scotland) Act 1991."

Rent (Scotland) Act 1984 (c. 58)

41. For section 25(1)(iii) substitute—
    "(iii) the Agricultural Holdings (Scotland) Act 1991."

Law Reform (Miscellaneous Provisions) (Scotland) Act 1985 (c. 73)

42. In section 7(2), in the definition of "agricultural holding," for "section 1 of the Agricultural Holdings (Scotland) Act 1949" substitute "the Agricultural Holdings (Scotland) Act 1991."

Agriculture Act 1986 (c. 49)

43. In section 14(a) for "the Agricultural Holdings (Scotland) Act 1949" substitute "the 1991 Act."

44. In section 16—

(a) in subsection (2), for "section 7 of the 1949 Act" substitute "section 13 of the 1991 Act"; and

(b) in subsection (7), for "section 86 of the 1949 Act" substitute "section 79 of the 1991 Act."

45. In section 18(6) for the words from "the absolute owner" to "1949" substitute "the owner of the dominium utile."

46. In section 19(4) for "the Crofters (Scotland) Act 1955" substitute "the 1955 Act."

47. After section 23 insert—

"23A. In this Act—

"the 1886 Act" means the Crofters Holdings (Scotland) Act 1886;

"the 1911 Act" means the Small Landholders (Scotland) Act 1911;

"the 1955 Act" means the Crofters (Scotland) Act 1955; and

"the 1991 Act" means the Agricultural Holdings (Scotland) Act 1991."

48. In Schedule 2, paragraph 1(1)—

(a) in the definition of "landlord"—

(i) in sub-paragraph (a), for "the 1949 Act" substitute "the 1991 Act" and for "section 93(1)" substitute "section 85(1)"; and

(ii) in sub-paragraph (c), for "the 1949 Act" substitute "the 1991 Act";

(b) in the definition of "tenancy," for "the 1949 Act" substitute "the 1991 Act"; and

(c) in the definition of "tenant"—

(i) in sub-paragraph (a), for "the 1949 Act" substitute "the 1991 Act" and for "section 93(1)" substitute "section 85(1)"; and

(ii) in sub-paragraph (c), for "the 1949 Act" substitute "the 1991 Act."

49. In Schedule 2, paragraph 3(1)(b), for "section 20 of the 1949 Act" substitute "section 11 of the 1991 Act."

50. In Schedule 2, paragraph 7—

(a) in sub-paragraph (2), for "the 1949 Act" where it first occurs substitute "the 1991 Act" and for "section 7 of the 1949 Act" substitute "section 13 of the 1991 Act"; and

(b) in sub-paragraph (4)—

(i) in sub-paragraph (a)(i), for "section 93 of the 1949 Act" substitute "section 85 of the 1991 Act";

(ii) in sub-paragraph (a)(iii), for "the 1949 Act" substitute "the 1991 Act" and

(iii) in sub-paragraph (b), for "section 93 of the 1949 Act" substitute "section 85 of the 1991 Act."

51. In Schedule 2, paragraph 10(1)—

(a) in sub-paragraph (a), for "the 1949 Act" substitute "the 1991 Act" and for "section 78" substitute "section 60(2)"; and

(b) for "section 75 (or, where the circumstances require, sections 77 and 87) of the 1949 Act" substitute "section 60(1) (or, where the circumstances require, sections 64 and 80) of the 1991 Act."

52. In Schedule 2, paragraph 11—

(a) in sub-paragraph (1)(a), for "the 1949 Act" substitute "the 1991 Act" and for "section 78" substitute "section 60(2)";

(b) in sub-paragraph (4)—

(i) for "section 75 (or, where the circumstances require, sections 77 and 87) of the 1949 Act" substitute "section 60(1) (or, where the circumstances require, sections 64 and 80) of the 1991 Act"; and

(ii) for "paragraph 13 of the Sixth Schedule" substitute "paragraph 14 of Schedule 7"; and

(c) in sub-paragraph (5), for "section 61 of the 1949 Act" substitute "section 50 of the 1991 Act."

53. In Schedule 2, for paragraph 12 substitute—

"Sections 65 and 75(1), (2), (4) and (6) of the 1991 Act (recovery of sums due and power of tenant to obtain charge on holding) shall apply in relation to any sum payable to the tenant under this Schedule as they apply to sums payable under that section.".

Housing (Scotland) Act 1987 (c. 26)

54. In section 256(1) and (3) for "Agricultural Holdings (Scotland) Act 1949" substitute "Agricultural Holdings (Scotland) Act 1991."

55. In section 338(1), in the definition of "agricultural holding," for "Agricultural Holdings (Scotland) Act 1949" substitute "Agricultural Holdings (Scotland) Act 1991."

56. In Schedule 8, Part IV, paragraph 13—

(a) in sub-paragraph (1)—

      (i) for "Section 8 of the Agricultural Holdings (Scotland) Act 1949" substitute "Section 15 of the Agricultural Holdings (Scotland) Act 1991;

      (ii) for "the said section 8" substitute "the said section 15";

(b) in sub-paragraph (2)—

      (i) for "paragraph 18 of Schedule 1 to the said Act of 1949" substitute "paragraph 18 of Schedule 5 to the Agricultural Holdings (Scotland) Act 1991";

      (ii) for "section 79" substitute "section 73";

      (iii) for "the said Schedule 1" substitute "the said Schedule 5";

      (iv) for "sections 51 and 52" substitute "sections 38 and 39";

      (v) for "section 49 of the said Act of 1949" substitute "section 36 of that Act."

Housing (Scotland) Act 1988 (c. 43)

57. In Schedule 4 in paragraph 6(a), for "Agricultural Holdings (Scotland) Act 1949" substitute "Agricultural Holdings (Scotland) Act 1991."

Section 87   SCHEDULE 12

TRANSITIONALS AND SAVINGS

Continuation of savings

1. The repeal by this Act of an enactment which repealed a previous enactment subject to a saving shall not affect the continued operation of that saving.

Construction of references to old and new law

2.—(1) Where an enactment contained in this Act repeals and re-enacts an earlier enactment—

(a) for the purpose of giving effect to any instrument or other document it shall be competent, so far as the context permits, to construe a reference to either enactment as a reference to the other;

(b) anything done or required to be done for the purposes of either enactment may, so far as the context permits, be treated as having been done or as something required to be done for the purposes of the other.

(2) In this paragraph, a reference to an enactment reenacted in this Act includes a reference to any such enactment repealed by the Agricultural Holdings Act 1923, the 1949 Act or the Agricultural Holdings (Amendment) (Scotland) Act 1983.

Savings for specific enactments

3. Nothing in this Act shall affect any provision of the Allotments (Scotland) Act 1922.

4. Section 21 of the Reserve and Auxiliary Forces (Protection of Civil Interests) Act 1951 (as read with section 24 of that Act) shall continue to have effect—

(a) in subsections (2) and (3) with the substitution for references to the Secretary of State of references to the Land Court; and

(b) with the reference in subsection (6) to section 27 of the 1949 Act being construed as a reference to that section as originally enacted.

Compensation

5. Notwithstanding section 16 of the Interpretation Act 1978, rights to compensation conferred by this Act shall be in lieu of rights to compensation conferred by any enactment repealed by this Act.

SCHEDULE 13

REPEALS AND REVOCATIONS

PART I

REPEALS

Chapter	Short title	Extent of repeal
1 Edw. 8 & 1 Geo. 6. c. 34.	Sheep Stocks Valuation (Scotland) Act 1937.	The whole Act.
9 & 10 Geo. 6. c. 73.	Hill Farming Act 1946.	Sections 28 to 31. Second Schedule.
11 & 12 Geo. 6. c. 45.	Agriculture (Scotland) Act 1948.	Section 52. In section 54, the definitions of "deer", "occupier of an agricultural holding" and "woodlands".
12, 13 and 14 Geo. 6. c. 75.	Agricultural Holdings (Scotland) Act 1949.	The whole Act.
14 & 15 Geo. 6. c. 18.	Livestock Rearing Act 1951.	In section 1(2)(b) the words "in paragraph (d) of subsection (1) of section 8 of the Agricultural Holdings (Scotland) Act 1949".
14 & 15 Geo. 6. c. 65.	Reserve and Auxiliary Forces (Protection of Civil Interests) Act 1951.	In section 24(b), the words from "for references" to "twenty-seven thereof".
6 & 7 Eliz. 2 c. 71.	Agriculture Act 1958.	Section 3. Schedule 1.
1963 c. 11.	Agriculture (Miscellaneous Provisions) Act 1963.	Section 21
1964 c. 41.	Succession (Scotland) Act 1964.	In Schedule 2, paragraphs 19 to 23.
1968 c. 34.	Agriculture (Miscellaneous Provisions) Act 1968.	Part II. Schedules 4 and 5.
1973 c. 65.	Local Government (Scotland) Act 1973.	Section 228(5).
1976 c. 21.	Crofting Reform (Scotland) Act 1976.	Schedule 2, para. 25.
1976 c. 55.	Agriculture (Miscellaneous Provisions) Act 1976.	Section 13 and 14.
1980 c. 45.	Water (Scotland) Act 1980.	In Schedule 10, Part II, the entry relating to the 1949 Act.
1983 c. 46.	Agricultural Holdings (Amendment) (Scotland) Act 1983.	The whole Act.
1985 c. 73.	Law Reform (Miscellaneous Provisions) (Scotland) Act 1985.	Section 32.
1986 c. 5.	Agricultural Holdings Act 1986.	In Schedule 14, paras. 25(8), 26(11) and 33(8).
1986 c. 49.	Agriculture Act 1986.	In Schedule 2, para. 1, the definitions of "the 1986 Act", "the 1911 Act", "the 1949 Act" and "the 1955 Act".

PART II

REVOCATIONS OF SUBORDINATE LEGISLATION

Number	Citation	Extent of revocation
S.I. 1950/1553.	The Agricultural Holdings (Scotland) Regulations 1950.	The whole Instrument.

Number	Citation	Extent of revocation
S.I. 1978/798.	The Agricultural Holdings (Scotland) Act 1949 (Variation of First Schedule) Order 1978.	The whole Order.
S.I. 1986/1823.	The Hill Farming Act 1946 (Variation of Second Schedule) (Scotland) Order 1986.	The whole Order.

TABLE OF DERIVATIONS

Notes: The following abbreviations are used in this Table—

1937	=	The Sheep Stocks Valuation (Scotland) Act 1937 (1 Edw. 8 & 1 Geo. 6. c. 34).
1946	=	The Hill Farming Act 1946 (9 & 10 Geo. 6. c. 73).
1948	=	The Agriculture (Scotland) Act 1948 (11 & 12 Geo. 6. c. 45).
1949	=	The Agricultural Holdings (Scotland) Act 1949 (12, 13 & 14 Geo. 6. c. 75).
1958	=	The Agriculture Act 1958 (c. 71).
1963	=	The Agriculture (Miscellaneous Provisions) Act 1963 (c. 11).
1964	=	The Succession (Scotland) Act 1964 (c. 41).
1968	=	The Agriculture (Miscellaneous Provisions) Act 1968 (c. 34).
1973	=	The Local Government (Scotland) Act 1973 (c. 65).
1976	=	The Agriculture (Miscellaneous Provisions) Act 1976 (c. 55).
1983	=	The Agriculture Holdings (Amendment) (Scotland) Act 1983 (c. 46).
1986	=	The Agriculture Holdings Act 1986 (c. 5).
S.I. 1950/1553	=	The Agriculture Holdings (Scotland) Regulations 1950 (S.I. 1950/1553).
S.I. 1978/798	=	The Agricultural Holdings (Scotland) Act 1949 (Variation of First Schedule) Order 1978 (c.I. 1978/798).
S.I. 1986/1823	=	The Hill Farming Act 1946 (Variation of Second Schedule) (Scotland) Order 1986.

Provision of Act	Derivation
1	1949 s.1; 1958 s.9(1).
2	1949 s.2.
3	1949 s.3; 1949 s.24(1).
4	1949 s.4, s.6(4).
5	1949 s.5.
6	1949 s.23.
7	1949 s.12; 1958 Sch. 1, Pt.II, para. 33.
8	1949 s.17.
9	1949 s.9; 1958 Sch. 1, Pt.II, para. 32.
10	1949 s.18.
11	1949 s.20; 1964 s.34(1), Sch. 2, paras. 19, 20 and 21.
12	1949 s.21; 1964 s.34(1), Sch. 2, para. 22.
13	1949 s.7; 1983 s.2.
14	1949 s.6(3).
15	1949 s.8.
16	1949 s.10.
17	1949 s.13.
18	1949 s.14.
19	1949 s.22.
20	1949 s.19.
21	1949 s.24; 1958 Sch. 1, Pt. II, para. 34.
22	1949 s.25; 1958 s.3(1), (3), Sch. 1, Pt. II, para. 35.
23	1949 s.27; 1958 Sch. 1, Pt. II, para. 37.
24	1949 s.26; 1958 s.3(2), (3), Sch. 1, Pt. II, para. 36; 1983 s.4(1).
25	1949 s.26A; 1983 s.3, s.4(2).

Provision of Act	Derivation
26	1949 s.28; 1958 Sch. 1, Pt. II, para. 38; 1989 (c. 15) Sch. 25, para. 12.
27	1949 s.30; 1958 Sch. 1, Pt. II, para. 40.
28	1949 s.31.
29	1949 s.32.
30	1949 s.33.
31	1949 s.34.
32	1976 s.14.
33	1949 s.36; s.47.
34	1949 s.37, s.41, s.42, s.43, s.44(4), s.45, s.48, s.53, s.54.
35	1949 s.11, s.46, s.55
36	1949 s.38, s.43, s.44(1), s.49, s.53.
37	1949 s.39, s.50.
38	1949 s.40, s.51.
39	1949 s.52; 1958 Sch. 1, Pt. II, para. 41.
40	1949 s.65.
41	1949 s.66; 1958 Sch. 1, Pt. II, para. 43.
42	1949 s.67.
43	1949 s.35.
44	1949 s.56.
45	1949 s.57, s.58.
46	1949 s.6(1), (2); s.57(3); S.I. 1950/1553.
47	1949 s.59.
48	1949 s.16.
49	1949 s.60.
50	1949 s.61.
51	1949 s.63; 1958 Sch. 1, Pt.II, para. 42; S.I. 1977/2007.
52	1949 s.15; S.I. 1977/2007.
53	1949 s.64.
54	1968 s.9, s.16, Sch. 5, para. 1.
55	1968 s.11.
56	1968 s.12, s.16.
57	1968 s.14; 1972 (c. 52) Sch. 21, Pt.II.
58	1968 s.15, s.16, Sch. 5, para. 5.
59	1968 s.16, s.17.
60	1949 s.74, s.78.
61	1949 s.68, s.75; 1973 s.228(5); 1983 s.5(1).
62	1949 s.68.
63	1949 s.76; 1971 c. 58 s.4.
64	1949 s.77, s.87(2); 1986 s.17(3).
65	1949 s.69.
66	1976 s.13.
67	1949 s.91; 1971 c. 58 s.4.
68	1937 s.1; 1946 s.28; 1985 c. 73 s.32; S.I. 1986/1823.
69	1937 s.2.
70	1937 s.3; 1946 s.29; S.I. 1986/1823.
71	1946 s.30.
72	1937 s.4.
73	1949 s.79.
74	1949 s.80.
75	1949 s.70, s.82; 1980 (c. 45) Sch. 10.
76	1949 s.83.
77	1949 s.84.
78	1949 s.85.
79	1949 s.86; 1968 s.17(3).
80	1949 s.87(1).
81	1949 s.88.
82	1949 s.89; 1975 c. 21 s.289; 1977 c. 45 s.31.
83	1949 s.73; 1976 s.14(6); 1976 (c. 21) Sch. 2, para. 25.
84	1949 s.90; 1985 c. 6 s.725(1).
85	1949 s.93.
86	1949 s.95.
87	1949 s.99(2).

Provision of Act	Derivation
88	1949 s.97.
89	1949 s.101.
Schedule 1	1949 Sch. 5.
Schedule 2	1983 Sch. 1.
Schedule 3	1949 Sch. 2.
Schedule 4	1949 Sch. 3.
Schedule 5	1949 Sch. 1; S.I. 1978/798.
Schedule 6	1949 Sch. 4.
Schedule 7	1949 Sch. 6; 1983 s.5(2).
Scheduie 8	1968 Sch. 4, Sch. 5, para. 6, para. 7.
Schedule 9	1946 Sch. 2; 1963 s.21.
Schedule 10	1946 Sch. 2; 1963; s.21.

INDEX

References are to sections and Schedules

55–137

55–138

APPENDIX

AGRICULTURE (SCOTLAND) ACT 1948 (c. 45)

Section 26   ## FIFTH SCHEDULE

RULES OF GOOD ESTATE MANAGEMENT

1. For the purposes of this Act, the owner of agricultural land shall be deemed to fulfil his responsibilities to manage it in accordance with the rules of good estate management in so far as his management of the land and (so far as it affects the management of that land) of other land managed by him is such as to be reasonably adequate, having regard to the character and situation of the land and other relevant circumstances, to enable an occupier of the land reasonably skilled in husbandry to maintain efficient production as respects both the kind of produce and the quality and quantity thereof.

2. In determining whether the management of land is such as aforesaid regard shall be had, but without prejudice to the generality of the provisions of the last foregoing paragraph, to the extent to which the owner is making regular muirburn in the interests of sheep stock, exercising systematic control of vermin on land not in the control of a tenant, and undertaking the eradication of bracken, whins and broom so far as is reasonably practicable, and to the extent to which the owner is fulfilling his responsibilities in relation to the provision, improvement, replacement and renewal of the fixed equipment on the land in so far as is necessary to enable an occupier reasonably skilled in husbandry to maintain efficient production as aforesaid.

Section 26   ## SIXTH SCHEDULE

RULES OF GOOD HUSBANDRY

1. For the purposes of this Act, the occupier of an agricultural unit shall be deemed to fulfil his responsibilities to farm it in accordance with the rules of good husbandry in so far as the extent to which and the manner in which the unit is being farmed (as respects both the kind of operations carried out and the way in which they are carried out) are such that, having regard to the character and situation of the unit, the standard of management thereof by the owner and other relevant circumstances, the occupier is maintaining a reasonable standard of efficient production, as respects both the kind of produce and the quality and quantity thereof, while keeping the unit in a condition to enable such a standard to be maintained in the future.

2. In determining whether the manner in which a unit is being farmed is such as aforesaid regard shall be had, but without prejudice to the generality of the provisions of the last foregoing paragraph, to the following:—

[A-1]

(a) the maintenance of permanent grassland (whether meadow or pasture) properly mown or grazed and in a good state of cultivation and fertility;

(b) the handling or cropping of the arable land, including the treatment of temporary grass, so as to maintain it clean and in a good state of cultivation and fertility;

(c) where the system of farming practised requires the keeping of livestock, the proper stocking of the holding;

(d) the maintenance of an efficient standard of management of livestock;

(e) as regards hill sheep farming in particular:—
    (i) the maintenance of a sheep stock of a suitable breed and type in regular ages (so far as is reasonably possible) and the keeping and management thereof in accordance with the recognised practices of hill sheep farming;
    (ii) the use of lug, horn or other stock marks for the purpose of determining ownership of stock sheep;
    (iii) the regular selection and retention of the best female stock for breeding;
    (iv) the regular selection and use of tups possessing the qualities most suitable and desirable for the flock;
    (v) the extent to which regular muirburn is made;

(f) the extent to which the necessary steps are being taken—
    (i) to secure and maintain the freedom of crops and livestock from disease and from infestation by insects and other pests;
    (ii) to exercise systematic control of vermin and of bracken, whins, broom and injurious weeds;
    (iii) to protect and preserve crops harvested or in course of being harvested;
    (iv) to carry out necessary work of maintenance and repair of the fixed and other equipment.